PRACTICING LITERARY THEORY IN THE MIDDLE AGES

PRACTICING LITERARY THEORY IN THE MIDDLE AGES

Ethics and the Mixed Form
in Chaucer, Gower,
Usk, and Hoccleve

ELEANOR JOHNSON

THE UNIVERSITY OF CHICAGO PRESS

CHICAGO AND LONDON

PUBLICATION OF THIS BOOK HAS BEEN AIDED BY A GRANT FROM THE BEVINGTON FUND.

The University of Chicago Press, Chicago 60637
The University of Chicago Press, Ltd., London
© 2013 by The University of Chicago
All rights reserved. Published 2013.
Paperback edition 2017
Printed in the United States of America

23 22 21 20 19 18 17   2 3 4 5 6

ISBN-13: 978-0-226-01584-2 (cloth)
ISBN-13: 978-0-226-52745-1 (paper)
ISBN-13: 978-0-226-01598-9 (e-book)

Library of Congress Cataloging-in-Publication Data
Johnson, Eleanor, 1979–
    Practicing literary theory in the middle ages : ethics and the mixed form in Chaucer, Gower, Usk, and Hoccleve / Eleanor Johnson
        pages. cm.
    Includes bibliographical references and index.
    ISBN 978-0-226-01584-2 (cloth : alk. paper) — ISBN 978-0-226-01598-9 (e-book)
1. English literature—Middle English, 1100–1500—History and criticism.
2. Ethics, Medieval, in literature.   3. Literature, Medieval—History and criticism.
4. Boethius, d. 524.   5. Chaucer, Geoffrey, d. 1400.   6. Usk, Thomas, d. 1388.
7. Gower, John, 1325?–1408.   8. Hoccleve, Thomas, 1370?–1450?   I. Title.
    PR275.E77J64 2013
    820.9′001—dc23   2012043148

♾ This paper meets the requirements of ANSI/NISO Z39.48-1992 (Permanence of Paper).

CONTENTS

ACKNOWLEDGMENTS

In its earliest stages, this project received generous fellowship support from the University of California, Berkeley; the Townsend Center for the Humanities at UC, Berkeley; the Northern California chapter of Phi Beta Kappa; and the Mabelle McLeod Lewis Fund. In its later stages, the book was awarded a Junior Faculty Grant from Columbia University. I am immensely grateful to the University of California, the Townsend Center, Phi Beta Kappa, the McLeod Lewis Fund, and Columbia University.

I have had more advisers, interlocutors, and champions than anyone should dare hope for. At Berkeley, Steven Justice's and Maura Nolan's sage and indefatigable counsels were invaluable in the early, middle, and late stages of the project, as well as in the daunting process of getting the manuscript ready for publication. I owe both of them a tremendous debt of gratitude. I also owe a great deal to Anne Middleton, whose perspicacity and rigor have helped me in this project and in many others. I am thankful to Lyn Hejinian and Geoffrey G. O'Brien for helping me remember questions of form at all points—how poetry works, not just what it says. And my humble thanks go to Carol Clover for her unflagging support, generous criticisms, and flair for all that's exciting about literary studies.

At Columbia, I have found a wonderful host of colleagues, friends, and advisers, many of whom have made significant and shaping comments about this book. Thank you, Paul Strohm, Susan Crane, and Chris Baswell, for helping me to realize that my book was trying to say something much larger than I initially thought it was, and for helping me to reframe the project to make that clearer. Thank you, Jean Howard, for your pointed questions about how I wanted to position the book in the field, and for your wise counsel on how to shape the book before sending it off for publication. Thanks to the wonderful members of my third-year review committee—

Kathy Eden, Molly Murray, Nick Dames, and, again, Susan Crane—for all your questions about and suggestions on the manuscript. I would like to thank Edward Mendelson for our many book-related conversations over hamburgers, Sharon Marcus for sharing with me her incredible knack for strategy, Julie Crawford for her encouragements and suggestions on a near-final version of the book, Erik Gray for his many insights both aesthetic and pragmatic, Jim Shapiro for his unflinching and insightful suggestions on readying the book for publication, Michael Golston for being an inexhaustible font of enthusiasm for enjambment, Marianne Hirsch for her incisive and supportive questions about what I wanted to achieve with the finished book, Sarah Cole for her inspiring attention to style, Rachel Adams for her willingness to listen to and advise about many stages of the process of book-making, Teo Barolini for her insights on Dante's poetic methodologies, Elisabeth Ladenson for her generous counsels and inimitable intellectual vivacity, Jesús Rodríguez Velasco for his invaluable clarity of perspective and his championing of medieval ethics as a category of study, Adam Kosto for his well-timed questions about Boethius's political significance, and Patricia Dailey for being my constant writing companion and interlocutor.

Among my excellent colleagues at neither Berkeley nor Columbia, I would like to thank Bruce Holsinger, whose comments and suggestions on an earlier version of this book as well as on its penultimate version helped bring my vision into focus and helped me to articulate my own principles of formalist scholarship more fully. For insights into the chapters of the book, for help untangling particular conceptual snarls, and for well-timed and helpful suggestions, I thank Seth Lerer, David Wallace, Rita Copeland, Michelle Karnes, Jessica Rosenfeld, Jessica Brantley, Amy Hollywood, Cathy Sanok, Claire Waters, Hal Momma, Martha Rust, Michael Sargent, Ethan Knapp, Mark Miller, Barbara Newman, Matthew Fisher, Sarah Beckwith, Peggy Knapp, Matthew Giancarlo, Seeta Chaganti, Mary Carruthers, and Aranye Fradenburg. My deep thanks also go to Christopher Cannon: your suggestions for final revision were extraordinarily useful, helping me to think through the mechanism of transmission of the formal trends I analyze in the book. Finally, I once again thank Lee Patterson, whom I will miss every time I read the *Canterbury Tales*, for having been so exacting about that paper on the Wife of Bath—happily for me, I still have not gotten over our conversations, though I wish we could have just one more.

I would also like to thank the faculties of English and medieval studies at Wellesley College and the University of Pittsburgh, for the generous feedback they gave at lectures I presented; the members of the New Chaucer Society, who responded warmly but exactingly to early versions of my second chapter in a conference talk; and Susanna Fein and David Raybin, the editors of the *Chaucer Review*, as well as Carolyn Collette, for helping me publish an early version of my book's chapter on the *Canterbury Tales*. And of course, a hearty thank-you to Randy Petilos, my wonderful and clear-sighted editor, to Susan Tarcov, and to the rest of the splendid staff at the University of Chicago Press.

Finally, with all my heart, I want to thank my friends and my parents. You have reminded me, always, that in this somewhat lonely process of making a book, I have never been alone.

New York
July 2012

∽

An earlier version of chapter 4 was published as "Chaucer and the Consolation of Prosimetrum" in *Chaucer Review* 43 (2009): 455–72.

∽

ON SPELLINGS AND TRANSLATIONS

Thorns and yoghs are normalized to modern English orthography. All translations are mine unless otherwise noted.

Formalism and Ethics:
The Practice of Literary Theory

MEDIEVAL LITERARY THEORY: FORM AND ETHICS

The relationship of literary writing and reading with the production of ethical learning is a dominant concern of early European literary theory. Horace's *Ars poetica* famously insists that literary writing can be either delightful or useful, but that it is best when it achieves both goals.[1] Several centuries later, Isidore of Seville underscores this Horatian lesson, specifying that the highest mode of literary experience is that which contributes to the moral understanding of its readers.[2] Later medieval commentaries pick up and expand upon this notion that good literature should work to improve readers' moral and ethical understandings. As Alastair Minnis and A. B. Scott have shown, between the twelfth and fourteenth centuries, a formidable Latin commentary tradition on literary writing

1. "Aut prodesse volunt aut delectare poetae / aut simul et iucunda et idonea dicere vitae . . . omne tulit punctum qui miscuit utile dulci / lectorem delectando pariterque monendo." Horace, *Satires* 478. (Poets wish either to delight or benefit us, or, at once, to speak words both delightful and useful to life . . . He who mixes the useful with the pleasant and who while delighting the reader simultaneously teaches him carries off every vote.) Horace's mandate on the moral utility and aesthetic pleasure of literary writing, as Glending Olson notes, ends up being "probably the most familiar literary commonplace in the Middle Ages," influencing the work of Latin, French, and English poets alike (*Literature as Recreation*, 21).

2. Some poems, Isidore notes, "ad mores hominum interpretati sunt" (*Etymologiae*, bk. 1, chap. 40, line 15) (are understood to pertain to men's morals). Glending Olson notes this passage as well and traces some of its influences on later writers (*Literature as Recreation*, 27–28).

emerges that praises those works that "pertain to ethics" and condemns those that, because lacking in ethical or moral instruction, are merely "lying fictions."[3] According to Latin medieval literary theory, literary writing should do some kind of ethical work if it is to be worth its ink.

But these theories that literature should do ethical work or "pertain to ethics" leave two lacunae. The first is how exactly we, as scholars of medieval literature, are to understand the "ethical work" of literature. In contemporary critical discourse on medieval literature, "ethics" tends, either implicitly or explicitly, to be understood as an intersubjective phenomenon, as the code of prosocial behaviors a person must embody in order to lead a good life.[4] There is, of course, ample reason for this understanding: in medieval philosophy, "ethics" encompasses political action, interpersonal action between intimates, and interpersonal action between fellow Christians.[5] But Jessica Rosenfeld's recent book reminds us that for medieval philosophers, commentators, and poets, the pursuit of individual happiness and fulfillment is, itself, construed as an ethical pursuit—indeed, the one from which the more "social" forms of ethics emanate.[6] Ethics is thus not exclusively concerned with political or interpersonal conduct

3. Commentaries on Avianus, Homer, Arator, Ovid, and Horace claim their authors' works "pertain to ethics." See Minnis and Scott, *Medieval Literary Theory*, 16, 17, 19, 20, 33. Conrad of Hirsau says of Aesop's fables, "In that they are made to relate to a moral end, and have been invented to give pleasure, Aesop's fables differ from the lying fictions of Terence, Plautus, and other similar poets" (*Medieval Literary Theory*, 47).

4. For instance, L. O. Aranye Fradenburg's analysis of desire and its relation to ethics implicitly understands ethics as relational, contributing to love between people and, in its darker manifestations, to interpersonal violence. See the introduction in *Sacrifice Your Love*.

5. David Aers's description of how faith and ethics interrelate in the late medieval *imaginaire* participates in this discourse. For Aers (*Faith, Ethics and Church*), faith is social, and therefore faith is ethical, because ethics is a sphere of social action and social thought. For a consideration of how fortune and chance affect a person's ability to be an ethical agent in and of the world, see Mitchell, *Ethics and Eventfulness*, 14, 28, 36.

6. Rosenfeld, *Ethics and Enjoyment*, 1–3. Within an Augustinian framework, ethical action, Rosenfeld notes, is what happens when "the highest goal of the human subject . . . coalesces in one perfected, eternal instance of love for the divine object" (17). The medieval philosopher John Buriden, perhaps following Augustine, takes as written that ethics is about the pursuit of happiness, construed both as knowledge of God and as love of God: "Again, happiness is held to consist in the perfect contemplation of God; but the perfect contemplation of God does not exist without love, nor does love without knowledge. But happiness is constituted from both" ("Questions on the Ten Books of the Nicomachean Ethics of Aristotle," 772).

but is also and perhaps primarily concerned with bringing oneself to a deeper understanding of one's own soul and closer to an understanding of universal truths—for it is in the gaining of such understanding that true happiness consists. Drawing on this notion, my own analysis understands the concept of "ethics" to encompass both the inward-focused and the outward-focused modes of right behavior, both the personally salvific and the prosocial.[7] Civic ethics, as we will see, is not segregable from spiritual ethics, so that the poets whose works "pertain to ethics" are often thinking first about the transformation of the human soul toward God or toward self-understanding and second about the possibility of ethically transformative action in a larger social arena.

The second lacuna is precisely *how* literature is supposed to do either of these two kinds of ethical work. In fact, how literary writing is supposed to communicate ethical learning to a readership is left wonderfully underspecified throughout Latin literary-theoretical works from the Middle Ages. I say "wonderfully" because this underspecification of how literary writing can work ethical transformation for a reader proves generative for late medieval vernacular writers, who, in the course of their writing projects, turn into literary theorists themselves. In particular, I will suggest that the great efflorescence of fictive literature in medieval England, between about 1380 and 1422, owes a great deal to an emergent will to experiment with how—and whether—literature can perform ethical work by virtue of its formal composition.

In this experimentation, "ethics"—both inward-focused and outward-focused—is explored not just through the thematic contents of individual works but also and more trenchantly through the aesthetic. By "aesthetic" I mean that which is perceptible to the senses, and, by extension, I mean the literary devices, forms, topoi, tropes, and styles by which a work engages with its readers' sense perceptions.[8] As we will see, the aesthetic

---

7. Isidore of Seville also notes the coincidence of inward- and outward-focused ethics, calling "ethics" equivalent to "morals," as the second part of philosophy. "Altera moralis, quae Graeci Ethica dicatur, in qua de moribus agatur" (*Etymologiae*, bk. 2, chap. 24, lines 25–26). Alcuin Blamires has suggested a different way of anatomizing medieval theories of ethics. To theorize the difference between inward-focused ethical conduct or the work of the spirit and outward-focused conduct in the social world, he makes a distinction between morality, which he understands as inward and Christian, and ethics, which he understands as outward and Aristotelian (*Chaucer, Ethics, and Gender*, 7–8). Throughout this book, I will use "ethics" to refer to both the inward- and outward-focused categories.

8. See *OED*, s.v. "aesthetic," etymology: "of or relating to sense perception."

power of literary language—its power to make ideation sensory and hence experiential through form and style—is fundamental to late medieval experimentation with ethically transformative writing.

This experimentation takes its motivating force from a late antique practice of couching ethically transformative narratives in one particular aesthetic form: *prosimetrum*.[9] Indeed, in the medieval works I will examine in this book, the mixed form of prose and meter is inextricable from the attempt either to provide ethical learning or to theorize how and whether it might be possible to do so at all in literary writing. Through medieval writers' sustained and various experimentation with the nature and limits of the mixed form, and with its relation—either natural or constructed— to ethical transformation, the association of the mixed form with ethical learning eventually animates an emerging body of literary-theoretical fiction. It animates, that is, a veritable *practice* of vernacular literary theory in the late Middle Ages.

To situate the late medieval mixed-form experiments with ethical writing, it is necessary first to review the two late antique mixed-form works that shape and inform the practices and theories of prosimetrum for subsequent centuries. Martianus Capellus's *De nuptiis Philologiae et Mercurii* is regarded by medieval commentators as the point of origin for prosimetrum as a recognizable literary mode.[10] Martianus uses the mixed form to narrate the wedding of Mercury to Philology, during which the gods, helped by the personified seven liberal arts, praise the virtues of Philology. One commentary on this work, composed around 1150, suggests that Martianus uses meter because of its musicality, which has the power

9. Peter Dronke has written on prosimetrum as a genre with its point of origin in Menippean satire. His study focuses on the macrocosmic form of prosimetrum, showing how the alternation of verse with prose provides a useful aesthetic template for Icelandic saga writers, as well as for late medieval mystics (*Verse with Prose from Petronius to Dante*).

10. As Danuta Shanzer notes, the Menippean satire is the first prosimetrum in Western European literature. Shanzer, indeed, has suggested that Martianus's prosimetrum is in dialogue with classical Menippean satire, though she suggests that one of Martianus's major interventions into this tradition is to amplify the amount of verse and promote it to a higher level of organizational significance in his work (*Philosophical and Literary Commentary on Martianus*, 29–32). Judson Allen acknowledges that despite the priority of Menippean satire, Martianus is seen in the Middle Ages as the originator of the mixed form (*Ethical Poetic of the Later Middle Ages*, 75). For a discussion of the prosimetrum genre in the Middle Ages, with Martianus at the origin, see Eckhardt, "Medieval Prosimetrum Genre," 27.

to activate man's higher capacities for contemplation.[11] Later, this same commentary associates the experience of music with the alleviation of ire and the bringing of sweetness and ease to the mind via the senses.[12] Half a century later, Alexander Neckham gives a similar explanation of the utility of the mixed form in *De nuptiis*, though his explanation, by recurring to Horatian principles of poetry writing, more specifically distinguishes the effect of prose from that of meter. Literary works are to be praised, Neckham reminds his readers,

> uel utilitatis causa uel delectationis uel utriusque, quod notat Oratius, ubi dicit: 'aut prodesse uolunt aut delectare poete', aut simul et iocosa et idonea dicere uite. His autem et utilitatem confert in prosis et delectationem in metris.[13]

> [because of either use or delight, as Horace notes, where he says: "poets want either to instruct or to delight," or else to be both funny and substantial. This work (*De nuptiis*), indeed, confers utility in prose and delight in meter.]

For Neckham, both Martianus's prose and his meter are important species of doing "poetic" work, but they differ in how they function: meter confers pleasure and delight, while prose is useful.

For Neckham, Martianus is a Horatian *Wunderkind*, aware of and able to execute Horace's mandate that literary writing should be, at once, pleasing and useful precisely by writing in the twinned form of prosimetrum. An early thirteenth-century commentary puts more pressure on the exact nature of prose's utility, nominating prose as the form appropriate to didactic action. Focusing on the switch between meter and prose that takes place in the frame of *De nuptiis*, when Martianus is singing to himself and then turns to speak—in prose—to his son, this commentary notes that "In hac enim prima prosa didascalicam eligit narrationem"[14] (Thus, he chose to put didactic narration in this prose). For this commen-

---

11. *Commentary on Martianus Capella's* De nuptiis Philologiae et Mercurii *Attributed to Bernardus Silvestris*, pp. 50–51, lines 36–63.

12. "Dat musica sonos et adimit iram, suggerit clementiam, suadet." Ibid., p. 54, lines 145–46. "Set cur nostro se nequaquam auditui suggerat hec ratio? In omnibus sensibilibus modulo et mensura egent sensus humani." Ibid., p. 51, lines 80–82.

13. Alexander Neckam, *Commentum super Martianum*, 5.

14. *Berlin Commentary on Martianus Capella's* De nuptiis Philologiae et Mercurii, book 1, p, 30.

tator, prose is the form most appropriate to teaching, which he assumes is the primary drive of Martianus's work: "In hoc autem quod didascalicam eligit narrationem et ad filium, lectorem reddit attentum, quia filium in nullo instrueret quod utilitatem non contineret"[15] (In this, moreover, because he chose narration that is instructive and is addressed to his son, he renders the reader attentive, because he would instruct his son in nothing that would not contain usefulness). The prosimetrum of *De nuptiis* has thus become a paradigmatic formal embodiment of Horatian poetics in the minds of its medieval commentators. To them, the mixed form has a power all its own, consisting in the dual action of meter's musical sensuality and prose's ability to be didactic.

Boethius's *Consolation of Philosophy* perceives and radically reinvents this approbation of the mixed form as a vehicle for ethical learning.[16] Making close associations between Martianus's prosimetric work and Boethius's on formal grounds is common in the medieval commentary tradition: in fact, commentators often derive Boethius's initial impulse to write in the mixed form directly from Martianus. In doing so, however, they sometimes make rather harsh judgments of Martianus's formal practices, as against Boethius's. One commentator intimates that Boethius imitates "Martianum Feliccem Capellam, qui prius libros de nuptiis Philologiae et Mercurii eadem specie poematis conscripserat. Set iste [Boethius] longe nobiliore materia et facundia praecellit, quippe qui nec Tullio in prose nec

---

15. Ibid.

16. A familiar figure to medievalists, Boethius is seen, throughout the Middle Ages, as an authority on nearly every branch of human knowledge. Boethius's translations and analyses of Plato's philosophical treatises and of Aristotle's *Categories* are the main conduit through which these Greek works reached Latin readers throughout the Middle Ages. His theological writings develop important theories on the Trinity, as well as on the eternity of God and the perpetuity of the world. His treatise on music, which I will discuss in detail in chapter 1, is as influential as Augustine's formidable *De musica*. For an overview of these works, see Chadwick, *Consolations of Music, Logic, Theology, and Philosophy*. For the original works, see Boethius, *De divisione* and *In categories Aristotelis libri IV* and *De institutione musica*, in Patrologia Latina 63; Boethius, *Quomodo trinitas unus Deus ac non tres dii* and *Utrum Pater et Filius et Spiritus sanctus de divinitate substantialiter praedicantur*.

Though all of Boethius's works are influential, it is his mixed-form *Consolation of Philosophy* that has the deepest and broadest impact on medieval writers and thinkers. For an analysis of the tremendous impact of the *Consolation*, see Courcelle, *La Consolation dans la tradition littéraire*, 1–12.

Throughout this book, all citations of the *Consolation* are drawn from *Boethii: Philosophiae consolatio*, ed. Bieler.

Virgilio in metro inferior floruit."[17] (Martianus Capellus, who had written the earlier work on the marriage of Philology and Mercury with the same type of poetry. But this Boethius holds forth his material and learning far more nobly, since he has written neither prose inferior to Cicero, nor meter inferior to Virgil.) The praise bestowed on Boethius is indicative of a larger phenomenon in later medieval commentaries: in the twelfth century and beyond, Boethius's work becomes, though not the recognized originator of the mixed form, its highest premedieval instantiation.[18]

Boethius's importance in this history of the mixed form as a formal vehicle for ethical writing originates not only in his excellent prose and poetic style but also and more fundamentally in a radical difference in genre between his work and Martianus's. Martianus's prosimetrum couches what is, thematically, an allegorical explication and defense of academic learning.[19] Although he appears at the beginning and end of his book, as a slightly inkhorn father who seeks to teach his son the virtues of the seven liberal arts, and although he makes a brief cameo in the book of grammar, Martianus is not a major protagonist within his narrative but is instead a passively narrating witness to the events it contains.[20] He learns about the

17. *Saeculi noni auctoris in Boetii Consolationem philosophiae Commentarius,* p. 4, lines 3–9.

18. This elevation of Boethian prosimetrum above and beyond Martianus's work is borne out in the tendency of Martianus's commentators retrospectively to associate Martianus's metrical successes—as at the end of Harmonia's disquisition or in his intial poem to Hymen—retrospectively with Boethian musical and metrical theory. Indeed, Bernard's commentary on musicality in Martianus's metrical practice makes explicit reference to Boethius as a touchstone, indicating that the later theorist has, at least as regards metrical and musical philosophy, overshadowed the earlier. "Prefatum ordinem attendens Boetius, cum de tota musica disserere curam suscepisset, ab instrumentali orsus est, succedenter dicturus de mundana, tandem humana . . . Et eundem ordinem observans Martianus primo instrumentalis indicat efficatiam, dicens, 'Tu quem psallentem,' et cetera" (*Commentary on Martianus Capella's* De nuptiis Philologiae et Mercurii *Attributed to Bernardus,* pp. 50–51, lines 54–57, 60–63). (Listening to the aforementioned order, Boethius, having undertaken to set in order all music, he begins with instrumental, he will next speak about worldly, and finally human . . . And observing this same order, Martianus indicates first the efficacy of instrumental, saying, "You, what psalm," etc.]

19. As William Stahl puts it, Martianus's story is best understood as a "handbook" on the seven arts ("To a Better Understanding of Martianus Capella," 102).

20. Bernard of Silvester not only commented on Martianus's prosimetrum but also wrote his own mixed-form work, the *Cosmographia.* Like Martianus's *De nuptiis,* the *Cosmographia* is an allegorical narrative containing gods as well as personified abstrac-

seven liberal arts by overhearing—rather than by interacting with—the allegorical figures whose debates and disquisitions he witnesses. A reader is meant to come away from his work having internalized how and why the seven arts are useful in human life. By contrast, the *Consolation* is, as Mikhail Bakhtin notes, autobiographical in its narrative frame, as it purports to narrate the imprisonment and internal struggle of its own narrating author, Boethius.[21] Because of its autobiographical frame, the *Consolation* is not simply a tale that imparts instruction or reveals the value of academic study. Instead, it shows the gradual process by which nourishing and salvific lessons take hold in the mind of a narrator-protagonist-author. Through the autobiographical persona of the gradually evolving Boethius, the *Consolation* enacts ethical transformation as a spectacle, as a real-time performance of Boethius's own psychological renewal.

In being constructed as a real-time spectacle of psychological transformation, the *Consolation* is designed not only to tell about Boethius's transformation but also to initiate a parallel process of transformative consolation for a reader by facilitating identification between that reader and Boethius himself. In so doing, the *Consolation* embodies a powerful answer to the mandate that fictive literature should "pertain to ethics." The *Consolation* is not simply *about* ethics. Instead, it promises to *do* ethics, to do the work of transforming the soul from miserably self-destructive ideation and affect to jubilantly self-healing ideation and affect. It is designed to catalyze ethical reeducation in its reader by modeling it in Boethius himself.

This modeling function of Boethius's transformation is central to medieval commentaries on the *Consolation*'s ethical value. According to William of Aragon, "Boethius wrote this book to console himself, but those things which are disputed in it clearly teach each of us to distinguish between the various goods and show which good men ought to direct their hearts and minds towards."[22] Nicholas Trevet notes that Boethius

---

tions and ideas, though Bernard's tale concerns the nature of the construction of the heavens and earth, rather than the the significance of the seven liberal arts. Bernard, like Martianus, takes a minute role in his own narrative, instead presenting his work in the third person. Because my book is concerned with mixed-form works that also depict the ethical transformation of their own narrator, it will not focus on Bernard's prosimetrum.

21. Bakhtin, *Dialogic Imagination*, 119, 144.

22. William of Aragon, "Commentary on Boethius," in Minnis and Scott, *Medieval Literary Theory and Criticism, 1100–1375*, 330. Trevet, *Exposicio Fratris Nicolai Trevethi Anglici Ordinis Predicatorum super Boecio "De consolatione,"* cited in

writes his autobiographical *Consolation* so as to inspire compassion in its audience—"intendit animum audientis mouere ad compassionem"—and sees that compassion as a foundation of the *Consolation*'s capacity to teach.[23] William of Conches in particular spends a great deal of energy explaining the ethical function of the *Consolation*, specifying that Boethius's work is designed to "show" and to "demonstrate" the truth of its transformative consolation by reason, and to specify in what things readers should take joy and in what things they should not. As his commentary continues, William weaves in a series of passive periphrastic constructions, to characterize normative emotional reactions that readers should have in encountering Boethius's *Consolation*: *laetandum, dolendum,* and *gaudendum* signal that a reader should be taking joy, overcoming sorrow, and rejoicing, along with Boethius himself. Finally, toward the end of his introduction to the *Consolation*, William integrates first-person-plural constructions—*extollamur* and *deprimamur*—to show that he understands Boethius's tale to be designed to model a transformation of understanding in its readers: "we" readers are supposed to be affected by "our" experiences of reading through Boethius's fiction of autobiographical transformation.[24]

Modern scholars often use the Greek term *protreptic* to categorize the *Consolation*'s combining of autobiographical framework and ethically transformative function, and I will follow suit throughout this analysis.[25] Protreptics are designed to teach ethical lessons, but not by the action of straightforward explication or exemplary embodiment. Rather a protreptic teaches ethics by facilitating identification between its reader and its nar-

---

Rosenfeld, "Doubled Joys of *Troilus and Criseyde*," 58 n. 33. The unknown commentator, who may be Johannes Scottus, says that Boethius, having suffered greatly himself, "intended his book to be consoling" (intendit hoc in opere consolari) to other sorrowing people. *Saeculi noni auctoris in Boetii Consolationem philosophiae Commentarius,* p. 5, line 10.

23. Rosenfeld, *Ethics and Enjoyment,* 143–44.

24. William of Conches, *Glosae super Boetium,* pp. 4–5, lines 33–50.

25. "Protreptic" works both as a noun and as an adjective: nominally, it designates the literary work itself (e.g., "The *Consolation* is a protreptic"); adjectivally, it describes the kind of effect that literary work has (e.g., "The *Consolation* has a protreptic effect"). The other form this word will take in my analysis is the noun *protrepsis,* which designates not the literary work but the psychological process of change (e.g., "Boethius undergoes protrepsis over the course of his protreptic narrative"). For further background in this genre, see Courcelle, *La Consolation dans la tradition littéraire,* 18; Rand, "On the Composition of Boethius' *Consolatio philosophiae*"; M. Jordan, "Ancient Philosophic Protreptic"; Cook, "Protreptic Power of Early Christian Language"; T. Smith, "Protreptic Character of the Nicomachean Ethics.".

rator who is also the protagonist of an ethical quest for truth. It teaches ethical transformation to a reader by modeling an ethical transformation in its own narrator. *Protrepsis*, the phenomenon that protreptic works produce, is thus the literary modeling of ethical transformation in a main character who is also the narrator of the work.

The use of prosimetrum as a vehicle for protrepsis comprises a key provocation for late medieval literary experimentation with the relationship between aesthetic form and ethical function in England. Geoffrey Chaucer, Thomas Usk, John Gower, and Thomas Hoccleve all manifest a sustained impulse to explore and question the power of mixed-form literary writing to create protrepsis. None are quite so sanguine about the mixed form's innate ethical powers as is Boethius himself, but each is nevertheless keen to consider, reinvent, and play with it as an experimental tool of literary ethics. In their sustained and sundry reinvestigations of prosimetrum and its relation to protrepsis, the works I examine body forth a tradition of literary experimentation with how aesthetic form and ethical function might intersect in literary writings.

By invoking the discourse of "tradition," I do not mean to suggest a straightforward, linear, or unidirectional line of influence that runs from Boethius to Chaucer to Usk to Gower to Hoccleve. In fact, I do not mean to suggest straightforward "influence" at all. During his writing career, Chaucer encounters a cluster of related literary experiments with the mixed-form—in the works of Alain de Lille, Dante Alighieri, and Guillaume de Machaut—as well as a cluster of contemporary theoretical ideas about the relative ethical powers of prose and poetry. Chaucer revisits and reinvents these experiments and theories over and over again in his ongoing effort to think through how and whether form and ethics intersect in literary writing. The slightly later Middle English writers I examine— Usk, Gower, and Hoccleve—are each in conversation with two or more of these earlier continental mixed-form writers and literary theories, and all are in conversation at least with Boethius and Chaucer. There *is* a tradition here, though it is not one as neat or tidy as can readily be accounted for by linear models of influence.

The tradition of experiments with the mixed form and its relation to ethical transformation in the late Middle Ages is more nearly rhizomatic: complex, intersecting, and shallowly buried lines of relationality run among a set of related literary works.[26] Each work is recognizably related

---

26. For an in-depth philosophical analysis of the interpretive utility of the concept of the rhizome, see Deleuze and Guattari, *Thousand Plateaus*, 3–28.

to others in the system, and all can be linked to one progenitor, but the various branchings of the buried network make the direct ascription of exclusionary filiation or linear hierarchy both impossible and misleading. The patterns of growth within this rhizomatic literary tradition are gnarled and recursive, rather than clean and linear. This rhizomatic tradition proliferates in two ways: first, when an individual work reinvents the paradigm of the mixed-form protreptic in combination with parallel reinventings in other individual works, and, second, when a work grafts onto its own roots other literary-theoretical strains, including late medieval theories of prose, late medieval ideas about *apologiae*, and late medieval practices of writing commentary on literary works. *Practicing Literary Theory in the Middle Ages*, in the end, offers a formalist literary history—an examination of the inauguration and rhizomatic evolution of a particular literary topos. In this case, that topos is the mixed-form protreptic as a means for theorizing the relation of ethical transformation to aesthetic experience.

To examine this literary evolution, *Practicing Literary Theory in the Middle Ages* asks "how" questions at least as often as "what" questions—it asks how particular formal choices work, how they resonate with medieval literary-theoretical ideas, and how particular poems and prose works meditate on the tricky business of modeling ethical transformation for a readership. In so doing, it addresses the aesthetic effects that particular formal choices have, on both small and large scales, and then moves to theorize how and why they matter in their particular historical contexts. The exploration of those "how" questions eventually leads to each work's implicit theory of how and whether literary work can or should prove ethically transformative, either for narrating author or for reader.

In seeking the formal strategies by which fictive works disgorge their own literary-theoretical investments, this study is concerned with moments of metapoetics and metacriticism—moments at which literary works step outside of themselves, to do the work of theoretical commentary and to enact meditations on the nature of literary experience itself. Indeed, *Practicing Literary Theory in the Middle Ages* shows late Middle English mixed-form protreptics to be critically savvy on their own terms and to be consciously conversant with the literary-theoretical works that preceded them. It shows these writings to perform—aesthetically—the work of literary theory, and it suggests thereby a way of merging formalist critical practices with a historically situated theoretical approach.

The medieval works in this book perform their literary-theoretical meditations both at the global level of overarching structure and at the local level of style and poetic device. That is, the works examined in this book all register that in order to produce a protreptic prosimetrum on a large scale, they must engage in particular kinds of stylistic work on a very small scale. For this reason, mixed-form protreptics provide both medieval writers and contemporary critics a framework within which to explore the relationship between macrocosm and microcosm in the study of literary form. In providing this framework, medieval prosimetrum speaks to the two different senses of "formalism" that Catherine Gallagher points up as a potential critical problem: one sense takes the overall structure of a work into account, while the other focuses on local elements of style.[27] The mixed-form experiments examined in this book all make plain that these two notions of form—the structural and the stylistic—are inseparable and that the former can be fully understood only in the context of the latter.

A BRIEF AND RECENT HISTORY OF FORMALISM

Practicing Literary Theory in the Middle Ages aspires to suggest new ways of thinking formally in the study of medieval literature. When considering formalism as a strategy of literary study, it is crucial to remember that formalism's ethical status is precisely what lies behind assertions of its limitations. In the late twentieth century, it was the entrenched ethical indifference and the valorization of taste and style over all other concerns that made formalists and New Criticism such easy targets of New Historicism and psychoanalytic criticism.[28] New Historicism offered itself as a more ethical way of reading, which would expose structures of power and ideological formations, without relying on judgments of literary value to do so. In Stephen Greenblatt's words, New Historicism sought to "turn away from the formal, decontextualized analysis that dominates new criticism" in favor of "the embeddedness of cultural objects in the contingencies of history."[29] Similarly, the psychoanalytic critical movement sought to ponder questions of intersubjective, social ethics as a driving critical telos,

27. "Formalism and Time," 230–31.

28. Taking T. S. Eliot as a prime exemplar of the formalism typical of high modernism, after which New Criticism patterned itself, Richard Halpern says that, in Eliot's writing, "literary works . . . are to be judged solely according to their own internal principles of order, consistency, and decorum—not according to how accurately they portray their own societies or how we may feel about their conventions." Halpern, *Shakespeare among the Moderns*, 31.

29. *Learning to Curse*, 163–64.

as opposed to pondering matters of style or taste.[30] Though both groups achieved tremendously important goals and radically reconfigured—for the better—the practice of medieval literary scholarship, New Historicists and psychoanalytic critics alike also marginalized formal reading as an ethically inert, politically disengaged, and fundamentally antiquated mode of engaging with literature.[31]

For over a decade, "New Formalists," as they are often called, have pushed back against this marginalization. As early as 2000, a special issue of *Modern Language Quarterly* showcased a number of essays that sought to reaffirm the importance of attention to form in both literary teaching and critical research; these essays also sought to suggest that formalism was in no way incompatible with historical attention and historical particularity. Susan Wolfson reminded her audience of Georg Lukàcs's dictum that "the truly social element in literature is the form" in order to suggest that the ascription of historical and ethical indifference to formalist methodologies was entirely unwarranted.[32] In a similar vein, Garrett Stewart suggested that "the formalist imperative is to read, to read what is written as a form (and formation) of meaning, both authorially designed and culturally inferred."[33] By the dawn of the twenty-first century, it seemed that "formalism"—newly conceived as ethical and historical—was already having something of a renaissance.

What it was not yet having was a Middle Ages. Early articles and essays that practiced and theorized the "New Formalism" centered on postmedieval literature. In the 2000 *MLQ* issue, for instance, all of the articles dealt with postmedieval, and nearly all post-Enlightenment, literary works or theories: modern novels, literary criticism, romantic poetry, the country house poem, eighteenth-century couplets, cultural studies, Austen's novels, and Victorian novels. As Marjorie Levinson later noted in her compendious review of New Formalism, "New-formalist work concentrates in the areas of early modern and Romantic period study."[34] Medievalists, in comparison with scholars from later historical fields, have been somewhat hesitant to embrace New Formalism as a methodology.[35] One probable rea-

---

30. Fradenburg, *Sacrifice Your Love*, 2–4, 9–12, 14, 28–41.

31. For an overview of this marginalization, see Wolfson, "Reading for Form," 5.

32. Ibid., 6.

33. "Foreign Offices of British Fiction," 181.

34. "What Is New Formalism?" 562.

35. This is not to say there has been no formalist scholarship; far from it, as Seth Lerer has shown, there have long been certain medieval literatures (notably lyrics) that have attracted tremendous formalist attention. But, as Lerer also notes, a renewed for-

son why is that in order to be a medievalist, one *must* be a serious historian; there is no getting around the historical method in medieval literary
studies, nor would anyone want there to be. For that reason, though it cut
its teeth in early modern studies, New Historicism has taken a strong and
steady hold of medieval literary studies. For good reason, medievalists are
unwilling to give up "the historical" as a primary analytic category.

Happily, we do not need to give it up; nor do we need to hold formalism
at arm's length. The way out of this methodological conundrum involves
scholars' recognition that form and historicity are kissing cousins.[36] A
prominent case in point, Christopher Cannon has suggested that "formalism" in medieval studies needs to orient itself historically, in Aristotelian notions of form. Cannon's mode of formalist criticism moves away
from New Critical assessments of value and style and instead toward a notion that, for medieval writers, form *is* matter—the real, tangible building
blocks and historical devices of the literary text.[37] This particular resituating of "form" allows Cannon to suggest that in the Middle Ages, forms
are not separate from history but are, as the real, substantial "matter" of
the literary text, imbued with their own contemporary historical environ-
ment.[38] Formalism is thus not belle-lettrism; it is not a denial of the presence of history in the world. Quite the contrary, it is a tool for handling

---

malist methodology—as distinct from the New Criticism—in medieval studies needs
to account for how and where ideology and aesthetics come together. As he puts it, "The
formalist approach to Middle English studies, then, should not be limited to classroom
close readings or mere appreciation. It should, as I have claimed here, reveal ways in
which our current, overarching historicism still contends with the legacy of formalism
and how, in that contention, certain groups of texts or classes of material may lose out.
But an attention to the forms of Middle English texts can show us something of their
material history: their presentation in manuscript contexts, their participation in the
politics of metrical choice, their own adjudications between form and history. But in
the end perhaps, in spite of the best efforts of historicists, whenever readers come to
texts that dare bewitch us with their poetry and song, there will be formalists to lead
us through that spell." Lerer, "Endurance of Formalism in Middle English Studies,"
10–11.

36. As early as 1989, Alan Liu argued that New Historicism itself, despite its overt
denials of the supervening importance of form in literary studies, was nevertheless
subtly indebted from its inception to "formalism" as a way of dealing with literature.
In Liu's view, "[I]t is simply not the case that the New Historicism is different from
formalism. It is more true to say that it is an ultimate formalism so 'powerful' that it
colonizes the very world as its 'text'" ("Power of Formalism," 754–55).

37. *Grounds of English Literature*, 1–15.

38. Ibid., 6.

the world, history, and all things material because it is, itself, the material of literature. Revising Lukàcs's dictum with Cannon's theory in mind, we might say that form is the truly *historical* element in literature.[39]

Practicing Literary Theory in the Middle Ages likewise understands form as inescapably historical, but it focuses on a history in which literary form is especially central: the history of how literary theories about ethics are put into practice in English between 1380 and 1422. During this narrow band of time, medieval writers find in form their primary tool for exploring the possibility of producing ethically transformative literature. *Practicing Literary Theory in the Middle Ages* discloses a formal, aesthetic logic by which a properly *literary* ethics emerges and evolves in late medieval literary culture, and it takes a particular literary topos—the mixed-form protreptic—as its test case.

ORGANIZATION OF THE BOOK

Once it establishes in detail how the mixed form works for Boethius, my first chapter shows how Alain de Lille, Dante Alighieri, and Guillaume de Machaut each reengage with the twin paradigm of prosimetrum and protrepsis. These continental literary experiments with transformative protrepsis and the mixed form of prosimetrum are far from naïve mimicry of an initial Boethian paradigm. Quite the contrary, the association of prosimetrum with ethical transformation provides the most fertile ground for literary experiment when medieval authors reinvestigate and often challenge the possibility that literature has any innately transformational ethical power, or that that power could inhere in aesthetic choices. Through these continental medieval writers' ongoing experiments with the relationship between protrepsis and prosimetrum, the association of mixed-form writing with transformative function becomes a laboratory for a vernacular practice of literary theory. It becomes a laboratory for thinking through how literature works, by thematizing protrepsis—ethical transformation—as a possible narrative goal and theorizing the relationship between form and function, between aesthetics and ethics.

Entering into this literary-theoretical laboratory, Chaucer experiments with the association between protreptic function and the mixed form

---

39. For other recent studies that think through the interdependence of form and history in similar terms, see M. Nolan, *John Lydgate and the Making of Public Culture*, 3–14; Trilling, *Aesthetics of Nostalgia*, 3–27; Chaganti, *Medieval Poetics of the Reliquary*, 155–69; Brantley, *Reading in the Wilderness*, 1–6, 301–6.

through much of his career, beginning with his translation of Boethius's mixed-form *Consolation of Philosophy* into his own Middle English prose *Boece*, moving through his *Troilus and Criseyde,* and culminating in his *Canterbury Tales.* As my second chapter shows, in his translation of the *Consolation,* the mixed form and its transformative function serve primarily as a challenge to think through the formal capacities of prose and to devise a practice of vernacular prose writing that could be equal to the aesthetically and ethically transformative goals of a Latin prosimetrum. The aesthetic prose that Chaucer develops ultimately stands up not only to the ethical mandates of prosimetrum but also to contemporary vernacular theories about the nature and function of prose as a vehicle for literary truth. But, as I explain toward the end of the chapter, Chaucer's experiments with a prose style that could be ethical and aesthetic in the same breath also lead him to some of his most innovative experiments with stanzaic verse form.

Building on the aesthetic experiments of the *Boece, Troilus and Criseyde* reaches deeper into the narrative and structural logic of the *Consolation,* to consider how a narrator's transformation can be represented in vernacular literary fiction and what kinds of formal and stylistic maneuvers might make that transformation exportable to a readership. My third chapter suggests that the poem does so by reconceiving prosimetrum as a dialectic between the narrator and his narrative, rather than between formal verse and prose. In so doing, the *Troilus,* picking up on the formal maneuvers and literary-theoretical investigations of Guillaume de Machaut's *Remède de Fortune,* reveals some of the chinks in Boethius's literary-theoretical armor, showing prosimetrum to be an artificially constructed topos of ethically transformative writing rather than a natural requirement for it. In the process, the *Troilus* also enacts an elegant and surprising defense of tragedy as an ethical mode.

Chaucer's most playful use of prosimetrum and most concerted experimentation with protreptic writing, however, arises in the *Canterbury Tales,* the earliest free-standing, fully fledged prosimetric work in Middle English, which stages and restages self-conscious concerns about literature's efficacy in provoking ethical renewal, and stages them as crises of form. But, as my fourth chapter demonstrates, these concerns prove liberating rather than crippling: when the *Tales* conclude, they have moved into an understanding of prosimetric literary practice and protreptic theory as sophisticated and supple methods for justifying a large-scale project of transformative fiction, as well as for setting that fiction on sure feet in literary history. Chaucer's career, then, manifests an internalization, interrogation, and reinvention of the twin paradigm of prosimetrum and ethical transformation—its movement from a paradigm for exploring the aesthetic nature of ethical learning to a recognizable mode of representing ethical transformation in a narrator who is also a protagonist and putative "author" of the stories he tells, and who is keen to theorize how and whether literary learning is truly exportable to an audience.

Writing contemporaneously with or shortly after Chaucer, and in dialogue with his works, Thomas Usk, John Gower, and Thomas Hoccleve understand both the seriousness of mixed-form narratives of ethical transformation and the possibility of demystifying classical ideas of literary transformation by reimagining those transformations in vernacular poetry. Engaging with and reinventing both Boethius's *Consolation* and Chaucer's *Boece*, Usk realizes the ethical potential available in the twin form as well as its utility in exploring how prose alone might be used to embody transformative writing. At the same time, my fifth chapter suggests, he also registers an apologetic and political force in Boethius's paradigm. This registering of apologetics and politics as elements of the ethical plan of the *Consolation* induces Usk to experiment with how prose form alone might create a *better* fiction of a narrator's transformation and a better vehicle for a broad-based, socially minded, and decidedly apologetic protrepsis than the mixed form could do—at least in the cultural context of late fourteenth-century English literary culture.

John Gower's *Confessio amantis*, in conversation not only with Boethius but also with Martianus Capellus, with Alain de Lille, and with Chaucer, reinvents the mixed form and its transformative function in its own terms—as an alternation of English vernacular narration with Latinate lyricism in the head verses. Though the *Confessio* seems, on the surface, rather somber, Gower's linguistic revision of the mixed-form modality of staging a narrator's transformation leans by degrees away from serious philosophy and toward a fluent and decidedly comical reengagement with the very idea of literary transformation, as well as with the idea that transformation should require any *forme fixe* for its realization. For Gower, the mixed-form paradigm for transformative writing has become available not only to meditations on the nature of literature's aesthetic powers but also to demystifications of those powers.

The final chapter shows that the demystification of the mixed-form framework for protreptic works continues into the fifteenth century, culminating in the works of Thomas Hoccleve, a reader and scribe of both

Chaucer's and Gower's literary production.[40] Hoccleve's engagement with
Boethius, too, is obvious thematically throughout his corpus, but nowhere
more than in his *Series*, in which formal and literary-theoretical gestures
toward Boethius are organizing, pervasive, and more iconoclastic than in
Gower's work or in Chaucer's. Hoccleve's work reveals the penetration of
Boethian literary theory into English literary consciousness, though his
particular deployment of that theory registers an interest in defamiliariz-
ing the idea of protrepsis and its relation to the mixed form. Indeed, judg-
ing by Hoccleve's works in particular, and by how the first two poems of
his *Series* set a reader up to encounter that work as a whole, the theory
and practice of transformative fiction and the mixed form have become
as valuable in the breach as in the honoring in late Middle English poetry.
The association of protrepsis with the mixed form has already proven an
explosively exciting provocation for medieval literary practice and theory.

In my conclusion, I suggest why this experimentation happens when it
does and how its study might offer up new ways of thinking about formal
topoi in literary history.

40. "Apparently to supplement his livelihood, Hoccleve joined with other professional scribes to copy and disseminate the works of Lancastrian poets such as John
Gower. By working jointly on a transcription of the *Confessio Amantis* with the
two scribes who also produced the landmark manuscripts of the *Canterbury Tales*—
Hengwrt, Ellesmere, Harley 7334 and Corpus Christi 198—Hoccleve took a hands-on
role in manufacturing the literary works by the authors whose standing at the head of
the English tradition he labored so diligently to promote." Bowers, "Thomas Hoccleve
and the Politics of Tradition," 356.

CHAPTER ONE

Formal Experiments with Ethical Writing: Prosimetrum and Protrepsis

If the evolution of the mixed-form topos of protreptic writing has a prime mover, as I have suggested, it is Boethius's *Consolation of Philosophy*. Part of what makes this work a particularly important initiator of the literary history that *Practicing Literary Theory in the Middle Ages* will tell is that it carefully teaches its readers how it should be read and experienced. The *Consolation* practices the literary principles that it theorizes, and it theorizes them explicitly as it practices them. It is thus a work of literary theory-in-practice. Throughout, the *Consolation* treats prose as the form that embodies rational thought and meter as the form that embodies sensuality and pleasure. Also throughout, prose is where dialogue—the back-and-forth Socratic conversation between Philosophy and Boethius—takes place. Meter, on the other hand, is where monologic lyricism occurs, where a single speaker—either Boethius or Philosophy—sings a song. The dual formal embodiment of reason and sensation in dialogic argumentation and monologic lyric is central to the ethically transformative function of the *Consolation*, as is made explicit by Philosophy's own statements throughout her conversation with Boethius. Repeatedly, she signals to him *why* she deploys the twinned forms of prose and meter when she does. In so doing, she foregrounds how meter works in a productive synergy with prose—how meter and prose are in fact mutually necessary to ethical reeducation, via their alternating action of logical dialogue and lyricism. In this foregrounding of the mutual necessity of prose and meter, Philosophy goes far deeper into the ethically transformative logic of the mixed form than did Martianus or his commentators.

Early on and explicitly, the *Consolation* cultivates a tension between prose and poetry—a tension that shows poetry in a decidedly negative light. The *Consolation* opens with a meter, a versified lamentation that

Boethius is forced to sing by poetic muses ("poeticas Musas") who, like vultures, circle around him while he lies imprisoned, prone and vulnerable, on his sickbed.[1] In response to his lamentation, Philosophy, styling herself as his spiritual doctor, makes her first appearance. She decries the poetic muses, claiming they do not promote his healing but merely deepen his pains with their sweet venom: "quae dolores eius non modo nullis remediis fouerent, uerum dulcibus insuper alerent uenenis"[2] (by no means do they support those in sorrow by any remedies but instead always foster sorrow by venomous sweetnesses). The poetic poisoning, Philosophy explains, has soured Boethius's affect and thus blocked him from access to rational thought: "Hae sunt enim quae infructuosis affectuum spinis uberem fructibus rationis segetem necant hominumque mentes assuefaciunt morbo, non liberant."[3] (These [muses] are they who injure the fruitful harvest of reason with the fruitless spines of affects. They get men's minds used to illness; they do not liberate them.) Since rational thought will be key in healing Boethius's addled soul, without further ado she banishes these poetic muses from Boethius's cell—and from the *Consolation*—permanently. Adding extra force to Philosophy's condemnation of the poetic muses, throughout her initial diagnosis of Boethius and her banishment of the muses, she has addressed Boethius in prose, suggesting in form what is implied in content: that the discursive form of rational healing is prose and that poetry is unhealthy and self-indulgent.

This joint valorization of prose and condemnation of poetry, however, quickly grows complicated. Philosophy's first attempt to reason with the desperate Boethius takes place in prose, but that attempt is a conspicuous failure. Seeing the ineffectiveness of her prose discourse, she switches to a metrical song—a surprising move for one who has just banished the "poetic muses" from her ward's bedside. After she sings this first song to Boethius, she asks a question that reveals the essential function of song and meter in Boethius's process of philosophical learning: "Sentisne, inquit, haec, atque animo illabuntur tuo?" ("Do you feel these things," she said, "and do they penetrate into your soul?").[4] Philosophy's diction suggests that she sees her song as a penetrative agent ("illabuntur") that Boethius can feel or sense ("sentisne"). This characterization first reveals

1. Bk. 1, pr. 1, sentence 7.
2. Bk. 1, pr. 1, sentence 8.
3. Bk. 1, pr. 1, sentence 9.
4. Bk. 1, pr. 4, sentence 1.

that Philosophy's healing song acts by penetration; song is useful when prose cannot—quite literally—get through to Boethius. Its piercing action breaks through the affective wall of his sorrows. Second, by evoking "sense," Philosophy's characterization suggests that meter penetrates by producing aesthetic experience—that which can be felt sensually, or perceived by the senses. Evidently, Philosophy needs to use the sensual penetration of metrical song in order to initiate the process of Boethius's philosophical transformation from despair to hope.

Once Philosophy has "pierced" into Boethius via song, however, she immediately recurs to prose, in which she conducts the rational argumentation that is meant to draw Boethius out of his despair. But it is still too soon for her to rely on the rational argumentation that her prose discourse embodies, so she switches once again into song. To explain why she does so, she deploys a medical metaphor that casts song as a poultice or compress that can ease Boethius's psychological pain:

Sed quoniam plurimus tibi affectuum tumultus incubuit diuersumque te dolor ira maeror distrahunt, uti nunc mentis es, nondum te ualidiora remedia contingunt. Itaque lenioribus paulisper utemur, ut quae in tumorem perturbationibus influentibus induruerunt ad acrioris uim medicaminis recipiendam tactu blandiore mollescant.[5]

[But since this multiplicity of tumultuous affects overwhelms you— sorrow, ire, and mourning tear you up—since you are now weak of spirit, stronger remedies cannot yet touch you. So let us briefly use gentler medicines, so that these affects that have hardened in you into a cyst may be softened by a milder touch, until the power of your illness will bear a harsher remedy.]

With this proffer of gentler medicines, Philosophy breaks into a metrical song. Thus, early on, the *Consolation* encourages a reader to see meter as a necessary means of penetrating into one's psyche via one's body, through the action of sensuality and palliation. This gentle palliation paves the way for the "stronger remedy" of rational argumentation in prose. In Philosophy's explicit theory of how prosimetrum has transformative efficacy, meter evidently helps prose do its rational work by easing the patient into readiness for ethical restructuring.

5. Bk. 1, pr. 5, sentences 11–12.

To understand how Philosophy can both banish the "poetic muses" and yet rely on meter's gentle medicinal properties, it is important to remember that in her initial banishment of the "poetic muses," Philosophy does not banish meter per se; she does not, that is, banish the form that poetry is usually written in. Instead, she specifically banishes the *poeticas musas*—whom she seems to understand as a dangerous subtype of metrical utterance that works exclusively by amplifying negative affect.[6] What she seems to find most objectionable in "poetry" is how it encourages indulgence in self-pity, which in turn contributes to false and deceptive beliefs. Poetry, for her, seems to be a designation of *content*, rather than a designation of form: the poetry Philosophy banishes, in effect, is tragic fiction—false, sorrow-inducing, antiphilosophical lamentation, not metrical song writ large. Apart from this affectively negative mode of song, Philosophy recognizes an ongoing and undeniable utility to song in both working and representing Boethius's transformation.

Even so, the *Consolation* also acknowledges that meter's transformative powers have their limits. Upon hearing a meter Philosophy has sung to ease his heart, Boethius again recognizes song's saving powers, but he now also laments that some sorrows lie too deep for song's aesthetic reach:

Speciosa quidem ista sunt, inquam, oblitaque rhetoricae ac musicae melle dulcedinis tum tantum, cum audiuntur, oblectant, sed miseris malorum altior sensus est; itaque cum haec auribus insonare desierint insitus animum maeror praegrauat.[7]

[These are beautiful utterances, I said, and are anointed with the honey sweetness of rhetoric and musicso that, when they are heard, they please. But for the wretched there is a deeper sense of misfortunes. And therefore when these pleasing things cease to sound in their ears, this deep-set sorrow wearies the spirit.]

Boethius recognizes that song brings pleasure while sung, but he insists that once the sweetness and beauty of the words have departed from the

---

6. Indeed the word *poetry* appears nowhere in the *Consolation* except in this opening scene; Philosophy's and Boethius's later metrical utterances are consistently referred to simply as "songs."

7. Bk. 2, pr. 3, sentence 2.

senses, one is left with one's agonies. Sensual pleasure is thus depicted as a necessary but limited tool for psychological transformation. With these assertions Philosophy agrees outright, saying that the sweetness of song is not a full remedy for Boethius's psychological ills, but insisting that it is nevertheless a critical part of his healing process, since it draws off his excessive sorrows.

[H]aec enim nondum morbi tui remedia, sed adhuc contumacis aduersum curationem doloris fomenta quaedam sunt; nam quae in profundum sese penetrent cum tempestiuum fuerit admouebo.[8]

[For these things are not yet remedies for your illness, but they are certain poultices for your sorrow, which is stubborn toward your cure. When the time comes, I will give you something that will get deep inside you.]

Song works sensually and pleasurably, to produce affective change in a hearer. That affective change—the removal of sorrow and introduction of pleasure—is necessary to the work of rational reeducation. Only after the senses are eased by pleasure can the real work of philosophical reasoning take place. That philosophical reasoning then takes place in prose. Prose is thus cast as the vehicle of serious philosophical interrogation in the *Consolation*, the intellectual substance to which the meter acts merely as sensory facilitator. Song is again cast as a necessary prerequisite to the "stronger medicines" Philosophy will administer later on in prose.

But the relation of prose to meter grows yet more nuanced as the *Consolation* continues. In book 4, Philosophy both reveals the true nature of prose argumentation and also deepens a sense of why meter is a necessary adjunct to it:

Sed uideo te iam dudum et pondere quaestionis oneratum et rationis prolixitate fatigatum aliquam carminis exspectare dulcedinem; accipe igitur haustum quo refectus firmior in ulteriora contendas.[9]

[But now I see that you are pressed down by the heaviness of my questioning and that you are fatigued by the prolixity of my reasoning and

8. Bk. 2, pr. 3, sentences 3–4.
9. Bk. 4, pr. 6, sentence 57.

that you await the sweetness of song; take this draft that will refresh
you and make you abler to wrestle with later matters.]

Philosophy again represents song as the space for pleasure, delight, and
sweetness; but now, that sweetness is used less to lighten Boethius's sorrows than to lighten what seems to be the innate burden of prose, where
heavy, wordy reasoning and onerous interrogations take place. Song's
sweetness evidently is useful not simply as a preparation for prose but also
as a reprieve from it. Thus, although meter is repeatedly suggested to have
slightly less power in producing true and salvific new understanding in
Boethius than prose, it is nevertheless clear that Boethius's transformation can dispense with the songful delight of meter no more easily than
with the heavy and sometimes onerous rational argumentation of prose.
By this point, *The Consolation of Philosophy* appears as a metapoetic
work, a work of literary theory-in-practice, foregrounding the formal con-
ditions by which it pursues its ethically transformative, protreptic end and
outlining distinct and seemingly innate functionalities for both prose and
meter.

    This explicit theory of how the mixed form achieves its transforma-
tive function is apparent to and made explicit by medieval commentators. William of Conches explains that song serves to draw off negative
affect and introduce positive affect, while prose is the appropriate space
for heavier, more linear, organized logical argumentation: "In prosa igitur
Boetius utitur ratione ad consolationem, in metro interponit delectatio-
nem, ut dolor remoueatur" (Therefore, in prose Boethius uses reason for
consolation; in meter he interposes delight, to remove sorrow).[10] William's
commentary notes that Boethian song has a sensual and palliative effect,
which then paves the way for the rational argument of prose. William
thus registers that the form of Boethius's writing is inseparable from its
consoling function, though he also apparently realizes that prose is the
more powerful form—what produces the actual "consolationem"—while
song is useful merely in removing unwanted affective blockages out of the
way. It is through this twin form that the ethical renewal of the *Consolation* takes place. In the *Consolation of Philosophy*, prosimetrum becomes
the form of philosophy, the form of comfort, the form necessary to produce Boethius's psychological transformation. In its crossing of prose and
metrical forms, it is construed by commentators as the aesthetic correla-

10. *Glosae super Boetium*, p. 6, lines 61–63.

tive of ethical transformation—being a crossing of forms, quite literally, a trans-formation.

THE CONSOLATION OF CAUSALITY: THE SENSIBILITY OF PROSE

But the affective and rational transformation programmed into Boethian prosimetrum is not the whole story of how his formal choices undergird the ethical transformation that his work models. Having laid out the skeleton of Boethian metapoetics, I will now demonstrate how prose and meter are styled differently at a local scale to create discrete aesthetic effects and, thence, to initiate soul-transforming understanding in Boethius. As I have noted, throughout the *Consolation*, prose is the form of dialogue, while meter is the form of monologue.[11] I use these terms literally: where there is prose, there are two voices, both Boethius and Philosophy, which are in conversation with each other. Where there is meter, there is a single voice, either Boethius or Philosophy, which sings a lyrical song that erupts out of the dialogic narrative. The dialogic proses pit Philosophy's Socratic questioning against Boethius's responses: they show Boethius's understandings and his misunderstandings, and they show Philosophy's measured and rational responses to them. In the ongoing conversation between teacher and student, the proses advance propositions, consider possible consequences and alternative understandings, formulate and reformulate questions, and eventually arrive at logical conclusions. Throughout the *Consolation*, then, dialogic prose is the form of rational argumentation.[12] Precisely how the proses are formally designed to render rational argumentation persuasive for Boethius and, by extension, for the reader is what we must next address.

As discussed above, Boethius represents meter as the form appropriate to the affective and sweetly sensual pleasure of protreptic transformation, while he represents prose as the form appropriate to its hard, rational work. To be sure, meter's capacity to afford aesthetic pleasure and engender positive affect is a necessary adjunct to the rational argumentation

---

11. Describing late medieval French mixed-form works, Maureen Boulton also notes that the lyrical interpolations are monologic in nature, even if the larger works in which they appear are dialogic (*Song in the Story*, 24, 22–23).

12. See also Scarry, "Well-Rounded Sphere," 103–5, and Wetherbee, *Platonism and Poetry*, 74–82, who note that argument is what happens in the prose sections.

of prose. But to read the meters as the only "aesthetic" passages of the work, because they are explicitly characterized as "sweet" and "delightful" to the senses, is to overlook the fact that the prose passages, too, are "aesthetic"—designed by their style to be sense-perceptible. In a question she asks Boethius immediately after a prose explication of universal order, Philosophy reveals that prose, like meter, creates feeling or sensation: "Tum illa: Cum haec, inquit, ita *sentias* . . ."[13] (Then she said, Since you sense these things . . .). She asserts not that he understands intellectually but instead that he can feel—can perceive in his senses—the truths she expresses in prose. Prose, like meter, is theorized as a verbal mode of engaging with sensation.

Sensation matters in Philosophy's practice of teaching ethics to Boethius because it ultimately produces "assent" and "consent" in him, literally the "feeling toward" and "feeling with" her assertions that are necessary to his learning. After Philosophy moves gradually through a series of prose propositions demonstrating that worldly happiness is false, she arrives at her conclusion: "Haec igitur uel imagines ueri boni uel imperfecta quaedam bona dare mortalibus uidentur, uerum autem atque perfectum bonum conferre non possunt." (Therefore these things [i.e., earthly wealth and power] either seem to be likenesses of true goodness, or else they seem to give to mortal people a type of goodness that is not perfect. But the good that is true and perfect, that is the good that they cannot give.) To this conclusion, Boethius simply assents: "Assentior"[14] (I assent). Later, in the twelfth prose of book 3, after a lengthy passage of Philosophy's reason, Boethius declares, "Uehementer assentior"[15] (I assent vehemently). In book 5, as Boethius's ethical transformation nears its culmination, his soul turns toward his teacher, and he grants, once again, his consent to her prose teachings: "Animaduerto . . . idque uti tu dicis ita esse consentio"[16] (My soul turns toward you . . . and I consent that it is as you say). The end of all of Philosophy's careful explication is to elicit from Boethius his assent, his agreement and submission to the transformative and salvific truth of her teaching. This dynamic is repeated time and again as Philosophy reshapes Boethius's consciousness through her prose reasoning. Prose, as much as meter, is theorized as sensory, operating on the senses to produce Boethius's assent and consent to be ethically renewed.

13. Bk. 3, pr. 12, sentence 9.
14. Bk. 3, pr. 9, sentences 30–32.
15. Bk. 3, pr. 12, sentence 15.
16. Bk. 5, pr. 2, sentence 1.

To fail to consider the possibility that the truths of the prose sections must actually be *felt*, must be sensed, if they are to produce assent in an audience is to overlook one of Boethius's central literary-theoretical insights and one of his primary provocations to later medieval prose stylists. But to consider this possibility raises a question: how does one cultivate a prose style that promotes some "sense," some aesthetic correlative, of the ethical contents of a work?[17] How, that is, does one use the particular formal capacities of prose to make ethical ideation tangible and thereby more efficacious in producing assent to conform to that ethos?

This assent, in Mark Miller's view, is produced "dialectically," by the ongoing back-and-forth dialogue between Boethius and Philosophy, during which the former is gradually brought around to the beliefs of the latter.[18] For Miller, the intensive focus on dialectical learning originates in Boethius's will to understand psychological phenomena "such as repression, disavowal, perversion, fetishism, and masochism."[19] But rather than focusing on the discrete beliefs associated with exploratory psychology, Miller contends that the most important question to ask of Boethius's work is how it "investigate[s] the problems that animate [it.]"[20] Miller's observation that the "how" questions are crucial to an understanding of Boethius's significance both internally and as an inspiration for later works of philosophical poetry seems to me entirely right, as does his insistence that the dialogic element of the narrative is central to its ethical efficacy. But I would like to drill deeper into how the local stylistic construction of the prose sections of the *Consolation*—the places in Boethius's work where dialogue takes place—produces assent.

The dialogic interactions between Philosophy and Boethius are persuasive ultimately because of how they lay out a particular sense experience,

17. This idea that intellectual understanding exists on a spectrum with sensation reflects a widely held medieval notion, phrased by Robert Pasnau thus: "both sensation and intellection are 'a kind of being affected'" (*Theories of Cognition in the Later Middle Ages*, 126). For a more detailed treatment of how Boethius's *Consolation* takes up the relation of physical sensation to intellectual knowing, see again Scarry, "Well-Rounded Sphere," 95–96. What Scarry calls the medieval "hierarchy of cognitive faculties," as thematized by the *Consolation*, runs from sense to imagination, from imagination to reason, from reason to insight.

18. "[I]t is this dialectical character that finally matters most both for an assessment of Boethius's philosophical achievement and for an assessment of that achievement's importance to Chaucer" (*Philosophical Chaucer*, 112).

19. Ibid., 113.

20. Ibid., 145.

one that is absolutely central to Philosophy's theory of salvation from despair. Throughout their arguments, Philosophy's and Boethius's comments
are styled to foreground the logical causality that underpins their ideation.
A typical prose passage begins with Boethius remembering Philosophy's
last point ("memento etenim corollarii illius"[21] [for I remember the corol-
laries to those previous things]. Then Philosophy turns to explain a number of consequences to Boethius's new understanding. These consequences
are marked by a series of "igiturs" (therefores) that convey a sense of the
causal relation among the ideas. ("Est *igitur* praemium bonorum . . . *igitur*
probes probitas ipsa fit praemium . . . Si *igitur* sese ipsi aestimareuelint . . .
Hoc igitur modo quidquid a bono deficit . . . Euenit *igitur* ut quem trans-
formatum uitiis uideas, hominem aestimare non possis").[22] These *igiturs*
are interspersed with other rhetorical markers of causality, such as "cui
consequens est" and "necesse est," so that the prose of this passage is rhetorically styled to foreground the causal relations among ideas through its
use of argumentative markers.[23]

The importance of causality to Philosophy's transformative consolation becomes explicit a few sections later, when she describes how the
elegant workings of the universe are bound together by an "indissolubili
causarum conexione"[24] (indissoluble connection of causes). This causal
connection, she explains, emanates from providence ("ab immobilis proui-
dentiae proficiscatur exordiis"[25] [it goes forth from the unchanging order
of providence]), which calls into being the ineluctable order of causes ("in-
declinabilem causarum ordinem").[26] According to Philosophy, nothing
emerges from nothing; all events in human life are caused and are fore-
seen by the unchanging order of the universe. Fortune is thus phantasmatic, a false understanding of the world, based on a failure to understand
that mankind is ultimately protected by providence. Philosophy recurs
to this idea and, at the end of the first prose of book 5, defines chance
or fortune explicitly as a failure to perceive causes, saying, "Licet igitur
definire casum esse inopinatum ex confluentibus causis in his quae ob
aliquid geruntur euentum"[27] (One may therefore define happenstance as

---

21. Bk. 4, pr. 3, sentence 8.
22. Bk. 4, pr. 3.
23. Bk. 4, pr. 3.
24. Bk. 4, pr. 6, sentence 19.
25. Bk. 4, pr. 6, sentence 19.
26. Bk. 4, pr. 6, sentence 20.
27. Bk. 5, pr. 1, sentence 18.

an unforeseen outcome, from the flowing together of causes, in situations which happened for some other purpose). The consolation of divine providence is that it secures order and causality in human life, whether human beings see it or not. Causality is part and parcel of Philosophy's consoling teaching; it is part and parcel of Boethian protrepsis.

Causality's centrality to Boethian protrepsis is why the *Consolation*'s prose is styled as it is: the *Consolation* makes causality available to Boethius aesthetically—sensibly—through dialogic, argumentative prose, through local style. Through their stylistic aestheticization of argumentative causality, the proses embody the divine order of which Philosophy reminds Boethius in the content of her discourse. Philosophy spells out this special function of prose explicitly when she distinguishes it from song: "Quodsi te musici carminis oblectamenta delectant, hanc oportet paulisper differas uoluptatem dum nexas sibi ordine contexo rationes"[28] (Although the pleasures of song delight you, you must forbear such pleasure for now, while I weave together for you a nexus of ordered reasons). Where song and music bring Boethius pleasure and delight, prose works by weaving reasons together by *order*. By sequencing logical propositions in order, showing each to be causally linked to the one that preceded it, prose models the causal order of the universe; prose is thus the aesthetic correlative of causal order itself. As such, prose argumentation enables Boethius to feel the consolation of causality, to discern the supervening divine vision that encompasses all things and grounds them in a meaningful order. Through prose dialogue, the *Consolation* aestheticizes the argumentative flow of its ideation, making sensory the very sequential, linear, continuous order that Boethius is supposed to feel and understand. By feeling his way through the causal order of his prose dialogue with Philosophy, Boethius is sensibly reformed and healed.

But the linear, dialogic order of the prose sections is not the only aesthetic lesson Boethius is meant to feel over the course of his reeducation. The meters, like the proses, embody a philosophical comfort, which, as I have shown, the *Consolation* sometimes describes as "sweet relief," sometimes as "gentler medicine" than the harsh tonic of prose. But there is another level of meaning in Boethius's theory and practice of meter, one that arrogates more immediate cognitive power to the meters themselves. Although the proses are the space for linear, sequential, causal order, they do not hold an exclusive monopoly on rational work. Indeed, by focusing too closely on the prose passages as "logical" and "rational," we

28. Bk. 4, pr. 6, sentence 6.

miss how the songs are deeply "rational" (i.e., capable of carrying coherent cognitive content) even if they are not "logical" (i.e., dialogic or argumentative). Meters, like proses, are designed to produce consent in an audience by engaging with their senses toward a production of intellective understanding.

THE CONSOLATION OF HARMONY: THE SENSE OF METER

After Philosophy has sung a meter to Boethius, midway through the *Consolation*, she asks him whether her song has persuaded him of the truths of her teachings. In response, Boethius says, "Assentior . . . cuncta enim firmissimis nexa rationibus constant"[29] (I assent . . . as these things stand woven together by most firm reasons). Not only does Boethius "assent"—suggesting again that he has felt or "sensed" the truth of Philosophy's song—but he assents because the song has bodied forth a sturdy interweaving of reasons. Evidently, songs, like prose, can mobilize reason sensibly in the service of understanding, inducing Boethius to "assent." Though it is not the linear, argumentative, sequentially ordered reason of logic that comes in the proses, the meters are nevertheless styled and designed to render a specific and decidedly "rational" kind of cognitive understanding.

The "rational" understanding that the metrical portions of the *Consolation* are designed and theorized to render is an understanding of musical harmony. Although it is not immediately obvious why this should be so—why one should think of the meters as designed to embody harmony and why Boethius might have expected his audience to grasp their ability to do so—it is important to remember that the *Consolation* frequently calls its meters "songs" or "music" and calls attention thematically to harmony and songfulness repeatedly over the course of its narrative.[30] As I will explain, this pinning of metrical form onto musical function is far from acci-

29. Bk. 3, pr. 11, sentence 1.

30. Seth Lerer provides a reading of Boethius's meter about Orpheus that highlights the paralleling of poetic form and musical function in the *Consolation* (*Boethius and Dialogue*, 154–60). Scarry also draws upon Boethius's theory of music in her analysis of how the meters in his *Consolation* work, though Scarry sees this musical, poetic mode as one eventually to be overcome by the higher cognitive work that happens in prose ("Well-Rounded Sphere," 102–3).

dental: the meters are verbal embodiments of music, and they, like music, constitute intellective events unto themselves, though they also remain decisively rooted in sensory experience.

To see how the meters contribute formally to Boethius's transformation, it is useful to turn to Boethius's most explicit theorization of the feeling and intellection of music, articulated in his *De institutione musica*.[31] According to this treatise, God has established proportions, numbers, and ratios to govern and regulate the entire created world. Music (or song) results from the balancing of these proportions, numbers, and ratios into patterns of like quantities.[32] Three types of music exist: cosmic, human, and instrumental. Cosmic music results from the proportionality of distances between stars and planets. Human music, which ties body and soul together, is produced by proportions and numbers within the soul itself. The third kind of music, instrumental, is produced by musical instruments and is built, like cosmic and human music, out of proportions, ratios, and numbers—this time, the proportions, ratios, and numbers of strings and pipe lengths. Crucially, the same proportions and numbers that exist between the stars exist in a song or piece of music, as well as in the human body and human soul. Thus, a single system of proportional numbers and ratios runs throughout all of God's creation, binding the universe together in a unified and unifying system of harmony.[33]

The perception of instrumental music's harmonious proportions is salutary because, in those proportions, human beings perceive the like proportions and ratios within their own souls. Through that perception of likeness, they perceive their own harmonious and rational likeness to the cosmos, the harmonious relationship they share with all of God's creation. Thus, the essential power of music is to produce an awareness of si-

31. *De institutione musica* was tremendously influential throughout the Middle Ages: see Chadwick, *Consolations of Music*, 80–101; Chamberlain, "Philosophy of Music"; Crocker, "Musica Rhythmica and Musica Metrica."

32. For an overview not just of Boethius's theory of music and harmony but also of the Platonic and Ptolemaic traditions with which it is engaged, see Chadwick, *Consolations of Music*, 80–101.

33. As Chadwick puts it, in his elucidation of chapter 2 of the first book of *De institutione*, "[Boethius] distinguishes three kinds of music: cosmic, human, and instrumental . . . Cosmic harmony also means the holding together in consonance and equilibrium of the four elements of earth, air, fire, and water . . . Harmonia in Greek never loses its root meaning of the fitting together of disparate, potentially conflicting elements" (*Consolations of Music*, 81–82).

militude, arising from the perception of a rational and harmonic likeness
between the soul, the universe, and God:

> Cum enim ex eo, quod in nobis est junctum convenienterque coapta-
> tum, illud excipimus, quod in sonis apte convenienterque conjunctum
> est, eoque delectamur, nos quoque ipsos eadem *similitudine* com-
> pactos esse cognoscimus.[34]

> [For when we hear what is properly and harmoniously united in sound
> in conjunction with that which is harmoniously coupled and joined
> together within us and are attracted to it, then we recognize that we
> ourselves are put together in its *likeness*.][35]

In a very real sense, human beings do not "like" music; music "likes" them,
precisely because it makes aesthetically perceptible their own proportional
and rational "likeness" to God. Instead of being logical, in Boethius's practice and theory music is fundamentally *analogical*: it arises from the perception of like ratios, balanced proportions, and measurements.[36]

This analogical function—music's power to aestheticize likeness—
engages both the rational faculty and the sensory. Music produces a sensory understanding of the harmonious nature of the universe, and does so
through the sensory perception of likeness.[37] Like prose argumentation,
music is both cognitive and aesthetic. But whereas prose argument works
by linear, sequential, dialogic order, music works by analogical harmony,

34. Boethius, *De institutione musica*, Patrologia Latina 63, col. 1168C–D. My
emphasis.

35. *Fundamentals of Music*, trans. Bower, 180 (1.1). My emphasis. As Chamberlain
explains, for Boethius, "the relationship between soul and body is clearly moral as well
as mathematical" ("Philosophy of Music," 83).

36. Indeed, "analogy" in Greek simply means "likeness of proportions." *OED*, s.v.
"analogy," etymology, "mathematical proportion, proportion in general, correspon-
dence, resemblance." Boethius was, among other things, a prolific translator from
Greek into Latin and would likely have been quite aware of this etymology.

37. Boethius acknowledges music as both a sensory and a cognitive mode later in
the treatise, saying, "Nulla enim magis ad animum disciplinis via, quam auribus patet.
Cum ergo per eas rhythmi modique ad animum usque descenderint, dubitari non potest
quin aequo modo mentem atque ipsa sunt efficiant atque conforment" (*De institutione
musica*, col. 1169A–B). (No path to the mind is as open for instruction as the sense
of hearing. Thus, when rhythms and modes reach an intellect through the ears, they
doubtless affect and reshape that mind according to their particular character.) *Fundamentals of Music*, trans. Bower, 3.

offering an aesthetic of likeness rather than of argumentative sequence. It is this kind of aesthetic experience that takes place in Boethius's meters.[38] Singing the meters that he sings and hearing the meters that Philosophy sings to him, Boethius is gradually healed by the feeling of analogic harmony. But how, formally, does that healing take place? What about the formal structure of the meters enables them to facilitate this recognition of harmonious likeness?

Writing a century after Boethius, Isidore of Seville provides a definition of classical meter that helps to explain how Boethius's meters work formally to reproduce music's ability to aestheticize harmony, likeness, and analogy as sources of philosophical consolation. According to Isidore, meter is verbal organization by a certain number of feet, each of a certain length. There are, he notes, a wide range of meters, in both Greek and Latin, from elegiac to heroic, and these consist of different types of feet, such as iambs, dactyls, and trochees. But regardless of which metrical pattern a metricist chooses, what makes for good meter is consistency of line lengths and metrical patterns within a song.[39] Conceived as the requirement of lines of like lengths and types and numbers of feet, meter has a signal cognitive and aesthetic function, one very close to that of music: it cultivates in the narrating Boethius a sensitivity to likeness itself.[40]

---

38. Chamberlain has suggested that the *Consolation* is a test case for the theory of music that Boethius outlined in *De institutione musica*. He sees Philosophy as a great *musicus*, or musician, because she not only uses music to delight Boethius but also subjects it to the discernments of cognitive understanding and rational assessment. Chamberlain's reading of the *Consolation* as a realization of *De institutione*'s theories focuses on the former's meters as *thematic* embodiments of the ideas in the latter, rather than as practical, formal demonstrations of those ideas ("Philosophy of Music," 86, 85, 88, 89).

39. *Etymologiae*, bk. 1, chap. 39, lines 28–30. "Metra vocata, quia certis pedum mensuris atque spatiis terminantur, neque ultra dimensionem temporum constitutam procedunt. Mensura enim Graece μέτρον dicitur." [Those things are called meters which are completed with a certain measure and space of feet and proceed by no other assembled dimension of times. Measures therefore in Greek are called "metron."]

40. Boethius's practice and theory of the mixed form foreshadow Roman Jakobson's theory of prose and poetry. Jakobson describes prose as a linear, logical, temporally diachronic form, while understanding poetry as a nonlinear, nonlogical, and synchronic form. For Jakobson, prose works metonymically, by relations of contiguity, whereas poetry works metaphorically, by relations of similarity. Moreover, Jakobson argues that the metrical regularities and "phonic equivalences" of poetry contribute to a reader's perception of similarity and/or contrast. Jakobson, "Two Aspects of Language and Two Types of Aphasic Disturbances," 91 and 95.

The perception of metrical analogy—the likeness of proportion in line lengths—cultivates Boethius's openness to other forms of analogy in metrical writing, just as musical "analogy" is supposed to cultivate a hearer's openness to feeling the supervening harmony of the universe. Meter's formal architectures of likeness—its rhythm, meter, rhyme, and proportions—create a sensitivity to other types of likeness and analogy in Boethius's mind, much as the experience of instrumental harmony produces an awareness of the rational harmonies in the hearer's soul. The alliterations, rhythms, line lengths, and likenesses create formal analogies, then, that body forth the idea of music set out in *De institutione musica*, but do so in meter, in rhythm, in sonic repetition, and in words. The metrical and rhythmical parity within a meter establishes an architecture of likeness in which to create cognitive experiences that are also always aesthetic experiences—intellectual understandings of likeness that come through visual and aural perception of likeness. The metrical experience of likeness facilitates a mode of learning whose "rational" character lies in its being meditative, analogical, and empathic rather than argumentative, logical, and disputative.[41] For Boethius, metrical song is, like music, a mode of reeducation, a mode of eliciting assent to psychological healing and renewal, which works via resonance and likeness, rather than by the causal reordering of prose argumentation.

This aestheticization of harmony undergirds and supports the intricate systems of thematic likeness that suffuse his meters. A case in point is the meter that begins "Quantas rerum flectat," which elucidates for Boethius that all things will naturally return to their own divine origins. The process of teaching begins with Philosophy's example of imprisoned Carthaginian "lions":[42]

> Quamuis Poeni pulchra leones
> uincula gestent manibusque datas

---

41. William of Conches's commentary on the Boethian meters emphasizes this logic of likeness and analogy in its unpacking of similes early on: in his commentary to an image in the second meter of book 1, for instance, William says, "Hoc dictum est per simile, quia sicut infirmi oculi solem non possunt aspicere, ita infirmi ratione caelestia non possunt contemplari" (*Glosae super Boetium*, pp. 48–49, lines 85–87) [This is said by simile, because just as weak eyes cannot gaze upon the sun, so the weak cannot gaze upon the heavens by reason].

42. The "lions" in question are probably a metaphoric stand-in for the Carthaginian people themselves.

captent escas metuantque trucem
soliti uerbera ferre magistrum . . .[43]

[The lions of Carthage bear the beautiful bonds of captivity, and eat
the food that is given them by hand, and though they fear their harsh
master with his whip they know so well . . .]

Here the lions' passivity under the yoke of oppressors is represented in
three successive phrases: they bear chains, they take food from captors,
and they fear cruelty. Although successive, these three phrases are not
causally related; they are not logically sequenced. Instead, they are apposed and collocative. Rather than entailing forward motion through argumentative propositions, like Boethius's proses, they thus cause the narrating Boethius constantly to revisit a single idea: the imprisonment of
the lions. Indeed, although the precise semantic meaning of each phrase
differs, the effect of each is quite similar: each refers back to the subject
"Poeni," the Carthaginian "lions," and evokes their powerlessness and
passivity. The apposition of these phrases produces a lingering in a single referent, rather than a moving forward through sequential and causal
clauses of argumentation. It represents and models a learning experience
more akin to a meditation than to an argument, based more on analogy
than on logic.

The next section of this song turns away from the violent imagery to
depict delicate birds singing songs. There is no logical or causal relationship stipulated between the lions and the birds; instead, there is again an
analogical relationship between the two, a relationship of likeness.[44] This
relationship between the Carthaginian lions and the birds inheres simply
in their physical apposition and in the analogy that emerges between them
as the depiction of the birds becomes more complex. The description of the
birds begins with "quae" (which), suggesting that this innocent description of a singing bird, "Quae canit altis garrula ramis / ales"[45] (the garru-

---

43. Bk. 3, m. 2, lines 7–10.

44. Scarry describes an analogical "binding" for Boethius's tome, which she unpacks as a numerical organization of the books and proses and meters of the *Consolation*, so that there is a balance of numerical "bonds" (based on the numbers of proses
and meters in each book, and also based on the total numbers of books themselves) that
organizes the *Consolation* as a textual "sphere" ("Well-Rounded Sphere," 124–33).

45. Bk. 3, m. 2, lines 17–18.

lous bird which sang on the branch), is meant not to stand on its own but to be modified. Indeed, the next line brings a modifier. The singing bird is captured and locked in a cage—"ales caueae clauditur antro . . . "[46] (the bird from the copse is confined in a cage). Now the relationship emerges between the birds and the lions, and it is a relationship of likeness: both suffer captivity. Another modifier follows, in which the human captors of the bird nourish and tend to him studiously ("huic licet inlita pocula melle / largasque dapes dulci studio / ludens hominum cura ministret"[47] [there, cups are slathered with honey / and ample food with sweet zeal / is ministered by the care of men]). The image of the bird being fed recalls the image of the lions eating from the hands of their captors and sets the narrating Boethius up to expect a rebellion on the part of the birds, having just been ushered through the rebellion of the lions. Although the violent lions and the freedom-seeking birds seem, on the surface, to have little in common, the song formally embodies the reality that they do share something, namely, the desire to return to their natural state, in freedom.[48] This common desire is something they also have in common with Boethius, although the relation is left unstated, allowed simply to work on his mind by analogy: like the lions and like the birds, Boethius is imprisoned, but he will return to his natural state if once reminded of it. That "natural state" is, for Boethius, his innate but alienated understanding of his connection to God, though the meter does not make these connections causally or argumentatively plain. Instead, the musical meters of the *Consolation* are designed, via the accretion of analogies, to produce a feeling of likeness in Boethius himself, an empathy with the other created beings of the universe and, by extension, with the universe itself and the divine goodness that created it. The analogies in the poem, then, are constructed to help Boethius *feel like* others and, from there, to remember himself as part of a universe created in harmony with divine intention. Crucially, all of these analogies are set into lines of proportional lengths, even meters, similar sounds, and regular rhythms. The formal architectures of likeness in the poem serve to highlight and make aesthetically available the lessons on likeness that the poem contains.

---

46. Bk. 3, m. 2, line 18.

47. Bk. 3, m. 2, lines 19–21.

48. In his analysis of this passage in the *Consolation*, Lerer observes that the two lines about the birds, "siluas tantum maesta requirit / siluas dulci uoce susurrat" (bk. 3, m. 2, lines 25–26), anaphorically render the thematic truth of the return to origins that the poem is about (*Boethius and Dialogue*, 142).

Through his experience of both the proses and the meters, then, Boethius is made to feel the dual reordering that will bring him out of his despair and restore him to spiritual wholeness—by causal, logical order on the one hand, and by musical, analogical harmony on the other. As medieval commentators on Boethius's work point out, Boethius's twin processes of reeducation via the sensual experience of song and the rational experience of prose were intended not only to convey his healing process but also to model it for his readership. When Philosophy calls attention to how the proses should work, or to how the songs are necessary to complement them, she not only teaches Boethius but also trains the reader in how to encounter the *Consolation* and to understand the protreptic function of the prosimetrum. In the Middle Ages, some of those readers, upon internalizing the literary theory and practice of mixed-form protrepsis, turn to write their own ethical works. The first such reader-turned-writer that I will examine is Alain de Lille.

THE MEDIEVAL RECEPTION OF PROSIMETRIC PROTREPTICS: ALAIN, DANTE, GUILLAUME

Alain de Lille's twelfth-century *De planctu naturae* enacts a protrepsis much like the one found in the *Consolation*, in which the narrator-protagonist gradually attains new and transformative understanding from a wise interlocutor.[49] Moreover, *De planctu* deploys prosimetrum to represent its narrator's transformation, carefully theorizing the role and function of the mixed form all the while. At the end of prose 4, the narrator's teacher, Nature, explains a switch from prose to meter as follows:

> idcirco sive certa descriptione describens, sive legitima diffinitione diffiniens, rem immonstrabilem demonstrabo, inextricabilem extricabo; quamvis ipsa nullis naturae obnoxialiter alligata complexionibus, intellectus indaginem non exspectans, nullius posset descriptionis signaculo designari. Ergo, circumscriptae rei haec detur descriptio, inexplicabilis naturae haec exeat explicatio; haec de ignoto habeatur

---

49. Barbara Newman (*God and the Goddesses*, 66–81) notes the affinities between the *Consolation* and *De planctu* and also details the ways in which Alain borrows from Bernard's *Cosmographia*, suggesting that the *Cosmographia* is the most immediate source for Alain's poem. Her analysis of the Bernardian themes in Alain's work is irreproachable, but my own analysis focuses more on the formal and literary-theoretical heft of Alain's work, which is more closely affiliated with Boethius.

notitia, haec de scibili comparetur scientia, styli tamen altitudine castigata.[50]

[Either by describing with reliable descriptions or defining with regular definitions, I will demonstrate the indemonstrable, extricate the inextricable, although it is not bound in submission to any nature, does not abide an investigation by reason, and thus cannot be stamped with the stamp of any one description. Let the following, then, be set forth as a delimiting of the unlimited, let this emerge as an explanation of a nature that is inexplicable, let this be regarded as knowledge of the unknown, let this be brought forward as a doctrine on the unknowable; let it, however, be refined by the sublimity of the writer's pen.][51]

Nature's prologue to her coming poem offers an important characterization of her theory of the literary and its relation to transformative learning. First, Nature takes as given that her words should be didactic, that they should "describe with reliable descriptions or define with regular definitions" how the universe works. Second, she claims to have the power to resolve paradoxes of pedagogy in her discourse: she will "demonstrate the indemonstrable"; she will "extricate the inextricable." But third, significantly and unexpectedly, she regards her unpacking of impossible knowledge as requiring the facilitation of "the writer's pen." That is, these impossibly possible teachings cannot be taught naturally, by "Nature" alone. Instead they need artifice—literary artifice—in order fully to meet their didactic mark. "Natural," didactic truth needs aesthetic ornamentation to get its job done, and Nature herself seems quite ready to admit her dependence on that artistry.

What follows Nature's pedagogical monologue on resolving the irresoluble via the artifice of the writer's pen, appropriately, is a highly wrought meter—replete with alliteration, assonance, consonance, and occasional end rhymes—which lists a vast series of apposed paradoxes that embody, in Nature's view, the fundamental character of love.[52] In offering this

50. Alanus de Insulis, *De planctu naturae*, col. 455A.

51. *Plaint of Nature*, trans. Sheridan, 148.

52. An excerpt from Nature's poem reads, "Pax odio, fraudique fides, spes juncta timori / Est amor, et mistus cum ratione furor. / Naufragium dulce, pondus leve, grata Charybdis, / Incolumis languor, et satiata fames. / Esuries satiens, sitis ebria, falsa voluptas, / Tristities laeta, gaudia plena malis. / Dulce malum, mala dulcedo, sibi dulcor amarus, / Cujus odor sapidus, insipidusque sapor. / Tempestas grata, nox lucida, lux tenebrosa, / Mors vivens, moriens vita, suave malum. / Peccatum veniae, venialis culpa,

impressively artificed meter, Nature performs in practice the very same artificial intervention to which she alludes in theory: she takes her own teachings and applies to them the artifices of the writer's pen. Amplifying the performativity of this moment, Nature alludes to it as soon as the meter has finished: "Jam ex hoc meae doctrinae artificio, cupidinariae artis elucescit theorica"[53] (Now from this artistic exposition of my teaching, the theory of the workings of Desire begins to become clear to you).[54] Evidently, Nature's meter performs some kind of artistic exposition on her theoretical teachings. Meter is thus cast as a necessary, if slightly subordinate, adjunct to prose, much as it is in commentaries on the *Consolation*, though now it seems that meter works by artificial elucidation, and not straightforwardly by using affective and sensual engagement to pave the way for or offer a reprieve from prose.

Having explicitly staked out mutually reinforcing roles for prose and meter, however, *De planctu* subtly implies a particular importance for the role of the mixed form in embodying Nature's teachings—an importance that moves decisively away from the philosophical ambitions of the *Consolation* and has consequences for how mixed-form transformative writing will be practiced in vernacular works of the later Middle Ages. Thematically, Nature nominates heterosexual marriage as the ethical ideal of her teachings; the protrepsis that the work drives toward is the appreciation and enforcement of heteronormative sexual ethics, rather than the

---

jocosa, / Poena, pium facinus, imo, suave scelus. / Instabilis ludus, stabilis delusio, robur / Infirmum, firmum mobile, firma movens. / Insipiens ratio, demens prudentia . . . Tydeus mollescit amore, / Fit Nestor juvenis, fitque Melincta senex . . . / Dives eget Crassus, Codrus et abundat egendo . . . / Ennius eloquitur, Marcusque silet; fit Ulysses / Insipiens, Ajax desipiendo sapit." *De planctu*, col. 455A–B. (Love is peace joined to hatred, loyalty to treachery, hope to fear and madness blended with reason. It is sweet shipwreck, light burden, pleasing Charybdis, sound debility, insatiate hunger, hungry satiety, thirst when filled with water, deceptive pleasure, happy sadness, joy full of sorrow, delightful misfortune, unfortunate delight, sweetness bitter to its own taste. Its odour is savoury, its savour is insipid. It is a pleasing storm, a lightsome night, a lightless day, a living death, a dying life, a pleasant misery, pardonable sin, sinful pardon, sportive punishment, pious misdeed, nay, sweet crime, changeable pastime, unchangeable mockery, weak strength, stationary movable, mover of the stationary, irrational reason, foolish wisdom . . . Tydeus grows soft with love, Nestor becomes a youth, Melicerta becomes an old man . . . The wealthy Croesus is in need; Codrus, the beggar, abounds in wealth . . . Ennius makes speeches and Marcus is silent; Ulysses becomes foolish; Ajax in his madness grows wise.) *Plaint of Nature*, trans. Sheridan, 149–51.

53. *De planctu*, col. 456B.

54. *Plaint of Nature*, trans. Sheridan, 154.

contemplative heights toward which the *Consolation* presses.[55] The heteronormative ideal appears concretely when Hymenaeus, god of marriage,
approaches Nature. Hymenaeus is accompanied by a host of musicians
who tune their instruments to promote ethical reform: "Tunc illi quibus-
dam prooemiis sua illicientes instrumenta, vocem deformiter uniformem,
dissimilitudine similem, multiformi modulo picturabant"[56] (Their instruments being tuned with what one might call proems, they proceeded to reproduce in oft-changing strains the sound that has uniformity amid mul-
tiformity, similarity amid dissimilarity).[57] With that promise to bring new
union to a fractured world, the narrative launches into a meter that praises
how poetic song works to produce harmony: "Dividitur juncta, divisaque
jungitur horum / Dispar comparitas cantus, concordia discors, / Imo dis-
similis similis dissensio vocum"[58] (The joined is divided, the divided is
joined together / Unlike made like, concordant discord, disunited agreement, united dissent of voices).[59] Thematically, this "unlike made like"
or "concordant discord" figures how heterosexual marriage works: a male
and a female, dissimilar, are joined into a single unified thing; they are
made similar, made "concordant."[60] It figures, that is, the central ethical
drive of the work.

But, formally, this image of "unlike made like" also describes how the
whole book functions. Prose and meter, dissimilar and formally disunified,
are drawn together and joined to create a single unified structure. Thus,

55. In all likelihood, Alain derives this thematic emphasis from his exposure to
Martianus's *De nuptiis*. James Sheridan notes that Boethius and Martianus both "had
a deep influence on Alan" (*Plaint of Nature*, 35). G. Reynaud de Lage also sees the three
works as manifesting a literary tradition (*Alain de Lille*, conclusion). See also Green,
"Alan of Lille's *De planctu naturae*," 653 and 667–69.

The question of whether Alain's shrill condemnation of homosexuality is to be
taken seriously or ironically remains open—some scholars see Alain as a serious,
unironic would-be reformer of sexual mores; others see him as someone keen to play
around with literary prose and meter and show what he could do in each form, and see
his choice of topic as, in some ways, incidental to that formal project. Incidental, in
other words, in that, "Alan chose the Nature story to give him scope for a Menippean
satire." See Alanus de Insulis, *Plaint of Nature*, trans. Sheridan, 46–47. See again Green,
"Alan of Lille's *De planctu naturae*," 673.

56. *De planctu*, col. 477B.

57. *Plaint of Nature*, trans. Sheridan, 208.

58. *De planctu*, col. 477D.

59. *Plaint of Nature*, trans. Sheridan, 211.

60. In Wetherbee's formulation, "Hymen's office is the reconciliation of opposites,
the balancing of potentially discordant forces" (*Platonism and Poetry*, 200).

the appearance and performance of Hymenaeus and his band of songsters reveal another important element of *De planctu*'s theory of form. Just as Nature has divided the sexes into male and female, so artifice has divided the world of literary writing into prose and meter. Hymenaeus, standing as a paragon of heterosexual union and thus as an endorser of the union of unlike things, simultaneously reveals his understanding of the ethical utility in the mixed form itself. Through this aria on creating unity from difference, the mixing of forms is implicitly cast as an aspirational goal for literary writers, formally akin to the ethically unimpeachable union of male and female in a heterosexual marriage.[61] *De planctu* uses the mixed form to enact a transformation of its narrator's understanding precisely by figuring the heteronormative sexual practices that it endorses in its explicit content.[62]

61. Alain's tendency to think through and represent the ethical mandate on heterosexual union in his work via literary, formal analogy has long been noted, though primarily in one vein: famously, Nature analogizes heterosexual union to good grammar and homosexual to bad grammar. "Humanum namque genus a sua generositate degenerans, in conjunctione generum barbarizans, venereas regulas immutando, nimis irregulari utitur metaplasmo: sicque homo a venere tiresiatus anomala, directam praedicationem in contrapositionem inordinate convertit. A Veneris igitur orthographia homo deviando recedens, sophista falsigraphus invenitur. Consequenter etiam Dioneae artis analogiam devitans, in anastrophem vitiosam degenerat; dumque in tali quaestione me destruit, et in sua phraenesi, mihi themesim machinatur." *De planctu*, col. 449C–D. (The human race, fallen from its high estate, adopts a highly irregular (grammatical) change when it inverts the rules of Venus by introducing barbarisms in its arrangement of genders. Thus man, his sex changed by a ruleless Venus, in defiance of true order, by his arrangement changes what is a straightforward attribute of his. Abandoning in his deviation the true script of Venus, he is proved to be a sophistic pseudographer. Shunning even a resemblance traceable to the art of Dione's daughter, he falls into the defect of inverted order. While in a construction of this kind he causes my destruction, in his combination he devises a division in me.) *Plaint of Nature*, trans. Sheridan, 133–34. The fullest treatment of the utility of grammar to Alain's ethical project remains Ziolkowski, *Alan of Lille's Grammar of Sex*. For a consideration of how Alain uses his poetic style, allegory, and personification to embody and render his ideas about ethical and sexual deviancy, see also Green, "Alain of Lille's *De planctu naturae*," 649–74.

62. Suggesting how "natural" heterosexuality may actually necessitate the artfully mixed style of Nature's poem helps to resolve a long-standing interpretive crux in *De planctu*, namely, what to make of the fact that Nature preaches the use of plain language, unartificed and natural, and yet permits the Lover to imitate her own high-flown and poetic style. Barbara Newman sets this crux out, suggesting, "Perhaps the clearest sign of Natura's 'fallenness' lies in her language . . . An austere, unadorned plain style

The impulse to reinterrogate Boethian form and function, and to do so in a sexualized, amatory framework, overflows from Alain's Latin work and into vernacular literature in the writings of Dante Alighieri and Guillaume de Machaut, though neither of these vernacular authors pushes the mixed form to quite the same ethical and aesthetic verge that it attains in *De planctu*, in which the mixed form comes actually to embody a particular ethical mandate for sexual conduct.[63] For both Dante and Guillaume, the mixed form becomes, more than anything else, an occasion for metacritical and metapoetic reflection—for reflection on how theory and poetry work together.

Dante's autobiographical *Vita nuova* narrates his passionate love for Beatrice, her death, and his gradual healing process from that loss. This project of narrating love, loss, and recovery begins in prose but is interspersed throughout with agonized and versified exclamations. Then, having presented both the story of Dante's love and the poetic works that encapsulate its emotional content, this prosimetrum ends with a staging of Dante's own ethical renewal: he vows to abandon writing about his love of Beatrice until he can compose more fitting words about her.[64] This turn from the *Vita nuova* to a higher mode of verbal engagement reads as a signal of the narrator's own transformation, his turn from obsessive, amatory self-narration to a more ethically sound mode of loving contemplation.[65]

---

is Nature's supposed ideal in matters rhetorical and sexual alike, since 'the corruption of language by irresponsible poets makes it impossible to conceive of the proper place of sexuality within the divinely ordered cosmos.' Yet, as this very example proclaims, *De Planctu Naturae* may well boast the most pyrotechnic Latin composed by any rhetor of its pyrotechnic age" (*God and the Goddesses*, 71–72).

63. Green sees one of Alain's fundamental changes to Boethius being, indeed, his designation of worldly love—sexual love—in place of spiritual love of the *summum bonum* as the ethical focus of his narrative ("Alain of Lille's *De planctu naturae*," 666–69).

64. Dino Cervigni and Edward Vasta call the culmination of the work Dante's attainment of "mystical understanding." See Dante Alighieri, *Vita nuova*, 18.

65. Numerous scholars have noted the Boethian resonances of the basic form of the work (Frisardi, *Vita nova*, xxi; Musa, "*Essay*," ix; Lerer, introduction, 15). Elsewhere in his corpus, Dante places Boethius in a lauded place in his hierarchies of literary and philosophical authority. In the *Paradiso*, for instance, he situates Boethius high in the orders of sainted souls, alongside Augustine: "Or se tu l'occhio de la mente trani / di luce in luce dietro a le mie lode, / già de l'ottava con sete rimani. / Per vedere ogne ben dentro vi gode / l'anima santa che 'l mondo fallace / fa manifesto a chi di lei ben ode. / Lo corpo ond' ella fu cacciata giace / giuso in Cieldauro; ed essa da martiro / e da essilio venne a questa pace" (*Paradiso* 10.121–29). (Now, if the eye of your mind is following, from light to light, my commendations, already you must be waiting for the eighth. For

But Dante's narrative of transformation reinvents the paradigm of prosimetrum and its relation both to a narrator's transformation and to readerly protrepsis. To be sure, the *Vita nuova* does tend to locate emotion and sensuality primarily in its poems, while reserving the prose sections for reasoned narration, just as medieval commentators say Boethius does in the *Consolation*. But the *Vita nuova* questions the Boethian tradition's surface allocation of innate powers—such as rational argumentation and sensual palliation—to prose and verse respectively. In the first prose section of his work, before any poetry is included, Dante informs his readers that he will be setting his memories to paper—that his narrative will be structured as a retrospective account of his own experiences. Second, still before any poems appear, he explains his first sight of his beloved Beatrice, in which she is clad in a crimson dress. Third, still in prose, Dante tells of a dream he had, in which "uno segnore" (a noble man) holds a small woman in a crimson dress in his arms, while also holding Dante's own flaming heart. The young woman is forced to eat a portion of the heart, and then the dream dissolves in weeping.[66] Upon awakening from his dream, Dante decides to compose "uno sonetto, ne lo quale io salutasse tutti li fedeli d'Amore" (a sonnet, in which I salute all of Love's faithful followers) that details this strange dream.[67]

With this announcement, the *Vita nuova* achieves two crucial goals. First, it frames Dante's poem, from the outset, as a mode of communicating with like-minded people—with others who have been struck by love.[68] In so doing, the *Vita nuova* creates Dante's inset poem as an engine for pro-

---

seeing every good, the blessed soul, who makes earthly falseness manifest to all who listen well to him, rejoices. The body from which that soul was chased lies down in Ciel D'Oro; he has come from martyrhood and exile to this peace.) Boethius is buried in Pavia, in the Church of the Ciel D'Oro. For further discussion of Boethius's influence on Dante, see also Gualtieri, "Lady Philosophy in Boethius and Dante," 141–50.

66. Dante Alighieri, *Vita nuova*, ed. Domenico de Robertis, 37–39.

67. Ibid., 40.

68. As Teodolinda Barolini and Manuele Gragnolari put it, "Nel sonetto *A ciascun'alma presa e gentil core* Dante si rivolge a due categorie di lettori: a tutti gli innamorati—tutte le anime 'prese,' cioè possedute, da amore—e a tutti i cuori 'gentili,' cioè nobili . . . Il lessico tecnico e cortese di cui il poeta si serve per indicare il gruppo ristretto a cui scrive gli servirà anche molto più tardi." Alighieri, *Rime giovanile e della Vita nuova*, ed. Teodolinda Barolini and Manuele Gragnolari, 81. (In this sonnet, Dante turns his attention to two categories of reader: to all the lovers—all the souls "captured," which is to say possessed, by love—and to all the "gentle," which is to say noble, hearts . . . The technical and courtly lexicon that the poet avails himself of to indicate the elite group to whom he writes will serve him again much later.)

moting identification between his own narrating persona and the psyches of his readers. The *Vita nuova* creates, that is, a protreptic framework, with an amatory inflection: as we watch Dante go through his love-wrung transformations, we are meant to identify affectively with him, transition along with him through his process of learning. Second, the *Vita nuova* represents the poem as something that was composed in real time, while Dante was immersed in the vision of Beatrice.[69] The prose section functions essentially as a retrospective synopsis of that experience, while the poem casts itself as a contemporary witness to it.

> Allegro mi sembrava Amor tenendo
> meo core in mano, e ne le braccia avea
> madonna involta in un drappo dormendo.
> Poi la svegliava, e d'esto core ardendo
> lei paventosa umilimente pascea:
> appresso gir lo ne vedea piangendo.[70]

> [Glad seemed Love to me, holding
> my heart in his hand, and in his arms he had
> my lady, wrapped in a cloth, sleeping.
> Then he roused her, and this burning heart
> he humbly fed to her, who was most afraid:
> then I saw him vanish, weeping.]

---

69. Though, as Barolini and Gragnolari have shown, many of the poems of the *Vita nuova*, including this one, were written not for Beatrice but for other occasions, with Dante having only subsequently reintegrated them into this larger work. "Le liriche prescelte non subiscono soltanto una revisione passiva durante la procedura di selezione, ma anche una revisione attiva grazie all'azione della prosa narrativa che le piega a un senso nuovo, consono all'ideologia della 'vita nuova' del poeta. Le modificazioni/distorzioni dell'intenzione originaria che ne resultano producono inversioni narrative: per esempio, poesie scritte per altre donne in altri contesti sono ora considerate scritte per Beatrice." *Rime giovanile e della Vita nuova*, 82. (The lyrics selected [from among his juvenilia to include in the *Vita nuova*] submit themselves not only to a passive revision during the process of selection but also to an active revision thanks to the action of the prose narrative which bends them in a new way, a way consonant with the ideology of the "new life" of the poet. The modifications/distortions of the original intentions [of these lyrics] that result produce narrative inversions: for example, poems written for other women in other circumstances are now considered to have been written for Beatrice.)

70. Alighieri, *Vita nuova*, p. 42, lines 12–17.

In the *Vita nuova*, the prose synopses introduce Dante's ideas and familiarize his readers with the events and emotions that have inspired his poetry—in effect, the proses serve to teach a reading audience how to read
and understand the poems, offering the former as de facto primers for the
latter.[71] The Boethian idea that meter paves the way for the sterner stuff
of prose argumentation is thereby undercut: in the *Vita nuova*, prose and
meter can cover the same ground, only prose does so in a prefatory, intro-
ductory way, while meter exudes an aura of authentically present affective
experience.

Dante complicates this picture of the relation of prose to poetry in his
work by bookending the individual poems in two different modes of prose.
First there are the initial proses that pave the way for the poems, usually
by giving their backstory. But second, there are prose sections—of a different type—that follow the poems. This second category of prose comments upon the poems, explicating their mechanics, their forms, and their
literary values. This second category of prose offers a space for metapoetic
reflection—a space for propounding vernacular literary theory about the
function and form of Dante's poetry.

> Questo sonetto in quattro parti si può dividere: ne la prima dico e sop-
> pongo che tutti li miei pensieri sono d'Amore; ne la seconda dico che
> sono diversi, e narro la loro diversitade; ne la terza dico in che tutti
> pare che s'accordino; ne la quarta dico che volendo dire d'Amore, non
> so da qual parte pigli matera, e se la voglio pigliare da tutti, convene
> che io chiami la mia inimica.[72]

> [This sonnet can be divided into four parts: in the first I say and sup-
> pose that all my thoughts are about Love; in the second I say that they
> are diverse, and I describe their diversity; in the third I say how all
> of them appear to work together; in the fourth, I say that, desiring to
> speak of Love, I do not know from where to take my material, and if I
> want to take my material from everywhere, I will have to call upon my
> enemy.]

71. Responding to the parity of content between prose and meter in many of
Dante's chapters, Mark Musa notes that "the effect made by the poem on the reader of
the *Vita Nuova* is 'recapitulative,' as if the poem were repeating the prose. The rest of
the poems deal not with the experience itself but with the ideas suggested and emotions inspired by the experience." Musa, "Essay," 91–92.

72. Alighieri, *Vita nuova*, 87–88.

This type of prose follows the poems and usually precedes a turn back to the more narrative prose that begins each of the forty-two chapters of the book. In each prosimetric juncture, Dante does not use poetry in a salvific synergy with prose, nor indeed does he show prose to be the space where the "real" reeducation takes place, with the meters serving a sensual, palliative function. In the *Vita nuova*, the mutual symbiosis between prose and meter becomes something other than ethically "consoling," and something other than an embodiment of its central thematic drive: it becomes a form that seeks to teach its readers how the real literary work—which, for Dante, is his poetry—should be read, understood, and interpreted. The *Vita nuova* becomes a metapoetic work, a work of literary criticism-in-practice, grounded in but reinventing the Boethian tradition of the mixed-form protreptic.

In its reinvention of this literary paradigm, the *Vita nuova* is tripartite rather than bipartite, consisting of two very different prose modalities, each of which flank and contextualize every interpolated poem. These two prose modalities help the reader to navigate the putatively real-time poetic artifacts, both by contextualizing the poems within Dante's lived experiences and by articulating his metapoetic investments. The proses that come before the poems work to familiarize readers with the poems' contents; the proses that follow work to unpack the poems' formal designs. By flanking them with supporting prose, the *Vita nuova* makes its poems the main event, providing a reader with the interpretive and formal tools he or she will need to understand and appreciate them. On the whole then, Dante's prosimetrum is a more explicitly literary-theoretical work than Boethius's *Consolation* or Alain's *De planctu*, designed to set off the poems in their clearest light, all the while posing as a protreptic narrative. Dante's formal and theoretical reengagement with the mixed-form, then, both endorses that form's importance to a work of literary transformation and rewrites the canonical commentaries on and reexplorations of the nature and effect of its binary structure.

The end of that rewriting is to assert the primacy of metrical writing in a mixed-form protreptic. Throughout the work, the lyrics contain the touch of the real; they are the essential distillation of Dante's supposed poetic selfhood, as it crystallized in the moment of his amatory ecstasies and agonies. The lyrics represent his real-time experiences of love for Beatrice, which must be worked through and pored over by the narration and commentary that take place in the proses. In the *Vita nuova*, the lyric is the center, while prose is the periphery; the lyrics are the text for which these explanatory proses are the contextualization and marginalia.[73] The *Vita nuova* may present Dante's own ethical transformation as one from amatory indulgence to divine contemplation, but it simultaneously re-imagines a readerly protrepsis as an inauguration of his readership into a new kind of literacy—one both vernacular and poetic. The lesson, for readers, is not how to overcome mournful love but how to read Dante's own poetry, both for its form and for its relation to what he claims as his real-life experiences.

This reading of the *Vita nuova* as a metapoetic work and a calque on Boethian form and function dovetails with Teodolinda Barolini's work on the *Divine Comedy*. For Barolini, whether a reader is to take Dante's truth claims seriously or whether he or she is to take Dante's work as "fiction" is of paramount concern in encountering his magnum opus, the *Divine Comedy*.[74] My grouping of the *Vita nuova* with the tradition of mixed-form protrepsis envisions a way in which a reader does not have

---

73. Barolini and Gragnolari argue that the individual poems, often composed for purposes quite different from those to which Dante attributes them, are given meaning and substance specifically by their association with the proses. "La prosa sapida e ricca di dettagli conferisce significato allo scarno scheletro poetico. Si comincia con un testo che non ci autorizza nemmeno a identificare "madonna" con Beatrice, e si finisce—tramite il lavoro ermeneutico della prosa—con un primo annunzio della morte de lei, reso possibile dall'aggiunta di ulteriori informazioni." *Rime giovanile e della Vita nuova*, 85. (The wise prose, rich with details, confers significance on the bony poetic skeleton. It begins with a text that does not even authorize itself to identify "my lady" with Beatrice, and it finishes—by means of the hermeneutic work of the prose—with the first announcement of Beatrice's death, made possible by the addition of the later information.) From a perspective of book history, this argument is unexceptionable: Dante made the poems mean something different and something more—in the context of his poetic vision of himself as author and suffering lover—by devising the proses. In that way, the proses seem, as it were, more powerful, perhaps more important, than the poems. But from within the fiction of the narrative, from within what Dante tells us to believe about his poems and how they were written, the superadded proses function merely as a facilitating device for the real visionary work that is accomplished in the poems. Thus, Dante manipulates our reading experience: by devising the prose sections, he makes the poems mean in ways they were not originally intended to do, showing the proses, by a certain measure, to be the most powerful part of the work; yet, paradoxically, by the way in which he introduces and contextualizes the proses among the poems, he makes the poems seem as if they have always already concerned the real-time experiences of his love of Beatrice, and so are the epicenter of the work.

74. Barolini, *Undivine* Comedy, 4.

to choose between a "truthful" Dante and a "fictive" one. Because of the well-established contours of the post-Boethian protreptic mode, in which supernatural events—such as the appearance of a luminous personified Philosophy or the disclosure of mysterious and prophetic dreams—are entirely de rigueur, Dante's fictive choices within his work do not at all detract from the seriousness or claims to supervening ethical truth of the main narrative. By viewing this autobiographical mixed-form work as a self-conscious reinvention of Boethian literary modalities, a mode of reading emerges in which transformative ethical truth is entirely compatible with—indeed, is radically dependent upon—aesthetic, artful writing.

Dante is not the only continental, vernacular writer of the fourteenth century to encounter and experiment with protrepsis and its embodiment in the mixed form, nor is he the only one to use the mixed form as an occasion for elevating the status of versified writing in such a narrative. Guillaume de Machaut reframes the transformative drama of Boethius's story in his *Remède de Fortune*, resituating that drama—as Dante does—as an amatory one. In his retelling, the narrator-protagonist of the poem, Guillaume himself, lovelorn and alone, is visited by the beautiful lady Hope, who guides him back to self-possession and, eventually, onward to a romantic relationship with his beloved lady.[75] This amatory transformation is worked, as in Boethius's *Consolation*, by a combination of careful argumentation and lyrical interludes. The narrator-protagonist plays a role throughout that is analogous to Boethius's; Hope plays a role analogous to Philosophy's; the beloved lady, to the *summum bonum* or love of God that is the ever-present end of Boethius's protreptic narrative. Thus, the *Remède* both revisits and revises the Boethian mode of ethical transformation, reconceiving the *Consolation*'s emphasis on transcending the world as a revindication of that world's legitimacy, a legitimacy embodied in his beloved.[76] For both Dante and Guillaume, then, one effect of experimenting with the mixed form is to arrive at a kind of transformation that succeeds in finding meaning in temporal love and desire, rather than turning away from them.[77] Philosophical contemplation, the *telos* for Boe-

---

75. Guillaume de Machaut, *Le jugement du roy de Behaigne et Remède de Fortune*, 37–38.

76. Katherine Heinrichs recognizes that Machaut is often parodic in his attitude toward Boethian discourse. In her view, Machaut goes so far as to insist that worldly love can—and sometimes should—be the goal, rather than the psychological foible to be extirpated by philosophy (*Myths of Love*, 320–34, 222–26).

77. Jessica Rosenfeld has suggested that this revindication of the world and worldly pleasures—particularly romantic love and friendship—as valuable in the ethical pursuit

thius, has been shunted through the sexual lens of Alain's complaint and has emerged as a triumph of amatory transformation in the mixed-form writings of these fourteenth-century continental vernacular poets.

Correlative with its reinvention of Boethius's philosophical protrepsis as an amatory one, though, the *Remède* also programmatically reinvents the mixed form itself, leavening a narrative composed in rhymed couplets with lyrical interpolations of various forms—complaints, ballades, rondelles, and chants royals. In so doing, the *Remède* participates in a long and rich tradition of French writing, typified by the mixed-form romances of the thirteenth and fourteenth centuries on the one hand and by vernacular song on the other.[78] Critics who study the French mixed-form tradition tend to engage with lyrics that appear in larger narrative structures in late medieval French literature as lyrical insertions, short verse works that are tipped into what is implicitly the dominant, supervening narrative. Even when they take these lyrical insertions as deliberate and important parts of the overall structure of a work, they are usually construed as borrowings, quotations, or evidence of the impulse to combine genres for the sake of hybridity alone.[79] As Maureen Boulton puts it, "Composed between 1342 and 1357, the *Remède* contains seven songs set to music. Not coincidentally, these include an example of each of the six genres then

---

of happiness is perhaps the most significant result of the late medieval absorption of Boethian and Aristotelian ethical thought (*Ethics and Enjoyment*, 1–14).

78. Ardis Butterfield and Maureen Boulton both work on these lineages and how they inform Guillaume's poetic practice. See Boulton, *Song in the Story*, 181–242. Butterfield says of Machaut, "The author who explores this rich potential of writing more sophisticatedly than any other in either century is Guillaume de Machaut, whose works provide a glittering display of literary and musical collaboration. His *Remede de Fortune* and *Le Voir Dit* are examples of writing where poetry and music forge together the sound of the page and the silence of the imagination. This partnership . . . is already presaged in the early decades of the thirteenth century with some of the first surviving records of vernacular song." Butterfield, *Poetry and Music in Medieval France*, 9.

79. Boulton, *Song in the Story*, 1–2. There are cases, such as *Aucussin et Nicolette*, that Boulton sees in a slightly different light: *Aucussin* "does not in fact fit our definition. Its sung passages are not independent songs, but laisses. The prose and verse passages occur in regular alternation, but neither could stand alone" (*Song in the Story*, 3). There is excellent reason for focusing on genre as a part of the story for why these various lyrics are grouped together in single larger works. As Ardis Butterfield has shown, there is an "increasing preoccupation in the late thirteenth century with genre and generic terms in the organisation of manuscripts and in manuscript indices," indicating that, at least for scribes, the local logic of organization was seen to be generic. See Butterfield, *Poetry and Music in Medieval France*, 172.

current: a *lai*, a *complainte*, a *chanson royale*, two *ballades*, a *virelai*, and a *rondeau*."[80] Although the *Remède* evidently seeks to showcase its fluency in multiple song forms, I would suggest that its inserted lyrics are inseparable from the *Gestalt* form of the larger project and should not be construed exclusively as discrete genre experiments within the work.

Given the therapeutic and dialogic framework of the narrative, that the *Remède* recreates the mixed form of prosimetrum specifically as a mixing of different *verse* forms indicates its will to explore the possibility of producing a verse-only protreptic. During a section of narration, Hope says in rhymed couplets:

> Or t'ay devisé et apris—
> Se retenu l'as et compris—
> Comment ta dame puet savoir
> Que tu l'aimes sans decevoir . . .
> Mes pour toy un petit deduire
> Et pour tes mauls a joie duire,
> Te vueil dire un chant nouvellet;
> Car chose plaist qui nouvelle est.[81]

> [Now I have set out and shown for you—
> if you have retained and understood it—
> how your lady can know
> that you love her without deceit . . .
> But to give you a little break,
> and to turn your ills to joy,
> I want to sing you a new song,
> because a new thing always pleases.]

From this offer, Hope launches into a *chant roial*. Rhymed couplets are, evidently, where she uses reason and discursive explanation; other verse forms, typically stanzaic, are where "song" happens. Rhymed couplets function as Cappelan, Boethian, Lillean, or Dantean proses; stanzaic lyrics function as their meters. The *Remède* uses rhymed couplets for dialogue; couplets are where reason and argumentation take place. It uses other po-

80. Boulton, *Song in the Story*, 188.

81. Guillaume de Machaut, *Le jugement du roy de Behaigne et Remède de Fortune*, pp. 275 and 277, lines 1935–38 and 1973–76.

etic forms—the lyrical interpolations—as de facto "meters," monologic, affective, sensual, and songful.[82] Through the process of moving through this alternately narrative and lyrical therapeutic intervention with Hope, the narrator of the work is transformed from despair to hope.[83] In reinventing transformative prosimetrum in this way, the *Remède* both engages with the idea that, in protreptic writing, the mixing of forms must do the twin work of reason and affective engagement and also disputes any idea that one of those forms absolutely must be prose. This reinvention of the mixed form suggests that any hard and fast divide between prose and meter is overdetermined; it suggests that verse is just as able to encapsulate dialogic narrative and rational argumentation as it is to encapsulate lyrical emotion and musicality.[84] Even so, simultaneously, it reaffirms a certain aspect of Boethian literary theory: namely, that both rational disquisition (here borne by the couplets) and emotional and sensual palliation (here borne by the song forms) are mutually necessary to the attainment of ethical transformation for a narrator.

But there is another element to Guillaume's reinvention of prosimetrum as a technique for representing a narrator's ethical transformation from despair to hope. Even though he does versify the "proses," thereby debunking the strict formal modus operandi of Boethian protrepsis, he goes farther, in a sense, than even Boethius—the theorist of music par excellence—in making his lyrical interpolations read conspicuously as *song*, and as the main event of the overall composition.[85] Guillaume, known to

82. Huot, "Guillaume de Machaut and the Consolation of Poetry." "Much of the literary oeuvre of Guillaume de Machaut can be seen as a response to the Boethian model" (170).

83. In Boulton's phrasing, "The *Remede de Fortune*, then, describes the transformation of an awkward young man into an accepted lover, at the same time that it demonstrates the role of poetry in that transformation" (*Song in the Story*, 192).

84. Machaut is not the only vernacular French writer to execute such a project; indeed, he may have derived part of his inspiration to do so from other vernacular sources. The mixed form, after all, occurs not only in *Aucussin et Nicolette* but also in the broader tradition of *chantefable*. Even so, these earlier mixed-form works have been shown to derive from Boethius's example. See Reinhard, "Literary Background of the Chantefable," and Hunt, "Precursors and Progenitors of *Aucussin et Nicolette*." For interesting and useful situatings of Boethius and this mixed form, see also Butterfield, "Chant/fable: Aucussin et Nicolette," *Poetry and Music in Medieval France*, 191ff.

85. Sarah Kay has argued that Machaut's lyrics are in fact the center of his work, much as I have suggested Dante's songs are the center of his *Vita nuova*: "Although it is framed as a first-person narrative, the Remede, like the Consolation, can also be said to

scholars at least as much as a musical composer as a versifier, includes
musical notation alongside his songful interpolations.[86] Ardis Butterfield
describes his manuscript layouts as follows:

> Music certainly represents the most striking visual expression of the
> difference between song and narrative: the difference between melody
> and speech being given strong visual emphasis by means of the red
> staves and the notation itself. The Machaut manuscripts illustrate this
> superbly, with the abrupt use of the whole width of a page, red staves
> and notes possessing their own calligraphic features, longs, breves, and
> semi-breves.[87]

Thus, while he shows that the work of prose—dialogic, rational argumentation—can be achieved easily in octosyllabic couplets, Guillaume carefully and programmatically associates the more heavily wrought and artificed poetic forms with musicality. Although the entire work is written
in verse, Guillaume registers and amplifies by manuscript layout a salient
division between the simpler, more prosaic couplet form and the more intricate and musical stanzaic form.

This division between musicality and argumentation in poetic form
has concrete and discernible consequences in how the *Remède* theorizes
protreptic transformation. For Lady Hope, sung lyric has two effects that
separate it from narration in octosyllabic couplets and that make it central to the work of literary protrepsis. She says, shortly before presenting a
lyric to her impassioned interlocutor,

> A Dieu te commant; je m'en voys.
> Mais ainçoys de ma clere voys
> Te diray une balladelle,
> De chant et de ditté nouvelle,
> Laquelle tu emporteras
> Et en alant la chanteras,

---

be framed by its inset lyrics . . . Although reproducing recognizable variants of the narrative structure of their model, the dits thus owe more to the verse of the Consolation
than to its prose. But more significantly, they transfer the burden of philosophy from
Philosophy's Latin prose to their own veranacular verse." *"Chansons de geste,"* 34, 36.

86. *Le jugement du roy de Behaigne et Remède de Fortune*, 39, and miniatures 3
and 24 of appendix 2.

87. Butterfield, *Poetry and Music in Medieval France*, 181.

Afin que tes cuers s'i deduise
S'il a pensee qui li nuise.[88]

[I commend you to God; I'm going away.
But first, with my clear voice,
I'll give you a balladelle,
in a new tune and with new lyrics,
which you'll take away,
and, while journeying, you will sing it
so that your heart will take delight
if it has any thought that hurts it.]

For Lady Hope, song—"words and music"—serves the dual purpose of being exportable because memorizable and being affectively engaging. Because of this dual purpose, her young pupil can "take away" the song to
use as an affective bolster whenever his heart grows heavy with hurtful
thoughts. Thus, even though the *Remède* shows that rhymed couplets can
embody rational argumentation, it also suggests both visually and discursively that in order to take its protagonist's ethical transformation away in
one's own heart, one must recognize the supervening importance of song.
Versified writing in couplets can do the hard work of rational argument,
but the exportable part of transformative reeducation takes place in an
even more artificed and aesthetic form.

The most important single change that these three continental prosimetra—Alain's, Dante's, and Guillaume's—together make to the twin paradigm of the mixed form and its protreptic function is to call into question
the theoretical effects of each form, as articulated in Boethius's work and
the commentaries on it, while simultaneously reaffirming some notion of
functional difference between how "proses" and "meters" work on one's
ethics. Whereas Boethius and his early Latin commentators take quite seriously the idea, first, that meter has certain innate sensual effects, while
prose argumentation embodies the hard work of rational reeducation, and,
second, that both forms are necessary to his own transformation and to
his modeling of protrepsis for his readership, Alain, Guillaume, and Dante
all explore how the attribution of any innately ethically transformative
powers to prose or meter per se is a constructed and conventional literary
association that can be reinvented and recast at will.[89]

88. *Le jugement du roy de Behaigne et Remède de Fortune*, p. 327, lines 2849–56.
89. Jeffrey Kittay and Wlad Godzich note an analogous desire to denaturalize

Even so, for each of these writers, the received correlation of prosimetrum with protrepsis provides a generative provocation for meditating on
how literary work might be ethically transformative. Alain sets prosimetrum up as an aesthetic correlative for the ethos of heterosexual marriage.
Dante's prose sections in the *Vita nuova* so deliberately and methodically
parse and analyze the meaning of his inset poems that the mystical ascription of any innate power to either prose or poetic form becomes nearly
impossible, and instead the mixed form becomes an occasion for his self-
fashioning as a vernacular protreptic poet. Guillaume's reinvention of prosimetrum as an interweaving of verse forms suggests that the fetishization
of "prose" as the rational, narrative component of producing ethical transformation in a narrator—much less as the only natural formal vehicle for
rational thought—is unwarranted. At the same time, his assertion of the
supervening importance of musicality, by creating musical scores alongside his lyrical compositions and insisting on stanzaic verse as more affectively charged and mnemonic than rhymed couplets, suggests that literary
transformation hinges more upon musicality and aesthetic ornamentation
than upon rationality or argumentation. Prose and meter, so carefully de-
lineated in their respective and mutually necessary protreptic effects by
Boethius and his commentators, become shifting and slippery categories
of ethical practice in the hands of these vernacular writers.

Thus, by the time Chaucer writes, prosimetric form and its protreptic
function have been extensively explored and exploited, both by late antique writers and by experimental, medieval writers, both in Latin and in
vernaculars. Martianus, Boethius, Alain, Dante, and Guillaume have, by
their experimentation, shown prosimetrum to be plastic, reappropriable,
and flexible—a scaffold for composing large-scale protreptics and for articulating metapoetic principles about the relation of aesthetic experience
to ethical learning. For later Middle English writers, then, prosimetrum
will be a formal choice with a complex and layered cultural resonance.
When they deploy prosimetric form and style, they agitate not only the
long-established cultural presence of Boethius, but also the recent and innovative presences of their vernacular near-contemporaries, both as literary writers and as practicing literary theorists.

---

various forms of discourse in the mixed-form work *Aucassin et Nicolette*. "What is
being staged at this juncture [of different forms and registers] of the text, and thematized in the play of request and refusal, is the nonnaturalness and, therefore, societal-
conventional basis, of forms of verbal interaction." *Emergence of Prose*, 99.

CHAPTER TWO

Sensible Prose and a Sense of Meter: Chaucer's Aesthetic Sentence in the *Boece* and *Troilus and Criseyde*

Like Alain, Dante, and Guillaume, Chaucer recognizes in the *Consolation* a powerful resource for vernacular literary experimentation with the relationship between aesthetic form and ethical function. He first puts this recognition into practice in his Middle English translation of the *Consolation*, the *Boece*.[1] His translation is, throughout, meticulously careful to render Boethius's original protreptic from Latin into accurate Middle English. At all points, the translation maintains the meaning of Boethius's Latin, and whenever that meaning is difficult to render into idiomatic English, the translation is supplemented by recourse to the French *Livre de Boice de Consolacion* by Jean de Meun or to Latin commentaries.[2]

Though he carefully maintains the content of Boethius's original work, the "father of English poetry" makes a bizarre and consequential change to Boethius's formal template. Rather than reproducing the mixed prose and verse form of Boethius's protreptic, he levels the metrical sections entirely, reproducing Boethius's Latin prosimetrum as one of the earliest literary works of Middle English prose. Puzzling over his leveling of the meters, some scholars suggest that Chaucer simply follows Jean de Meun's aforementioned earlier French translation of the *Consolation*, which is

---

1. According to Rita Copeland, the *Boece* is such a careful translation of the *Consolation* that it becomes Chaucer's source text for his later Boethian poems. "Within Chaucer's own canon of writings, the *Boece* effectively displaces its sources, to substitute itself for them as the point of departure for later Boethian efforts" (*Rhetoric, Hermeneutics, and Translation*, 145).

2. See Machan, *Techniques of Translation*, 4–6. On the sources and glosses of Chaucer's *Boece*, see Minnis and Machan, *Sources of Chaucer's 'Boece,"* 9–11; see also Minnis, *Chaucer's "Boece" and Medieval Boethius*.

also composed in prose.[3] As an alternative, I have suggested elsewhere that Chaucer may flatten the meters because of his awareness that the type of meter Boethius composed—quantitative—is not reproducible in English.[4] It is also possible that Chaucer, before translating the *Consolation*, internalized its identification of prose as the "stronger remedy" for philosophical illness and promoted that emphasis to the level of compositional mandate in his own translation.

Although all three explanations are likely part of the story, none fully accounts for Chaucer's turn to an all-prose form, for two reasons. First, though he evidently uses Jean's prose work as a guide to his Middle English redaction of the *Consolation*, there is no reason to assume Chaucer would not feel able to render the Boethian meters in verse just because Jean does not.[5] Second, although Chaucer may well be aware of his inability to reproduce the metrical form of Boethius's Latinate songs in English, his decision to versify select Boethian meters at other points in his career, in the so-called Boethian lyrics as well as in Troilus's famously Boethian "song," indicates both that he can and that he wants to experiment with converting Latin poetry—and specifically Boethius's Latin poetry—into English poetry.[6] The presence of the Boethian lyrics in his corpus also suggests that he continues to think of metrical form as an important vehicle for philosophical work, not to be unilaterally abandoned in favor of prose. His reason for rendering the *Consolation* into prose, then, must have another origin.[7]

3. The authoritative work on the relationship between Jean's *Boece* and Chaucer's remains that of Dedeck-Héry. See "Jean de Meun et Chaucer," 967–91, and "Le *Boèce* de Chaucer," 18–25. The editors of the Riverside Edition of the *Boece* think that "[i]t was probably Jean's example that persuaded him to 'degrade' the poetical parts to prose." Hanna and Lawler, "*Boece*," 397.

4. Eleanor Johnson, "Chaucer and the Consolation of Prosimetrum," 462–63. Bruce Holsinger has suggested, in his analysis of "Sumer is icumen in," that Middle English poets do find a way to experiment with quantitative verse in English. ("Lyrics and Short Poems," 187–90).

5. Indeed, as Copeland points out, Chaucer's translation differs from Jean's in a number of ways and is not a mere imitation of Jean's work (*Rhetoric, Hermeneutics, and Translation*, 142–49).

6. Holsinger, indeed, has suggested that Chaucer composes his Boethian lyrics precisely to atone for his all-prose rendering of the *Consolation* ("Lyrics and Short Poems," 203).

7. Carolyn Eckhardt notes that no one knows why the *Boece* is in prose, despite the prosimetric form of its source, and despite the fact that Chaucer seems to have pre-

This chapter suggests that his leveling of the Boethian meters has its origin in his engagement with three conflicting bodies of early literary theory. The first is an aforementioned aspect of Boethius's theory of prose: namely, his insistence that prose should produce sensation in a reader that leads toward the creation of assent to a new ethical understanding. For Chaucer, as for Boethius, prose must be aesthetic if it is to be protreptically useful. The second is a body of emergent, vernacular, fourteenth-century theories and practices of prose. The third is a well-established Latin tradition of theorizing and practicing prose style. His engagement with these three bodies of prose theory enables him to create his *Boece* not only as a translation of the *Consolation* but also as a meditation on the relation of aesthetic form to ethical content in its own right, a meditation that is situated in its own cultural moment and conversant with contemporary literary-theoretical controversies. Prose form in the *Boece* is thus neither an obeisant nod to Jean nor an admission of poetic inadequacy. Instead, it is a deliberate formal and stylistic choice, rooted in a desire to experiment with the aesthetic possibilities of prose form, and with how prose aesthetics might produce ethically transformative assent on its own, independent of metrical action.

THE VERNACULAR IDEA OF PROSE
IN THE LATE MIDDLE AGES

In being designed to be aesthetic—to produce sensory effects via literary form and style—Chaucer's prose *Boece* debunks an emerging, polemical division that vernacular prose theorists make between prose and meter. By the late fourteenth century, many vernacular literary theorists have become skeptical of meter as a formal vehicle for didactic and truthful writing. Studying the emergence of prose historiographies in France, Gabrielle Spiegel finds that vernacular historiographers come to see meter as an innately deceptive and misleading vehicle for narration. This formal prejudice emanates from their awareness of meter and rhyme as artificial constraints, into which an author must shoehorn his ideas: because a versifier's first obligation is to form, rather than to content, meter is inevita-

---

served the labels "prose" and "meter," which appear in the manuscripts. She also notes that it is problematic to assume that Chaucer was simply following Jean de Meun and suggests that Chaucer seems to have preferred prose as a vehicle for "open" translation ("Medieval Prosimetrum Genre," 21–22, 30–32).

bly a less truthful mode than prose. For this reason, medieval historiographers, keen to represent "truth" as accurately as possible, turn to prose as the obvious and necessary form for historical writing.[8]

Though it is first discernible in France, this turn toward prose as the natural vehicle for "true" writing happens in England as well. In the 1380s, John Trevisa makes clear that prose is preferable to verse because it is easier and clearer, and because it privileges the sense or "matire" of the work. As he himself puts it in the prologue to his translation of Ranulph Higden's Latin history, the *Polychronicon*, "nought sotilte of sentence, nother faire florischynge of wordes, but swetnesse of deuocion of the matire schal regne in this book."[9] The idea that meter, because of its artifice, is intrinsically prone to inaccuracy and even falsehood has crystallized in English historiographical culture by the late fourteenth century; with this crystallization, prose becomes the preferred form for carrying "sentence," or the meaning of an utterance, simply and without "sotilte" of ornament.[10]

The most explicit English association of prose with accuracy and meter with inaccuracy appears in the Wycliffite Bible's preface to Jeremiah. This preface acknowledges that the original was composed in Hebrew "to the mesure of metre and vers."[11] It then goes on to note that the attempt to reproduce original Hebrew meter and verse in Latin has muddled the translation: "the whiche [i.e.: the original Hebrew Jeremiah] . . . han yolden to the mesure of metre and vers. Therfore the ordre of viseouns, that anent Grekes and Latynes outerli is confoundid."[12] The "therefore" in this passage is particularly important: in the mind of the Wycliffite preface writers, the measure of meter and verse is an intrinsic formal obstacle to ac-

---

8. "Finding the poet's search for rhyme and measure to be incompatible with the historian's pursuit of truth and need for exactitude of narration, laymen increasingly sought to satisfy their curiosity about the past in new ways." These "new ways" were prose chronicles. Spiegel, *Romancing the Past*, 2. See also Parkes, "Literacy of the Laity," 555, and Spiegel, "Forging the Past."

9. Trevisa, *Polychronicon*,15.

10. "Sentence" usually denotes the meaning or ideational content of an utterance, rather than the grammatical unit that contains that meaning, as it has come to denote in modern English. *MED*, s.v., "sentence," 5 a–g. However, there are instances in which "sentence" means the grammatical unit that contains the thought. *MED*, s.v., "sentence," 5 h.

11. "Prolog to Jeremiah," 342.

12. Ibid.

curate translation—to translation motivated by a wish to produce "open" and clear writing.[13] The Jeremiah preface goes on to assure its readers that the present retranslation—into English—remedies the Latinate disorder. It does so by rendering the entire original work into English prose. The English *ars prosaica* of the late fourteenth century is, in essence, more matter, less art. Or, to be more precise, the less art, the more matter.[14]

Chaucer's own prose writings bear witness to this emergent idea of prose as a more innately truthful mode than verse, simply through their contents and genres. His *Treatise on the Astrolabe* is a nonfictive, didactic translation and is composed in prose; the same is true of the sermonic and ethically stringent *Parson's Tale*. The prose *Tale of Melibee*, another explicitly and self-consciously didactic work, is a close translation of the French *Livre de Prudence*.[15] When he seeks to translate true, didactic literature, he, like his contemporaries, seeks to render content as accurately as possible.[16] When he seeks to render content accurately, he, like the

13. For a treatment of "openness" as an ethic of translation, and of what that "openness" signifies in practice for the Wycliffites and other early prose stylists, see Mueller, *Native Tongue and the Word*, 40–55.

14. J. D. Burnley's analysis of "curial prose" in late medieval England is consonant with these findings; he demonstrates that the defining characteristics of curial style—namely, lexical doublets, specifiers, and deixis—are designed to clarify sense above all else ("Curial Prose in England," 596–99). As I will demonstrate, however, curial prose style was not the only mode of artful prose practiced in late medieval England.

15. For a comparison of the sources of *Melibee* with *Melibee* itself, see Bornstein, "Chaucer's Tale of Melibee as an Example of the 'Style Clergial.'"

16. Indeed, as Andrew Cole has demonstrated, Chaucer's later writings, notably the prologue to the *Treatise on the Astrolabe* and the treatise itself, were directly influenced by his exposure to Wycliffite writings on translation. According to Cole, Chaucer read the Wycliffite prologue to the Bible and responds to it in the *Astrolabe* prologue ("Chaucer's English Lesson," 1140, 1150–53). In Cole's words, "[T]he Wycliffite General Prologue would provoke Chaucer not only to adopt a new critical language geared toward translation in English (not French or Italian) but to write a prologue on English translation in the first place, thereby adding his voice to a contemporary, local conversation about translation and adopting a form by which he could rank himself amoung a group of innovators in English" (1141). My own analysis suggests that Chaucer was actively participating in a self-conscious group of literary theorists and vernacular translators already by the time he wrote the *Boece*, and that this text, although not prefaced by a translator's prologue, manifests a keen awareness of contemporary literary-theoretical controversies and ideas. Chaucer's interest in bringing Latin language, Latin knowledge, and Latin forms into an experiment with metaliterary concerns is discernible before he would have had access directly to the Wycliffite prologues—probably in

Wycliffite translators and vernacular historiographers, turns from verse to prose.

The *Boece* is no exception to this rule. Examining the *Boece* in the context of Chaucer's other translations, Tim Machan shows that Chaucer's overwhelming concern is conceptual fidelity to Boethius's original. In Machan's view, so consumed is Chaucer with the precise and meticulous transmission of Boethian ideas that he is simply not interested in executing any overarching stylistic design in his Middle English translation. The observation that Chaucer's writing strategies are motivated primarily by a desire to be faithful to thematic content is unassailable: as Machan demonstrates, Chaucer routinely draws in disambiguating synonyms for complex words and unpacks complex Latin constructions. And, moreover, throughout the *Boece*, Chaucer adds glosses and explanations, sometimes drawn from Latin commentaries on Boethius's work, and sometimes drawn from Jean de Meun's French translation. These additions alone suggest that Chaucer seeks to make Boethius's ideas, as abstruse and difficult as they can be at times, easy and accessible to a contemporary reading audience. Chaucer's *Boece*, like his other prose works, and like the other self-consciously true, open, clear, and "matire"-driven prose translations of the late fourteenth century, is intended to be didactic and accurate. Thus, it has no business being composed partially in verse.

Chaucer's formal commitment to conceptual accuracy does not, however, bring with it the programmatic resistance to artifice and ornament that characterizes many other late Middle English practices and theories of prose. Quite the contrary, the *Boece* is full of conspicuously artful, aesthetic writing. Reflecting its wrought artistry, a prominent strain of Chaucer scholarship regards the *Boece* as the high-water mark of Chaucer's stylistic achievements.[17] The challenge, then, in thinking about the theory and practice of prose that animates the *Boece* is to account for the intermittent but pronounced aesthetic richness of the work while remain-

---

1395–96, according to Cole (1154). Chaucer is an active participant in a thriving group of literary-theoretical experimenters and experimental translators by the time he writes the *Boece* in the 1380s.

17. See Saintsbury, *History of English Prose Rhythm*, 72; Baum, "Chaucer's Metrical Prose"; Schlauch, "Chaucer's Prose Rhythms". Recently, Peggy Knapp has said of the eighth meter of book 3: "I cannot read this passage even now, after many years of acquaintance with it, without a thrill I can only describe as delight in beauty." "Aesthetic Attention and the Chaucerian Text," 244.

ing focused on the evident commitment Chaucer has, throughout, to conceptual accuracy.

As I will demonstrate, Chaucer invents and displays a pointedly sensory style—an aesthetic prose—in the *Boece*. This aesthetic prose is designed to be painstakingly faithful to the *Consolation*'s ideation while also making that ideation sense-perceptible and hence more persuasive in its communication of ethical truths and its production of assent. In devising a prose style that magnifies—rather than derogating from—the truth of its contents, Chaucer responds to the contemporary vernacular trend toward prose as the optimal vehicle for true, accurate, and didactic translation. But he does so, significantly, not by conforming to the easy and simple style of Trevisa, or to the "open" prose of the Wycliffites. Instead, he imports into vernacular prose two Latin techniques, deploying each in a way that enables him to make sense—the meaning of his writings—available to the senses. In so doing, he revisits the *Consolation*'s emphasis on making ethical learning happen via aesthetic effects, but he reinvents that emphasis not as a function of the mixed form but as a function of a new form of English artful prose, one textured by Latin prose stylistics.

THE LATIN THEORY OF PROSE

Contemporaneous with the vernacular enshrining of prose as the preferable mode of "true" writing and translating, many vernacular prose stylists, including Chaucer, become keenly interested in the aesthetic possibilities inherent in prose.[18] For Chaucer in particular, this interest arises through his exposure to the *artes dictaminis*, or Latin manuals on the writing of formal letters. Since formal letters were usually written in prose, these guides to epistolary style constitute a Latin corpus of prose theory. Fully to understand what Chaucer is after in his *Boece*, it is crucial to unpack

18. For analyses of Latin influences on Lydgate and Chaucer, see again Burnley, "Curial Prose in England"; for Lydgate and Usk, see Schlauch, "Stylistic Attributes of John Lydgate's Prose". For general treatments of Usk's prose style, see Krapp, *Rise of Early English Literary Prose*, 30; Skeat, introduction, xix; Hayton, "Many Privy Thinges Wimpled and Folde"; and Turner, "'Certaynly his Sayinges Can I Nat Amende'." For analyses of prose stylistics in works of vernacular theology, see especially Chambers, "On the Continuity of English Prose," and Johnson, "Feeling Time, Words, and Will." It is worth noting that many of the most famous examples of high Middle English prose style, notably the prose vernacular theological works of Richard Rolle and Walter Hilton, are framed explicitly as epistles.

and consider how this Latin body of theory understands the project of artful prose.

In these guides, the first principle about the form of prose is, quite simply, that prose is not metrical. Thomas of Capua, a prominent dictaminist
of the thirteenth century, makes this assertion, insisting that prose, by
definition, must be written without being constrained to fit a particular
meter:

> Prosaicum dicitur a proson grece, quod latine significant longum, quia
> in prosa licet alicui longius et latius aut quantumlibet castigatius eva-
> gari. Metricum denominatur a metron grece, quod est mensura latine,
> quia sub certa pedum et syllabarum mensura constitit.[19]

> [Prose is said to come from the Greek "proson," which means in Latin
> "long," because in prose you may wander off farther and wider or,
> as much as you please, be more restrained. Meter is named from the
> Greek "metron," which is "measure" in Latin, because measure con-
> sists in certain feet and syllables.]

Though prima facie obvious, the observation that prose is not metrical has
consequences that are both surprising and significant: prose's lack of meter
allows prose to accommodate the expository needs and desires of authors
better than meter can—authors may "wander off farther and wider or, as
much as you please, be more restrained." The constraining, all-determin-
ing measure of meter is absent in prose; ergo, according to dictaminists,
a prose writer is freer to express his ideation and intention howsoever he
chooses than is a poet. This perception of prose's superior suitedness to
the encapsulation and embodiment of ideation likely informs the vernacular theorists' collective emphasis on prose's innate truthfulness and explains further why prose comes to be the preferred mode of nonfictive vernacular translation: prose's fluid and flexible formal construction allows
a writer relative freedom in articulating ideation precisely and accurately.
Prose is the form in which ideation leads, rather than follows, aesthetic
artistry.

In contrast with prose, which is the form best able to capture and relate
the precise shape and order of a writer's ideation, meter gains a rather un-
savory status in certain dictaminal writings—much as in later vernacular

19. Thomas von Capua, *Die ars dictandi*, 14.

writings and prefaces—precisely for its overly ornate formal strictures and constraints. Another prominent dictaminist, Bernard of Silvester, expands on Capua's theories, limning how metrical composition can vitiate ideation. He opposes prose to meter, defining the former as the continuous writing of speech, unbound by metrics:

> Prosaicum dictamen est litteralis edicio, a lege metrice differens, longa congruaque continuatione procedens . . . Prosa, ut ait Beda in Arte Metrica, est longa oratio a lege metri soluta, quia extra metricam non debet quantitatem mutilari.[20]

> [Prose publishing of a letter is a type of writing, different from metrical rules, proceeding in a long and meet continuity . . . Prose, as Bede says in *The Art of Meter*, is continuous speech unbound by metrical rule, because it should not be mutilated by metrical quantity.]

For Bernard, the difference between metrical and prosaic writing, though still originating in a formal difference, has taken on an ethical valence: since he claims that prose is not "mutilated" by meter, not bound by metrical rules, it seems that he sees prose as a privileged form. These Latin dictaminists, then, manifest an attitude toward prose and meter that resembles—and may indeed inform—that of the Wycliffites: meter, by dint of its stringent and artificial rules, deforms verbal content.

But there is a crucial difference between vernacular theories of prose as "truthful," "clear," and "easy" and what is found in the *artes dictaminis*. The dictaminists' recognition of prose's formal freedom to express ideation accurately does not mean that they see prose as necessarily unartificed. Quite the contrary, the sheer profusion of manuals on how to write prose epistles indicates beyond doubt that there were numerous rules and stylistic considerations to bear in mind when composing in prose. But there is one aspect of how prose style is theorized that bears extra scrutiny. Pushing the theorization of prose's formal relation to meter to its logical limit, many dictaminists suggest that prose, like meter, does consist of "feet," but that the "feet" of prose work differently from those of meter:

> in prosaico dictamine non utimur nisi duobus illis [pedibus] tantummodo, scilicet spondeo et dactilo, nec hos pedes iudicamus secundum

metricam racionem, id est secundum productionem et correptionem sillabarum, sed ex cursu quod habent dictiones.[21]

[in prose dictamen, we use only two of them [feet], namely, spondees and dactyls, but we use those feet not according to metrical rule, that is, according to the production and linking together of syllables, but according to the course that belongs to speech.]

The units of prose are "feet," but the feet of prose are determined not by the production or drawing together of syllables according to the proportions of meter but from the natural course of spoken utterances. Theories of prose understand it as a written reflection of a spoken form.[22] But, crucially, they understand that written reflection of speech as representable by specific formal conventions—prosaic "feet." In practice, this assertion has tremendous consequences for the evolution of literary prose, both in Latin and in Chaucer's Middle English *Boece*.

John of Garland takes the idea that prose obeys certain formal constraints further, noting that spoken utterances—the putative bases of prose composition—are formally organized into clauses: "Dicatur quid sit prosa. Prosa est sermo sentenciosus ornato sine metro compositus, distinctus clausularum debitis intervallis."[23] (Let it be said what prose is. Prose is sententent speech, composed without metrical ornamentation, distinguished by the necessary intervals of clausules.) Like meter, prose is "composed" and "ornate"; the difference is that the fundamental formal units of prose are "clausules"—units of sense and syntax—rather than metrical feet. Prose "feet," determined by the "natural course of utterance," are delimited by syntax. The theory of formal, Latin prose is that the basic formal unit of prose, the clause, is "necessary," because it is determined by syntax—the formal representation of the natural course of spoken utterance—rather than by the artificial constraints of meter. Since prose's fundamental unit is syntactic, it is theorized as the form that thought naturally takes when enfolded into language.

What the dictaminists do with the notion that prose is free from meter and hence free to encapsulate ideation clearly and without fetters, however, is quite different from what the Wycliffites and historiographers do.

21. Bernard of Silvester, introduction to "Il 'Dictamen,'" 194.
22. Mueller, *Native Tongue and the Word*, 1, 5, 7–8.
23. John of Garland, *Parisiana poetria*, 4.

Rather than insisting on prose as an open, natural, easy, and unartificed form, they devise a system of ornamentation that recognizes the "necessary" clausal construction of prose writing and capitalizes on it as a scaffold for aesthetic effects.[24] Since dictaminists recognize clauses as the basic units of prose composition, it is at the level of the clause that they place the characteristic adornments of prose: "Est enim dictamen litteralis edicio, clausulis distincta, verborum et sentenciarum coloribus adornata" (Dictaminal publishing of letters is therefore adorned with distinctness of clausules, and colors of words and sentences).[25] Crucial to the theory of prose style in these manuals is that prose ornamentation, when it occurs, should be necessitated by syntax, not arbitrarily mandated by metrical exigency.

The primary mode of such syntactic ornamentation is *cursus*.[26] Also called cadencing, *cursus* is a system of prose adornment at the ends of clauses, sentences, and sections of argument. It is created when a work of prose deploys one of four prescribed rhythmical patterns to demarcate syntactic units from each other. The first such rhythm is *planus*, in which the final syllables of a clause follow the stress pattern $/ \sim \sim / \sim$, where / represents stress and ~ unstress. The second is *tardus*, so called because it retards the stress patterning of the *planus* by adding an extra unstressed syllable after the second stress: $/ \sim \sim / \sim \sim$. The third is called *velox*, because it introduces a weak stress (`), which accelerates the pace of a clause: $/ \sim \sim \grave{} \sim / \sim$. The fourth pattern, the *choriamb*, is a *planus* with the final unstressed syllable lopped off: $/ \sim \sim /$.[27] By deploying these rhythmical patterns, a prose author can alert his readers to the coming conclusion of a

24. Thus, the dictaminists bear out Kittay and Godzich's assertions about prose and "naturalness": noting how scholarship, both medieval and modern, construes prose as "natural" and unornamented, Kittay and Godzich remind us that "anything communally considered to have the status of natural is most likely the locus of powerful semiotic mechanisms" (xi).

25. John of Garland, *Parisiana poetria*, 98.

26. Indeed, according to Margery Morgan, "Cursus is probably rightly regarded as the most distinctive feature of official letter-writing in the later medieval period" ("Treatise in Cadence," 158).

27. For a thorough treatment of *cursus* and an explanation of it in practice, see Schlauch, "Chaucer's Prose Rhythms." For a more general overview of the *cursus* and its role in dictaminal writings, see Murphy, *Rhetoric in the Middle Ages*, 248–53. Sherman Kuhn describes the basic forms of English *cursus* and analyzes the role and evolution of *cursus* stress patterns even in Old English works ("Cursus in Old English").

clause, sentence, or passage of argumentation and can set off successive clauses from one another.[28] In essence, *cursus* provides its practitioners a mode of nonorthographic, aesthetic punctuation; it deploys sensory patterns of sound and rhythm to mark off the ends of clauses, sentences, and units of argumentation.[29] Prose, as much as meter, is an artificial form of verbal communication, governed by formal conventions. The difference is that the formal conventions of prose originate in syntax, rather than in an "artificial" meter.

In rendering Boethius's work into Middle English prose, Chaucer draws extensively upon the *artes dictaminis* and upon their understanding and practice of artful cadencing. Given that the syntactic practice of prose ornamentation developed in curial courts and is largely associated with Latin documentary culture throughout the high Middle Ages, not with vernacular literary writing, and given also that the practice of formal letter writing declines over the course of the Middle Ages, so that by the time Chaucer writes, cadencing is an obsolescent literary technique, why

28. John of Briggis emphasizes the importance of pacing in the use of *cursus*. See *Compilacio de arte dictandi*, 95: "Item, cavendum est ne duos aut plures dactilos simul ponas, quia multe dicciones celeres simul iuncte deformitatem inducunt. Exemplum: 'Illius ingenium ad nichilum proficit qui viciis deditus minime se corrigit.' Nec eciam simul ponantur dicciones multe nimis tarde, quia impediunt ornatum loquele." (Also, be warned not to put two or more dactyls at once, because many fast cadences together lead to deformation. For example, "ILLius inGENium ad NIchilum proFICit qui VIciis DEditus MInime se corRIgit." Also, do not put together too many slow cadences, since they impede the ornateness of the passage.) For further treatment of *cursus* and its effects, see also Peter of Blois, *Libellus de arte dictandi rhetorice*, 46–47; Thomas Merke, *Formula dictandi et usitati dictaminis*, 134–35; Thomas Sampson, *Modus dictandi*, 163–64.

29. By "nonorthographic," I mean that it is not coded into the work visually, through signs or symbols such as obtain in modern writing: quotation marks, question marks, semicolons, commas, etc. In modern systems of punctuation, a reader sees a question mark and understands from that orthographic mark that the phrase she reads is interrogative; if she sees an exclamation point, she understands exclamatory; if semicolon, a break between independent clauses. *Cursus*, although not as programmatically subdivided and tailored to individual kinds of grammatical and syntactic shifts, similarly achieves punctuation effects, though it does so in an entirely different manner. This idea is borne out by the work of Margaret Schlauch and Margery Morgan. Schlauch suggests that for medieval prose stylists, "[*Cursus*] served, indeed, as a kind of aesthetic punctuation based on rhythm" ("Chaucer's Prose Rhythms," 572). Morgan, too, gestures toward the possibility of reading *cursus* as a mode of punctuation ("Treatise in Cadence," 17 n. 2). For a thorough treatment of the development of orthographic (notational) punctuation, see Parkes, *Pause and Effect*.

should we postulate that Chaucer's prose style would have any relation to the practice of formal Latinate letter writing?[30] First, this diminution of Latin *cursus* may be precisely what makes it available for integration into a vernacular work—just as many other Latin literary forms seep into vernacular use in the same period.[31] But more importantly there are concrete reasons—both explicit and implicit—to think Chaucer is aware of and interested in the practice of *cursus* and in its applicability to vernacular literature.

The explicit reasons emerge in Chaucer's poetry. First, in *The House of Fame*, Chaucer's Dantean eagle urges him "To make bokes, songes, dytees, / In ryme, or elles in cadence."[32] As Margaret Schlauch notes, through his use of the disjunctive "or elles" construction, he draws a distinction between "ryme" and "cadence," or between verse and rhythmical prose.[33] Second, he manifests an interest in the technical aspects of writing formal letters in *Troilus and Criseyde*, when he describes Troilus's first letter to Criseyde. His description can be broken down into the five major parts of a Latin epistle: the *salutatio*, the *captatio benevolentiae*, the *narratio*, the *petitio*, and the *conclusio*.[34] Troilus's *salutatio* reads:

> First he gan hire his righte lady calle,
> His hertes lif, his lust, his sorwes leche,
> His blisse, and ek thise other termes alle
> That in swich cas thise loveres alle seche.[35]

After these salutations, Troilus "gan hym recomaunde unto hire grace," thus performing a vernacular *captatio benevolentiae*.[36] The third part of a letter, the *petitio*, immediately follows, including the word "preyde," an Englishing of *peto*, from which *petitio* derives: "And after this ful lowely he hire preyde / To be nought wroth, thogh he, of his folie / So hardy was

---

30. See Richardson, "Fading Influence of the Medieval *Ars dictaminis* " and "Dictamen and Its Influence."

31. For primary sources that instantiate the medieval awareness of the rise of the vernacular, see Wogan-Browne, *Idea of the Vernacular.*

32. From *House of Fame* in *Riverside Chaucer*, lines 622–23.

33. See Schlauch, "Chaucer's Prose Rhythms," 572–74 and 576.

34. For a discussion of the five parts of a formal letter, see Dalzell, introduction, 19–20.

35. Chaucer, *Troilus*, bk. 2, lines 1065–68.

36. *Troilus*, bk. 2, line 1071.

to hire to write."[37] Troilus then moves into the fourth canonical part of a letter, the *narratio*, or main story the letter seeks to tell, signaling this subpart by his choice of verb ("telle" Englishes *narro*, the root verbal form of *narratio*): "And after that than gan he telle his woo."[38] Finally, we read Troilus's *conclusio* or leave-taking: "And seyde he wolde in trouthe alwey hym holde; / And radde it over, and gan the lettre folde."[39] Through Troilus's meticulous performance of the rules of *dictamen* writing, the *Troilus* evinces an interest in epistolary modes of writing and in rendering those modes into English.[40] Since the overwhelming majority of dictaminal manuals devoted attention to *cursus* as the sine qua non of epistolary prose style, this passage from the *Troilus* also serves as an oblique indication that cadencing would be of interest to Chaucer in his compositional strategies.[41]

The passages from the *House of Fame* and the *Troilus* are not the only indications that Chaucer might have known about and cared to experiment with *cursus*; his prose practice constitutes another, though more implicit, indication. Margaret Schlauch has shown that *cursus* pervades Chaucer's prose corpus and that, in keeping with dictaminal mandates, his use of *cursus* varies according to the stylistic level of the work: his less formal prose writings (*Astrolabe, Parson's Tale, Retractions*) use less, his more formal (*Boece, Melibee*) use more.[42] In prose practice, then, as well as in Troilus's epistolary performance of dictaminal theory, Chaucer manifests a serious and sustained interest in the techniques and mandates of formal Latin prose.[43] But that interest is nowhere more clear, or more re-

37. Cf. *OED*, s.v. "petition," etymology, and *MED*, s.v. "preien," 1. *Troilus*, bk. 2, lines 1072–74.

38. Cf. *OED*, s.v. "narration," etymology, and *MED*, s.v. "tellen," 1a and 1b. *Troilus*, bk. 2, line 1082.

39. *Troilus*, bk. 2, lines 1084–85.

40. For descriptions and overviews of the canonical parts of a letter, see Thomas von Capua, *Die ars dictandi*, 16; Transmundus, *Introductiones dictandi*, 60–65; Peter of Blois, *Libellus de arte dictandi rhetorice*, 52–53; Thomas Merke, *Formula moderni et usitati dictaminis*, 123–41.

41. Monica McAlpine also registers the narrator's seeming awareness of the conventions of letter writing, basing her argument on lines 1067–68, which read, "thise other termes alle / That in swich cas thise lovers alle seche," but she does not track this conventionality onto the *artes dictaminis* (*Genre of Troilus and Criseyde*, 38–39).

42. She notes, indeed, that the *Boece* contains a 25 percent rate of *cursus* at the ends of clauses and sentences. See Schlauch, "Chaucer's Prose Rhythms," 582–85.

43. This reading of Chaucer's interest in Latin prose theory dovetails with and reconfirms Andrew Cole's argument about Chaucer's prologue to the *Treatise on the*

velatory of his literary-theoretical ambitions, than in his *Boece,* where he shows himself to be a self-conscious *dérimeur* of the highest order, keen to show how ethically transformative ideation could be rendered sensible through the formal artifice of *cursus.*[44]

CHAUCER'S INTEGRATED PROSE THEORY AND PRACTICE: THE AESTHETIC SENTENCE I

Before I analyze how and why *cursus* matters to the formal composition of the *Boece,* I will review how cadencing translates from Latin into English vernacular practice in broad strokes. Although not a particularly familiar device to a modern reader, *cursus* is readily perceptible as a stylistic device: one generally need only read with reference to the stress patterns of modern English and listen for the four prescribed rhythmic patterns.[45] For example, in the passage "O ye, my frendes, what or wherto avaunted ye *me to be weleful?* [planus] For he that hath fallen stood noght in *stedefast degree* [choriamb]," "me to be weleful" would be stressed on "me" and "wele" and would be unstressed on "to be" and "ful," just as in modern

---

Astrolabe, in which Cole suggests that Chaucer's interest in translation as a literary and cultural challenge leads him to devise "a novel version of *translatio studii* that recognizes the utility and prestige of the European vernaculars" ("Chaucer's English Lesson," 1135). Chaucer's reworking of Latin *cursus* patterns into English prosody reflects his investment in experimenting with the intricacies of translation into the vernacular.

44. "Derhymers" are what Kittay and Godzich call the French medieval writers who took versified works and rendered them into prose (*Emergence of Prose,* 27–28).

45. By and large, I follow the rules for stress espoused by Burrow and Turville-Petre, who place primary stress "on a word's first syllable unless that syllable is an unstressable prefix." As they note, "Since this is also modern English practice, the reader will encounter no difficulty with most words." See *Book of Middle English,* 13–14. In words imported into English from French, however, I follow Halle and Keyser, who argue that Romance rules trumped Germanic rules. See "Chaucer and the Study of Prosody." There is, though, a difference between Chaucer's use of *cursus* in English and Latin tradition. In canonical, Latinate *cursus,* the stress patterns were to be divided among bisyllables and trisyllables; monosyllabic words were not endorsed as part of good *cursus* endings. But Chaucer's *cursus* includes short words, as the syntactic and linguistic particularities of the English language require. Latin *cursus* is free from the rhythmical constraints imposed by articles and prepositions and so can be structured consistently on bi- and trisyllabic words. As Margery Morgan notes, "English vocabulary would lack the great number of polysyllables found in Latin, so that we must not expect to find the identical *cursus*-patterns familiar in Latin texts" ("Treatise in Cadence,"163).

English.[46] As in modern English, "stedefast" would receive stress on its first syllable, and "degree" on its second. In this phrase, by using *cursus* endings, conventional to formal prose style and grounded in the natural stress patterns of the English language, Chaucer makes the ends of clauses perceptible to the senses, marking off grammatical units of ideation from each other through sonic patterning.

To show *cursus* in action, I will focus on the eighth meter of book 2 of the *Boece*. I will break this passage into clauses and purge all editorial punctuation, to allow the punctuating effect of *cursus* to emerge more readily.

                                                              /   ~~   / ~ ~

1. That the world with stable feyth varieth ac*cordable chaungynges* (tardus)

2. that the contrarious qualites of elementz holden amonge hemself
      / ~ ~ / ~~
    ally*aunce perdurable* (tardus)

3. that Phebus the sonne with his goldene chariet bryngeth forth the
    / ~ ~ /
    rosene day (choriamb)

                                           / ~ ~ / ~

4. that the moone hath comaundement *over the nyghtes* (planus)
                                      / ~ ~   / ~

5. whiche nyghtes Esperus the eve *sterre hath broughte* (planus)
                                             /   ~ ~

6. that the see gredy to flowen constreyneth with a certein *eende his*
    / ~
    floodes (planus)

                                        /   ~ ~ `

7. so that it is nat leveful to strecche his brode termes or *bowndes uppon*
    ~ /   ~
    the erthes (velox)

                       / ~ ~ ` ~ / ~

8. that is to seyn to *coveren al the erthe* (velox)[47]

46. Chaucer, *Boece*, in *Riverside Chaucer*, bk. I, m. 1, lines 29–32. All further citations from this work will be drawn from this edition.

47. In situations where a clause and *cursus* pattern end with a final, unstressed -*e*, I follow the guidelines outlined in Ian Robinson's theory of Chaucer's prosody. To wit, I generally assume that final -*e* is elided when the following word begins with a vowel (*Chaucer's Prosody*, 100). The exception I make, as in the case of the -*e* at the end of

            /   ~   ~   /~

9. al this accordaunce and ordenaunce of thynges is *bounde with love* (planus)

            /   ~ ~   `   ~

10. that governeth erthe and see and hath also co*mandement to the*

 / ~

 hevene (velox)

      / ~   ~   / ~ ~

11. and yif this love *slakede the bridelis* (tardus)

        /   ~   ~ / ~

12. alle thynges that now *loven hem togidres* (planus) ("loven" syncopated to avoid three consecutive unstressed syllables)

      / ~ ~ / ~ ~

13. wolden make ba*tayle continuely* (tardus)

       /   ~   ~   /   ~

14. and stryven to fordo the fas*soun of this worlde* (planus)

          / ~   ~ / ~

15. the which they now leden in accordable feith by *fayre moeuynges* (planus)

         / ~ ~ /

16. this love halt togidres peples joyned with *an holy boond* (choriamb)[48]

       / ~ ~   `   ~ / ~

17. and knytteth sacrement of mari*ages of chaste loves* (velox)

      / ~   ~ / ~

18. and love enditeth lawes to *trewe felawes* (planus)[49]

    / ~   ~   /   ~

19. o weleful *were mankynde* (planus)

      / ~ ~   / ~ ~   / ~   ~   `   ~ / ~

20. yif thilke love that *governeth hevene* (tardus) *governed yowr corages* (velox)[50]

---

this line, is when the following word seems to begin a new sentence and not just a new clause. By contrast, the *-e* at the end of "hevene" in line 10 elides with the *a-* of the following line, as does the *-e* at the end of "bonde" in line 16.

48. I stress the word "an," because, in this passage, Chaucer is emphasizing the unity, the oneness, of God's creation; thus, the word "one" should receive strong stress. In doing so, I again follow Robinson's principles, in which sense, ultimately, should lead stress (*Chaucer's Prosody*, 124, 130–31, 175).

49. Here, I want to note that "felawes" should probably be stressed on its second syllable, because doing so produces a medial word-rhyme between "lawes" and "felawes."

50. Bk. 2, m. 8, lines 1–27.

This passage, a meter in Boethius's original Latin *Consolation*, cadences the end of every clause, culminating in the final line, which contains two concatenated *cursus* endings. This pervasive cadencing allows each syntactic unit to stand on its own, marked off not only as a unit of sense but also as a unit of sensation. Although this former Boethian meter does not reproduce meter per se, its cadencing of clauses is so pervasive that clauses and sentences become de facto units of measure, in which the measured item is meaning, thought, and ideation, rather than syllabic lengths or feet. Through this prosodic and syntactic meter, through its programmatic calling of attention to clauses as formal units of composition, the ethical meaning of the passage becomes aesthetically perceptible. Syntax becomes an aesthetic mode of ethical meaning-making. Vernacular prose form, adopting Latin prose stylistics, becomes a technique of protreptic transformation, a technique for making the ethical sense of Boethius's *Consolation* sensible to a vernacular readership.

Nowhere else does the *Boece* deploy this clausal, prosaic "meter" with the consistency of book 2, meter 8. Indeed, when Tim Machan acknowledges that *cursus* appears in the *Boece* but stresses "how rare such passages are," he is right: long stretches in the *Boece* are quite light on cadencing.[51] But this lack of pervasiveness does not detract from the literary-theoretical salience of the ornament; quite the contrary, Chaucer's choice to cadence this particular passage so heavily reveals an essential element of his *ars prosaica*. He was captivated by this passage, retranslating it twice again into verse in his *Troilus and Criseyde*.[52] Its subject is the intrinsic and ineluctable connectedness of creation, revealed as the divine order and patterning that embraces and governs all life. By cadencing the end of every clause, Chaucer creates a stylistic reflex of the thematic of connection and likeness at the core of Boethius's original meter—he shows how ornamented prose can make Boethius's philosophical meaning sense-perceptible, in essence, by devising a prosodic meter. This passage of Chaucer's *Boece* is designed to create aesthetic effects that augment meaning, rather than, borrowing the phrasing of the dictaminists, "mutilating" it.

Cursus is one solution to the problem of creating aesthetic ornamentation in conceptually accurate English prose, but the *Boece* recognizes and

51. Machan, *Techniques of Translation*, 108.

52. The proem to book 3 and Troilus's "song" in book 3 of the *Troilus* are both, as Stephen Barney notes, adaptations and translations of this meter. See *Troilus and Criseyde*, ed. Barney, 149 n. 2.

cultivates a similar capacity in alliteration. The *Boece*'s use of alliteration is neither more regular nor more pervasive than its use of *cursus*, but is instead driven by the conceptual content of a passage, appearing only when warranted by sense. If Chaucer used alliteration pervasively in his translation, choosing words consistently to conform to a preexisting pattern of alliteration, he would sacrifice the conceptual precision of his translation to an arbitrarily imposed form. By using alliteration irregularly and sparingly instead, he contrives a system of ornamentation that always follows, and never leads, ideation—a system that dovetails with and supplements his cadencing by creating sonic likenesses between words.

Although alliteration appears at intervals throughout the *Boece*, some of the densest alliteration in the work appears in the very first former meter, when Boece bewails his fate:

> For eelde is comyn unwarly uppon me, *hasted* by the *harmes* that Y *have*, and sorwe *hath* comandid his age to ben in me. *Heeris hore* arn schad overtymeliche upon myn *heved*, and the *slakke skyn* trembleth of myn emptid body . . . Allas, allas! With how *deef* an ere *deth*, cruwel, turneth awey fro *wrecches* and nayteth to closen *wepynge* eien . . . Fortune cloudy *hath chaunged* hir deceyvable *chere* to meward, myn *unpietous* lif *draweth* along *unagreable duellynges* in me.[53]

In this passage, the agent of the passive second clause, "harmes" alliterates with its verb, "hasted." A few lines later, "heeris" is made to alliterate with "hore," the adjective that describes the "heeris," and with the "heved" on which they are found. Boece's "skyn" is described as "slakke," and the "deefness" of "deth" is accentuated by a *d* alliteration; Fortune's "chere" is said to "chaunge"; and Boece claims his "unpietous" life "draweth" "unagreable" "duellynges" in him. In each case, alliteration serves to highlight semantic relationships among words, creating an architecture of sonic likeness to subtend and shore up the sense of the passage.

One might assume that the alliteration affiliates the *Boece* with the long-standing tradition of insular literary ornamentation, stretching back to the alliterative prose of Old English writers.[54] This assumption is doubt-

---

53. Bk. 1, m. 1, lines 13–17, 20–23, 26–29.

54. Bruce Holsinger associates Chaucer's rare but pointed alliterative impulses, for instance in the *Parlement of Fowles*, with his awareness of and eagerness to register, though not consistently deploy, the presence and pressure of contemporary insular aes-

less true to a degree: Chaucer would recognize alliteration as a particularly suitable mode of ornamentation for his Englishing of Boethius's *Consolation*, since he would have been able comfortably to rely upon a certain
degree of audience familiarity with the form.[55] But the use of alliteration
in the *Boece* draws more immediately on the formal example of Boethius's
own Latin stylistics, and thus constitutes another aesthetic choice, along
with cadencing, that originates in Latin but transfers admirably into English. Boethius deploys alliteration frequently in his meters, as in his second meter, when he interweaves *m* and *p* alliterations, and concatenates *t*
alliterations and *s* alliterations.

> Heu, quam *praecipiti mersa profundo*
> *mens* hebet et *propria* luce relicta
> *tendit* in externas ire *tenebras*
> *terrenis* quoties flatibus aucta
> *crescit* in immensum noxia *cura* . . .
> quin etiam *causas* unde *sonora*
> flamina *sollicitent* aequora ponti,
> quis uoluat *stabilem spiritus* orbem
> uel cur Hesperias *sidus* in undas
> casurum rutilo *surgat* ab ortu.[56]

The *Boece*'s translation of this passage similarly interweaves alliterations,
though many of the alliterating letters are different from those in Boethius's Latin. The *Boece* replaces the interlaced *m* and *p* alliterations with
th and *d* alliterations:

> Allas how the *thought* of this *man, dreynt* in ouer*throwynge dep-
> nesse, dulleth* and forleteth hys propre clerenesse, *myntynge* to gone in
> to foreyne *dirknesses* as ofte as hys anoyos bysynes waxeth withoute
> mesure, that is dryven with *werldly wyndes* . . . he was *wont* to *seken*
> the causes whennes the *sounynge wyndes* moeven and bysien the
> *smothe watir* of the *see*; and what *spirit* turneth the *stable* hevene;

thetic conventions, such as he might have encountered in Langland's *Piers Plowman*'s
opening lines ("Lyrics and Short Poems," 191–93).

55. For more on Chaucer's possible aesthetic affiliations with the Old English alliterative tradition, see Cooper, "Chaucer's Poetics," 31–50.

56. Bk. 1, m. 2, lines 1–5, 13–17.

and why the *sterre* ariseth out of the rede est, to fallen in the *westrene wawes*.[57]

As the passage goes on, it, like the *Consolation*, deploys an extended pattern of *s* alliterations, on words nearly identical to (indeed, often cognate with) the words in Boethius's Latin: "sounynge," "spirit," and "stable" all follow the Latin closely—"sonora," "spiritus," and "stabilem." But, in addition to the *s* alliterations and the *th* and *d* alliterations, the *Boece* introduces new alliterations to the passage. It adds the term "westrene" to create a final alliteration between noun and modifier on "westrene wawes" that harks back to the "werldly wyndes" just a few lines before. It also creates alliteration between the noun "man" and its modifier "myntynge." Chaucer thus not only reproduces but also augments the alliteration he finds in Boethius's Latin, taking a relatively minor aspect of Boethius's metrical creation of architectures of likeness and converting it into a major aspect.

Alliteration appears not just in the passages that are metrical in the Latin but also in the renderings of Boethius's prose sections. Thick alliteration appears in the first former prose of book 1. Boece looks up "aboven the heyghte of [his] heved" to see Philosophy, who looms far above "the myghte of men."[58] Here, alliterative doublets underscore how incredible Philosophy's sheer height is, and they then continue throughout this prose section: "holden hertes," "myne muses," "abassyched and astonyd."[59] But, as the description goes on, the alliteration takes on a more specific purpose: Boece notes that "sometyme it semede that sche touchede the *hevene* with the *heghte* of *here heved*. And whan sche *hef hir heved heyere*, sche perced the selve *hevene*."[60] Here, the alliterative practice of the *Boece* produces not only emphasis but also an aural contiguity among words that are contiguously related in the narrative; that is, as Philosophy heaves her head higher into the heavens, Chaucer aestheticizes the semantic linkages among those words by highlighting them with alliteration. What is striking about Philosophy's stature is that her head reaches into the heights of the heavens; what is striking about Chaucer's prose style is that it renders that reaching aesthetically available, showing her head to be sensibly con-

57. Bk. 1, m. 2, lines 1–6, 15–21.
58. Bk. 1, pr. 1, sentences 4, 7.
59. Bk. 1, pr. 1, sentences 58, 72, 81.
60. Bk. 1, pr. 1, sentences 15–19.

nected to the heavens themselves, "heaved" up to their "heights." Chaucer's alliterative practice in this section, too, originates with Boethius:
"nunc uero pulsare *caelum* summi uerticis *cacumine* uidebatur; quae cum
altius *caput* extulisset ipsum etiam *caelum* penetrabat."[61] But Chaucer
once again carries the alliteration much further than Boethius, adding the
phrase "hef hir heved heyere," in place of Boethius's "caput altius extulisset." Chaucer takes Boethius's delicate alliterative pattern and promotes it
to a much higher level of aesthetic salience, using it as a formal rendering
of semantic contiguity.

This alliterative practice, driven by semantics and inspired by Latin,
takes on a self-analyzing force in the final former meter of book 1. After describing the human spirit, ruled by passions, the passage reads, "For
cloudy and derk is *thilke thoght*, and *bownde* with *bridelis*."[62] Here, the
second alliteration, "bownde with bridelis," describes the first alliteration, "thilke thoght," but also sonically enacts the binding described—the
letters being bound together by the bridles of sound. Through this formal
architecture, readers recognize the binding taking place in the work itself, the binding done by letters linked together, and they experience that
binding as an aestheticization of Philosophy's conceptual point through
sound.

Chaucer's expanded use of alliteration makes a reader feel the relationships between words and ideas; it makes those relationships sense-
perceptible. Throughout these alliteratively rich passages, how Chaucer
chooses to promote alliteration is crucially important to his artful prose
style and again reveals his *ars prosaica*. His alliteration is not random
but specifically linked to the meaning of the translated passage. In his
hands, alliteration reinforces semantic relationships between words, making sonic connections between nouns and adjectives, pronouns and nouns,
verbs and nouns. He uses sound to forge a sense of contiguity within a
passage. He uses the aesthetic field to underpin the ethical contents of the
work that he translates.

His use of alliteration thus dovetails with his use of *cursus*, in that
both are designed to work as modes of aesthetic punctuation, of making
Boethius's ethically restorative meaning available to the senses.[63] Cadenc-

61. Bk. 1, pr.1, sentences 8–11.
62. Bk. 1, m. 7, lines 19–20.
63. Similar usages of alliteration occur in the prose writings of Aelfric, which Anne
Middleton describes as "rhythmical prose." In her assessment, such prose deploys a
regularity of alliteration to consistent stylistic and rhetorical effect: "As each modifier

ing works by bounding and delimiting units of syntax; alliteration works by reinforcing semantic relationships within and among syntactic units and by creating a sonic architecture of likeness. Indeed, some of the most powerful passages in the *Boece* come when he combines alliteration and *cursus*, making "sentence," or meaning, a matter not only of aesthetic syntax but also of aesthetic semantics. This combination occurs notably in the aforementioned eighth meter of book 2. As I noted earlier, every clause in this passage ends with a *cursus* ending, creating a de facto syntactic meter. To that dense cadencing, Chaucer adds a number of alliterative elements that are not present in the Latin original.

> And yif this love slakede the bridelis, alle thynges that now loven hem togidres wolden make batayle contynuely, and stryven to *fordo* the *fassoun* of this world, the which they now leden in accordable *feith* by *fayre* moevynges. This love halt togidres peples joyned with an holy boond, and knytteth sacrement of mariages of chaste *loves*; and *love* enditeth *lawes* to trewe felawes. O *weleful weere* mankynde, yif thilke love that *governeth* hevene *governed* yowr corages.[64]

Here, the binding together of semantically related words through alliterative likeness reduplicates sonically and visually the binding together of the universe by divine love and works in concert with the syntactic ligatures afforded by *cursus*. This cadenced alliteration aestheticizes the meaning of his work, making sense a matter of form and style by cultivating aesthetic likenesses. *Cursus* works as a mode of punctuation that aestheticizes the boundaries between syntactic units and creates rhythmical echoes among them; alliteration reinforces semantic relationships among words, making them seem naturally bound to each other.

Because it is designed to render meaning available to the senses via the structures of syntax and semantics, I would term Chaucer's alliterative and cadenced style in the *Boece* "aesthetic sentence." It is a style of writing geared to render ethical meaning accurately not by omitting aesthetic artifice but instead by making that meaning sense-perceptible, through the joint deployment of alliteration and cadencing as two mutually reinforcing techniques of literary expression, the one making se-

---

is bound in place by alliteration and a rhythmic symmetry of some kind, it seems necessary and just . . . he uses it to promote moral as well as aesthetic assent" ("Aelfric's Answerable Style," 88).

64. Bk. 2, m. 8, lines 16–27.

mantic relations sense-perceptible, the other making syntactic boundaries sense-perceptible. Chaucer's aesthetic sentence is a response both to
the competing literary theories and practices of his historical moment and
to Boethius's commitment to making sense sensible. It reveals Chaucer's
reconciliation of the idea of prose as a truthful, accurate form, freed from
the "mutilating" strictures of meter, with the Boethian notion that a philosophic work should be rendered aesthetically available through its formal
devices. By ornamenting his writing at the level of the clause, Chaucer
allows a unit of syntax and ideation to be the basic aesthetic and formal
unit of his composition. In thus conforming to dictaminal mandates, he
seamlessly joins ethical content to aesthetic experience, sense to sensibility, what medieval writers called "sentence" (meaning) to what modern
writers call "sentence" (whole grammatical units).

Indeed, Chaucer's stylistic drive to make meaning sense-perceptible
through the sentence locates him at the cusp of a significant shift in the
definition of "sentence," as it moves from denoting meaning (content) to
denoting the formal structure of syntactic and grammatical wholeness.
Thus, the *Boece* asserts that the aesthetic experience is essential to the
conveyance of ethical teaching; it asserts that there is no meaning without form. In the *Boece*, style is nothing short of the aestheticization of
ethical meaning—the rendering sense-perceptible of a protreptic narrative. In Chaucer's lifetime, while prose works its way into cultural consciousness increasingly as the form of veracity, accuracy, and naturalness,
the *Boece* stands as witness to the possibility—indeed the necessity—of
maintaining an attention to the aesthetic, and even to the formally ornate,
in prose. Indeed, it is in the late medieval tradition of protreptic literature
that discernibly aesthetic prose comes into its own in Middle English—as
I will discuss further in my fifth chapter's discussion of Thomas Usk's
Testament of Love.[65]

65. With the partial exception of prose romances, prose form, prior to the end of the
fourteenth century, was primarily a vehicle for nonfictive writing (manuals, treatises,
sermons, saint's lives, history, devotional manuals) or for translations. For analyses of
the stylistic and ideational continuities in these nonfictive genres, see Chambers, *On
the Continuity of English Prose*. I call prose romances a "partial" exception because, as
Gabrielle Spiegel has shown, the increasing prestige of romance as a "true" and "nonfictive" historiographical discourse is intimately linked with its increasing appearance
in prose form. That is, the emergent ideology of romance as a nonfictional form of writing, a form of writing concomitant with historiography, coincides with the transition of
that genre from verse form to prose (*Romancing the Past*, 1–10, 57, 59–61).

RIME ROYAL AND HETEROGLOSSIA:
THE AESTHETIC SENTENCE II

Chaucer's experiment with aestheticizing syntax in the *Boece* is not an isolated event, even in his own body of works. He returns to the problem of rendering meaning sense-perceptible later in his career, reexploring the boundaries, both theoretical and practical, of the aesthetic sentence. This ongoing experimentation occurs in the rime royal form of *Troilus and Criseyde*. Despite its wrought metrical and rhythmical patterning, which would seem a surefire way to "mutilate" meaning by superimposing excessive metrical regularity, rime royal proves an ideal ground for testing how one might versify the aesthetic sentence and thereby create a poetic reflex of the experiment with aesthetic prose in the *Boece*.

To explain how and why rime royal relates to aesthetic prose, it is useful to review the overt structures of the form. Rime royal closely resembles the *ottava rima*, an eight-line stanzaic form with a rhyme scheme of *abababcc*. Since this is the form of Boccaccio's *Il filostrato*, the Italian poem that the *Troilus* translates, it is tempting to assume that rime royal had simply to do with Chaucer's wish to remain close to Boccaccio's formal example—it is tempting, that is, to assert the verse equivalent of the hypothesis that Chaucer chose prose for the *Boece* simply because Jean de Meun chose it for his French *Livre de Boice de Consolacion*. There is considerable metrical and rhythmical reason to make this assertion: Chaucer's verse practices in the *Troilus*, and in his other rime royal works, do indeed owe much to the Italian *ottava rima*.[66] But Chaucer's particular use of the rime royal form in the *Troilus* goes far beyond mere mimicry of Boccaccio's poem.

To show how, I will first explore the differences between Chaucer's use of rime royal in the *Troilus* and Boccaccio's use of *ottava rima* in the *Filostrato*. David Wallace has observed that Boccaccio's verse is more apt to overflow its linear boundaries than Chaucer's, noting that Boccaccio's lines frequently are not end-stopped but continue into the next line. Chaucer, by contrast, end-stops most lines, fitting clauses and sentences neatly into metrical patterning and into rhythmical units. Syntax that overflows from one stanza into the next, as Wallace notes, is extremely rare in the *Troilus*, in comparison with what is seen in Boccaccio's poem. When a

---

66. For a thorough analysis of the relationship of Chaucer's rime royal with the Italian and French antecedent forms, based largely on use of caesuras, see Duffell, "Craft so longe to lerne," 271, 282 and 283.

stanza contains two sentences, the first sentence almost always termi-
nates at the end of a line, so that both sentences in the stanza terminate
at a sonically and rhythmically marked point, in an end rhyme after a run
of five stresses. From these observations, Wallace concludes that Chaucer
makes his poem more conspicuously lyrical and more fully poetic than
his source, tailoring each unit of syntax and ideation as carefully as possible to the metrical unit of the line.[67]

Building on these observations, I would suggest that in tailoring
clauses and sentences to lines and stanzas, the *Troilus* revisits and revises
the central formal experiment that animated the *Boece*: the creation of an
aesthetic sentence—a system of ornamentation by which syntactic boundaries could be rendered sense-perceptible. The *Troilus*'s rime royal stanzas
force metrical and rhythmical units to coincide with syntax, using stanzas as boundaries or bumpers for sense. The rime royal stanzaic form thus
privileges the entire sentence as a formal unit, as a structure of meaning that must be folded neatly into the seven lines and thirty-five stresses
of the rime royal stanza. The management of sentences and clauses into
stanzas and lines thus constitutes an aesthetic means of calling attention
to units of thought, just as cadencing did in the *Boece*.[68]

By being aesthetically managed in this way, the poem becomes more
readily navigable.[69] Rime royal aesthetically alerts a reader not just to
clauses but also to the units of plot, dialogue, and argumentation that the
poem is built around, as when Troilus laments the loss of Criseyde to the
Greek camp:

"O verrey lord, O Love! O god, allas!
That knowest best myn herte and al my thought,
What shal my sorwful lif don in this cas,
If I forgo that I so deere have boughte?
Syn ye Criseyde and me han fully broughte

---

67. See Wallace, *Chaucer and the Early Writings of Boccaccio*, 106–40.

68. "Chaucer's special genius, his unique contribution to the rime royal form,
is that he applied the French ballade stanza to narrative in *Anelida and Arcite, The
Parlement of Fowles, Troilus and Criseyde*, and four stories in *The Canterbury Tales*."
Dean, "Chaucer, Gower, and Rime Royal," 252.

69. Owen, "Thy Drasty Rhymyng." In analyzing Chaucer's use of rime royal in
the *Troilus*, Owen asserts, "Chaucer plays the stanza (rime royal) for many effects. The
commonest . . . is simply an unobtrusive decoration of language that impedes narrative
as little as possible" (543).

Into youre grace, and bothe oure hertes seled,
How may ye suffre, allas, it be repeled?"[70]

In this lamentation, nearly every line is syntactically end-stopped, providing a rhythmical architecture in which Troilus's syntax can be perceived
and in which the breaks in his ideation can be anticipated. The first line of
the stanza contains his address to Love; the second contains a subordinate
clause modifying that address. Lines 3 and 4 contain, respectively, the
two clauses of a conditional question. Line 5 syntactically overflows into
line 6, but the two lines together are end-stopped and form another whole
syntactic unit, the first subordinate clause of a question. Line 7 contains
the independent clause of that same question. The line endings and end
rhymes coincide with the natural pauses of sense and syntax, affording a
sonic architecture in which units of thought become rhythmically perceptible. Through this rhythmical managing of syntax, the *Troilus* recreates
the *Boece*'s "aesthetic sentence" experiment in verse. This recreation destabilizes the dictaminal notion that prose is the natural form of clauses,
sentences, syntax, and, hence, meaning, while meter is all for artifice, to
the mutilation of sense. The *Troilus* makes plain that verse can aestheticize meaning via the structures of syntax—via thought units—just as
readily as prose could in the *Boece*.

But the *Troilus*'s verse experiment with syntax goes farther than did
the prose aesthetic sentence experiment of the *Boece*. Frequently, the *Troilus* uses its rhythmical architecture to differentiate between speakers and
to separate the narrator from the characters in the story. For instance, in
book 5, the formal structure of rime royal facilitates shifts between speakers, when Troilus expresses his hope that Criseyde will return to him, and
Pandarus both tries to comfort Troilus outwardly and also thinks lamen-
tative thoughts to himself.

"Allas, thou seyst right soth," quod Troilus;
"But, hardily, it is naught al for nought
That in myn herte I now rejoysse thus;
It is ayeyns som good I have a thought.
Not I nat how, but syn that I was wrought,
Ne felte I swich a comfort, dar I seye;
She comth to-nyght, my lif that dorste I leye!"

70. Bk. 4, lines 288–94.

Pandare answerde, "It may be, wel ynough,"
And helde with hym of al that evere he seyde.
But in his herte he thoughte, and softe lough,
And to hymself ful sobreliche he seyde,
"From haselwode, there joly Robyn pleyde,
Shal come al that that thow abidest heere.
Ye, fare wel al the snow of ferne yere."[71]

Here, the poem enfolds Troilus's entire utterance into one stanza and Pandarus's into the second. This enfolding uses stanzaic structure to separate speakers from one another and to render voicing perceptible in the rhythmical architecture of rime royal form.

Within stanzas, the rime royal form further parses the content of this passage: all of Troilus's clauses are tucked neatly into individual lines, providing his utterance with syntactic predictability via metrical regularity, while Pandarus's stanza is somewhat more varied. The first lines contain a whole sentence, which reports his external statement. The switch between lines (here, between lines 2 and 3) then manages a switch into the interior world of a character: lines 3 through 7 all recount Pandarus's "thought." Within his "thought," his syntax remains carefully tailored to line lengths, so that, again, units of ideation are also units of form and ornamentation, marked by rhyme, rhythm, and meter. In the stanza preceding these, there is a closer yoking of the two voices of Troilus and Pandarus, but they are still kept aesthetically distinct by being segregated across lines. The passage begins with Troilus speaking:

"We han naught elles forto don, ywis.
And Pandarus, now woltow trowen me?
Have here my trouthe, I se hire! Yond she is!
Heve up thyn eyen, man! Maistow nat se?"
Pandare answerde, "Nay, so mote I the!
Al wrong, by God! What saistow, man? Where arte?
That I se yond nys but a fare-carte."[72]

Here, Troilus's speech is limited to the first four lines, the *abab* section of the stanza, and Pandarus is restricted to the final three lines, the *bcc*. Within these two sections, Troilus's speech is carefully tailored to his in-

71. Bk. 5, lines 1163–76.
72. Bk. 5, lines 1156–62.

dividual lines: lines 1 and 2 encompass the two lines of a question, line 3 encompasses two full sentences, and line 4 encompasses an exclamation and a question. Not just the stanzaic form, then, but also the rhyme scheme's marking off of clausal units by lineation helps to render voicing more parsable by rendering it more sensory, and, thereby, to render the complex multivocality of the poem more navigable for readers. Even when the enclosure of Troilus within the quatrain of the stanza and of Pandarus in the tercet is partially frustrated by the fact that the switch in their voicing ruptures a rhymed couplet—the *bb* of lines four and five—the metrical form still facilitates the reading of dialogue. The effect of this split couplet is to create the sense of closeness between Pandarus and Troilus—quite literally, the sounds of their speech echo each other in rhyme. Thus, the space between stanzas typically serves to aestheticize differentiation between speakers; the space within the stanzas, while keeping Pandarus and Troilus distinct, also serves to draw them together.

A yet more intricate instance of rhythmical parsing of dialogue comes in book 3, when Criseyde and Pandarus and Troilus are all talking together, after Pandarus has brought Troilus to Criseyde in the night. The passage begins with four lines of omniscient narration, which contain four syntactic units. It then moves into Pandarus's voice when the *abab* quatrain slips into the *bcc* tercet, sonically and rhythmically marking the shift from narration to direct speech:

> Therwith his manly sorwe to biholde
> It myghte han mad an herte of stoon to rewe;
> And Pandare wep as he to water wolde,
> And poked evere his nece new and newe,
> And seyde, "Wo bygon ben hertes trewe!
> For love of God, make of this thing an ende,
> Or sle us both at ones er ye wende."[73]

But, as in the previous example, the shift of voicing between lines 4 and 5 also divides a rhymed couplet, here on "newe" and "trewe." Just as the previous split couplet made the closeness and empathy between Troilus and Pandarus aesthetically available, this split makes a likeness between Pandarus and the narrator aesthetically available; the shift from quatrain to tercet facilitates the shift in voicing, while the couplet shared between them makes a *full* separation of Pandarus from the narrator impossible.

73. Bk. 3, lines 113–19.

In the subsequent stanza, there is a far greater degree of complexity in voicing, as Criseyde and Pandarus alternate in speaking. That greater degree of complexity is again made more readily parsable by the poem's careful management of clauses into sense-delimited, decasyllabic, rhymed lines:

> "I, what?" quod she, "by God and by my trouthe,
> I not nat what ye wilne that I seye."
> "I, what?" quod he, "that ye han on hym routhe,
> For Goddes love, and doth him nought to deye!"
> "Now than thus," quod she, "I wolde hym preye
> To telle me the fyn of his entente.
> Yet wist I nevere wel what that he mente."[74]

Although a dialogically intricate passage—not least because Pandarus mimics Criseyde, beginning his speech with, "I, what?"—the passage retains a careful separation of speakers. That separation is maintained not only by the "quod she" and "quod he" but also by the rhythmical and rhyming architecture of the lines, as well as the fact that each clause ends at a line end. Criseyde's first utterance is enfolded into the first two lines; Pandarus's is enfolded into the second two. His utterance is rhythmically crafted to convey—perhaps ironically—his sympathy with her, not only because his statement lasts as long as hers and echoes her stress patterns, but because he precisely echoes her first two words. The first four lines thus convey a separation between the two speakers as well as, again, a kinship between them, much as shared couplets did in my previous example. And indeed, there is a shared couplet in this stanza as well, when the voicing shifts from Pandarus back to Criseyde, whose utterance occupies the final three lines. In this passage, Criseyde is gradually shifting in her attitudes and perspectives toward Pandarus—gradually giving in to his ideas and demands, reshaping her own desires to his. This intricate rhyme scheme renders her psychological shifting sense-perceptible via sound, showing how Pandarus, by mimicking her speech, insinuates himself into her rhyme scheme and, thence, into her confidence. As in my previous examples, rime royal form both individuates characters and shows the interlocking of their lives and perspectives, exploiting the seven-line structure of the stanza both to draw together and to hold apart the different characters in his narrative.[75]

---

74. Bk. 3, lines 120–26.

75. Owen reads this scene and its overlaying of syntactic parallel onto rhyme as a figuration of the awkwardness between Criseyde and Pandarus. He reads the scene,

Throughout the history of *Troilus* studies, a great deal of attention has been devoted to the "naturalness" and "realism" of the dialogue.[76] Often, these traits are ascribed to Chaucer's profound grasp of human social interaction, or to his dramatic flair. As early as the 1890s, Thomas Price said, "he has made each spoken word of each character . . . spring as by inevitable necessity, by force of the circumstances he has invented, from the soul of the character he has imagined."[77] Much more recently, Mark Lambert has noted that "One feature of Chaucer's technique which deserves special attention both for its contribution to our sense of texture in the poem and for its intrinsic interest is his mastery of dialogue. In *Troilus and Criseyde*, talk is vitality."[78] Lambert goes on to assert that the stanzaic form of the *Troilus* is intimately linked to what he calls the "vitality" of talk; in his view, the stanzas elegantly constrain and give shape to the dialogues, in a way that neither prose nor couplets could do in a manner so "truly exhilarating."[79] Lambert's central observation seems to me absolutely correct: stanzaic form contributes to the impression of the vibrancy and realism of dialogue in the *Troilus*. But the question of how the stanzas so productively contribute to the dialogue remains unanswered in his analysis.

Part of their productive contribution, as I have suggested, inheres in how rime royal works as a verse structure in which units of thought, via syntactic units and semantic connections, can be rendered aesthetically. Rime royal works, that is, as a verse form that feels as carefully based on what dictaminists identify as "the natural course of speech" as is the aesthetic prose in the *Boece*. But the particular deployment of rime royal in the *Troilus* not only reengages with the aesthetic sentence of the *Boece* but also improves upon it in a way that specifically improves the poem's ability to represent dialogue and multivocality. The ordering and regulating of syntax into the highly regular form of rime royal set up in a reader a rhythmical and sonic expectation of the ends of thought units; because

that is, as being metrically designed to convey a particular emotional valence, rather than to play with the boundaries between the two speakers' syntactic and semantic "sentences" ("Thy Drasty Rhymyng," 553–54).

76. For a general treatment of the *Troilus*'s realism, see Wimsatt, "Realism in *Troilus and Criseyde*."

77. See Price, "*Troilus and Criseyde*, a Study in Chaucer's Method of Construction," 310. Francis Utley also discusses the seeming naturalness and necessity of dialogue in the *Troilus* ("Scene-Division in Chaucer's *Troilus and Criseyde*").

78. Lambert, "Telling the Story in *Troilus and Criseyde*," 82.

79. Ibid., 83.

the metrical and stanzaic form is so regular, and because syntax is enfolded into it so carefully, a reader comes to expect clauses to end at line ends, and sentences at stanza ends.

Because it is so metrically regular, rime royal instills in a reader a paradigm by which she can anticipate breaks in syntax and ideation—such as shifts between speakers between lines 4 and 5 of a stanza. The regularity of rime royal and the *Troilus*'s careful tailoring of it to syntactic and dialogic breaks enable a reader to internalize a sense not just of when probable breaks in ideation will occur but also when changes in speaker are likeliest. Through the regularity of rime royal, readers come to expect line ends and, especially, stanza breaks to coincide with sense and character shifts. As a result of this rhythmical anticipation, those shifts seem more natural.[80] This naturalness and anticipation draw readers into the poem and make them feel, on some level, that they already know how the poem works. The regularity of the verse form, then, in relation to syntax, creates intuitive expectations in the reader that ultimately produce a kind of aesthetic empathy between the reader and the poem—an empathy that will be of the utmost importance to the poem's larger protreptic goals.

In the entire poem, there are only a few exceptions to the rule that stanzas end with sentence endings. The most conspicuous instance comes when Troilus meets with Criseyde in book 3 and initially attempts to explain to her his abject, heartsick, and swooning devotion. This explanation encompasses the longest single sentence in the poem, a sentence that spans three successive stanzas and contains a good number of enjambments:

"What that I mene, O swete herte deere?"
Quod Troilus, "O goodly fresshe free,
That with the stremes of youre eyen cleere
Ye wolde somtyme frendly on me see,
And thanne agreen that I may ben he,
Withouten braunche of vice on any wise,
In trouthe alwey to don yow my servise,

80. When Owen analyzes the structural importance of rime royal, he gets close to this observation, but he does not address why exactly the rhythmical demarcation of syntax in this poem feels natural or, in his phrasing, "unobtrusive," nor does he address why this naturalization of syntax and semantics would have seemed an interesting project to Chaucer in composing his most thematically Boethian poem. Instead, Owen simply says, "Rhyme has been given a structural as well as a decorative role. It defines the stanza. It reinforces the meaning. It remains for the most part unobtrusive" ("Thy Drasty Rhymyng, 554).

"As to my lady right and chief resort,
With al my wit and al my diligence;
And I to han, right as yow list, comfort,
Under yowre yerde, egal to myn offence,
As deth, if that I breke youre defence;
And that ye deigne me so muchel honoure
Me to comanden aught in any houre;

"And I to ben youre—verray, humble, trewe,
Secret, and in my paynes pacient,
And evere mo desiren fresshly newe
To serve, and ben ylike diligent,
And with good herte al holly youre talent
Receyven wel, how sore that me smerte;
Lo, this mene I, myn owen swete herte."[81]

By its sheer length, its overflowing syntax, this single sentence conveys to the audience a sensible awareness of the overflowing emotion Troilus feels for Criseyde and his unbounded will to possess her. This deviation from the supervening rule of stanzaic syntax has its effect—of making the reader feel the tremendous passion of Troilus's emotions—precisely because the rest of the poem cultivates an aesthetic awareness of ideation as controlled, bounded and delimited by syntax, made aesthetically available in the structures of meter, rhythm, and stanza.[82]

The aesthetic structuring of rime royal thus works on readers at an almost preconscious level; its regular line stops and stanza breaks become part of the audience's working knowledge about the poem, and they reassuringly promise that—except in cases of extreme emotion—whatever change occurs at the narrative level, the stresses, rhymes, and stanzas that structure the poem will continue unchanged, providing a scaffolding of anticipation for the reader. The enfolding of dialogue into metrically and rhythmically regular lines, then, produces not a stilted and inert dialogue but rather a vivacious and sensory one. Formally, rime royal in Chaucer's *Troilus* is designed to continue and perfect the work that began in the aesthetic prose of his *Boece*, but to do so with a decidedly new literary-theoretical agenda: the *Troilus* shows how verse, though belittled by some

---

81. Bk. 3, lines 127–47.
82. Owen notes how the regularity of rime royal can be fractured for dramatic ends, usually to heighten the emotionality of a passage ("Thy Drasty Rhymyng," 553).

prose theorists as a form that "mutilates meaning," can convey meaning *more effectively* than prose, via the very metrical, rhythmical, and stanzaic artifice—its formal constraints and artificial regularity—that Latin and vernacular prose theorists alike would condemn.

There is, to be sure, an effort to use form to differentiate between speakers and discrete discursive events in the *Boece*. After all, in the *Boece*, cadencing often comes in particularly high density toward the end of a section of prose or meter, and thus serves to demarcate one type of discourse (monologic song) from another (dialogic argumentation). Sometimes, the demarcations between prose and meter also coincide with a shift in speaker—as when Philosophy finishes a song, and Boece responds to her in prose. But in the dialogues of the *Boece*, as in the *Consolation*, there are always only two speakers talking to each other; in the meters, there is always only a single voice. As a result, the problem of voicing in the work is relatively uncomplicated. The *Troilus*, by contrast, is decidedly polyvocal, including several scenes in which multiple characters speak back and forth among one another. Thus, in the *Troilus*, the burden of cadencing, the burden, that is, of delimiting syntax in a sense-perceptible way, is greater: rime royal needs to make a heteroglossic poem, written centuries before the invention of the quotation mark, aesthetically parsable into recognizable speakers. By its far greater regularity of rhythm, rime royal is designed specifically to be better able to manage heteroglossic "sentence" than the artfully cadenced prose of the *Boece*.

The recreation of and improvement upon *cursus* via rime royal is not, however, the poem's only reengagment with the problem of how to make ideation sense-perceptible in verse. The *Troilus* adds to its stanzaic syntax another form of aesthetic punctuation, again like what occurs in the *Boece*. At intervals throughout the *Troilus*, there appear passages of dense alliteration. One occurs in the proem to book 3, in the narrator's apostrophe to Venus, which again renders the eighth meter of book 2 of the *Consolation*:

> O *blisful light* of which the *bemes* clere
> Adorneth al the thridde heven faire!
> O sonnes *lief,* O Joves *doughter deere,*
> Plesance of *love,* O goodly *debonaire,*
> In gentil hertes ay redy to repaire!
> O veray cause of heele and of gladnesse,
> Iheryed be thy myght and thi goodnesse.[83]

83. Bk. 3, 1–7.

Throughout this first stanza runs an interlocking system of alliterations: the "bemes" light is described as "blisful," Venus is termed Jupiter's "doughter deere" and as "debonaire" in the following line, the "love" that is the ultimate referent of the passage alliterates with the "light" that expresses its presence on earth and is called that light's "lief," or beloved. In the second stanza, the reader encounters "hevene and helle" being sonically linked together, demonstrating their mutual subjection to love's might. This formal linking together of words by sound serves a crucial metacritical and thematic purpose: first, thematically, it sonically underscores how the concepts that the related words represent are ultimately linked together by love. Second, on a metapoetic level, the linking of words together shows how the poet's own might is a central binding force in the poem, without which the boundness of the universe is less sense-perceptible, less aesthetically available in the poem.

The outstanding instance of this use of alliteration as a formal figure both for universal love and for poetry's unique power to represent it occurs in Troilus's second song, which reworks, yet again, the famous eighth meter from book 2 of the *Consolation*, which seems to have been so central to Chaucer's aesthetic experimentation in both the *Boece* and the *Troilus*. In this passage, alliteration occurs first as a clausal front rhyme, wherein "Love" leads off the first three and the fifth lines of the poem:

> "*Love*, that of erthe and se hath governaunce,
> *Love*, that his *hestes hath* in *hevene hye*,
> *Love*, that with an *holsom* alliaunce
> Halt peples joyned, as hym lest hem gye,
> *Love*, that *knetteth lawe* of *compaignie*,
> And *couples* doth in vertu forto dwelle,
> Bynd this acord, that I have *told* and *telle*."[84]

In addition to the anaphoric "loves" and, indeed, manifesting the work of binding and "coupling" that love is said to do, this first stanza of the passage weaves in the quadruple *h* alliteration on "hestes," "hevene," "hye," and "holsum." These *h* alliterations aesthetically perform the assertion in line 5 that "love . . . knetteth lawe of compagnie," which, itself, involves an interweaving double alliteration, in which "love" alliterates with "lawe," and "knetteth" alliterates with both "compaignie" and "couples." This stanza is again alliteratively ornamented to render in form the ideas

---

84. Bk. 3, lines 1744–50.

it expresses in content, and all the while to show how aesthetic form can work a "binding" of its own, which in turn sets the binding of the universe by love into sharper relief.

As Troilus's song progresses, the intensity of his alliterations approaches frenzy. Most lines contain an alliterative pair that binds together two related terms—either a noun and its modifier or a noun and its verb—to show again how love links together the elements and forces of the universe.

> "That, that the se, that gredy is to flowen,
> Constreyneth to a certeyn ende so
> His *flodes* that so *fiersly* they ne growen
> To drenchen *erthe* and al for *evere* mo;
> And if that *Love* aught *lete* his bridel go,
> Al that now *loveth* asondre sholde *lepe*,
> And *lost* were al that *Love* halt now to hepe."[85]

And in the final stanza of Troilus's song, though "love" and "liste" are twice made to alliterate, the most aesthetically salient line is the fourth, in which three related words—the noun "wight," its verb "wiste," and its direct object "wey"—are made to alliterate with each other, aesthetically underscoring the power and inescapability of the bond of divine love that the passage describes.

> "So wolde God, that auctour is of kynde,
> That with his bond *Love* of his vertue *liste*
> To cerclen hertes alle and faste bynde,
> That from his bond no *wight* the *wey* out *wiste*;
> And hertes colde, hem wolde I that he twiste
> To make hem *love*, and that hem *liste* ay rewe
> On hertes sore, and kepe hem that ben trewe!"[86]

As does the *Boece*'s rendering of the second meter of book 8, this passage uses semantically based alliteration to embody in form how the universe is bound together by love. The effect of all of this attention to alliterative patterning is, indeed, to aestheticize the "bond of love" that Troilus—like the narrator in the previous proem—now understands as the organizing

---

85. Bk. 3, lines 1758–64.
86. Bk. 3, lines 1765–71.

force of the universe. Troilus's song reveals the poem's ongoing engagement with Boethius not just as a thematic source but also as a stylistic inspiration and a resource for metapoetic reflection. The *Troilus's* alliterative rime royal verse is thus a virtuosic reengagement with the aestheticization of meaning that Chaucer discerned in the *Consolation* and initially explored in the *Boece* through his combined use of *cursus* and alliteration.

The *Boece* should be read as the prose and the *Troilus* the meter of a single, unified stylistic project, in which Chaucer reinvents how Boethius's prosimetric *Consolation* renders meaning aesthetically available. In the *Boece*, it is easy to see why he would do so: as a translation of the *Consolation*, it narrates an ethical transformation in its main character and hopes to model one for a reader. In the *Troilus*, notionally a fictive poem and not obviously protreptic in nature, Chaucer's motivations are harder to intuit. Why would he have sought to recreate the aesthetic sentence of the *Boece* in this poem through his deployment of rime royal stanzas? What ethical end does the careful aestheticization of meaning ultimately serve?

The next chapter will suggest that the *Troilus* is not simply a half prosimetrum but an experimental work of literary theory and practice, intended to explore the protreptic possibilities inherent not just in prosimetrum but in an all-verse protreptic. *Troilus and Criseyde* is not a "protreptic" work in the same way that Boethius's *Consolation* is, of course, nor should it be read as a strict formal prosimetrum. But the *Troilus* is most decisively a poem *about* literary protrepsis and about how dialectical formal construction works to convey that protrepsis. The *Troilus*, that is, evokes the mixed form and its putatively transformative effects as a recognizable literary mode that is everywhere under pressure in the poem. The rime royal scaffolding of aesthetic sentence is merely the first step in a much larger project of literary philosophy: the *Troilus* asks to be read as an experiment with how and whether ethical transformation can be represented and modeled in dialectically structured vernacular English poetry.

CHAPTER THREE

The Consolation of Tragedy:
Protrepsis in the *Troilus*

On many levels, *Troilus and Criseyde* can be read as an organized and sustained response to the *Consolation of Philosophy*, as scholars of the poem have long recognized. At least one medieval Chaucerian, Thomas Usk, cites the *Troilus* as a Boethian crib as early as 1386, in his semi-autobiographical work *The Testament of Love*. Exasperated with Usk's failure to understand how God could have perfect foreknowledge and yet not be the "maker and auctour of badde werkes"—a decidedly Boethian problem—Usk's interlocutor steers him toward Chaucer as a Boethian glossator, saying,

> [M]yne owne trewe servaunt, the noble philosophical poete in English . . . in a treatise that he made of my servaunt Troylus, hath this mater touched, and at the ful this questyon assoyled. Certaynly, his noble sayenges can I not amende; in goodness of gentyl manlyche speche, without any maner of nycite of st[o]rieres ymagynacion, in wytte and in good reason of sentence he passeth al other makers. In the *Boke of Troylus*, the answere to thy question mayste thou lerne.[1]

Evidently, in the late 1380s, a writer keen to dig deeply into the philosophical wealth of the *Consolation* need go no further afield than the vernacular, poetic *Troilus*, as a fictive elaboration of Boethian ideas. More recently, many other Chaucerians have contributed their own assessments of the *Troilus*'s Boethianism, showing it to be a pervasive and organizing force

---

1. Thomas Usk, *Testament of Love*, bk. 3, chap. 4, lines 230–31, 235–40.

throughout the poem.[2] As an index of the perceived depth of Chaucer's debt to Boethius, John Fleming calls the *Troilus* a "crooked" translation of the *Consolation*, in apposition with the "straight" translation Chaucer composed in the *Boece*.[3]

Although useful in establishing the pervasiveness of Boethian echoes in the *Troilus*, most such studies share an assumption that the poem's engagements with the *Consolation of Philosophy* are exclusively thematic: like the *Consolation*, the *Troilus* works through issues of fate versus free will, the possibility of achieving happiness in human life, and the role of fortune in shaping the created world. The critical consensus on the *Troilus* is that the poem uses Boethius as an ideational springboard, a way of grounding its own amatory history in high-order philosophical discourse.

Although the thematic affinities between the *Consolation* and the *Troilus* are as indisputable as they are pervasive, the overall *effect* of these thematic interpolations on how the poem can be read has been largely overlooked.[4] The poem's citations of ideas and themes from the *Consolation* and even certain elements of Boethian literary functionality and form are not ends unto themselves but instead serve to make Boethian literary modes and logics available as a familiar body of literary philosophy within the poem. As in the *Consolation*, *Vita nuova*, and *Remède de Fortune*, the narrative surface of the poem teaches its readers how to read and understand its practiced, deep-structural, formal logic by thematizing how literary experience works upon the human psyche. Through this thematic familiarization, the poem anchors its far larger experiment with a vernacular poetic practice of using literary dialectics—of narrative and lyric,

---

2. Stroud, "Boethius' Influence on Chaucer's *Troilus*"; Jefferson, *Chaucer and the Consolation of Philosophy of Boethius*; Patch, *Tradition of Boethius* and "Troilus on Determinism"; Owen, "Significance of Chaucer's Revisions to the *Troilus and Criseyde*"; Huber, "Troilus' Predestination Soliloquy"; Elbow, "Two Boethian Speeches in *Troilus and Criseyde* and Chaucerian Irony." Ida Gordon reads the *Troilus* as an ironic secularization of the thematics of the *Consolation* (*Double Sorrow of Troilus*, 24–60). John Steadman sees the end of the *Troilus*, and Troilus's famous ascent into the heavens, as a reworking of and commentary on Boethius's ascent through the spheres (*Disembodied Laughter*, 1–20). Alice Kaminsky sets out the *Troilus*'s thematic debts to Boethian philosophy and reviews critical assessments of the thematic relation of the *Troilus* to the *Consolation* (*Chaucer's* Troilus and Criseyde *and the Critics*, 41–53).

3. Fleming, *Classical Imitation and Interpretation in Chaucer's* Troilus, 84.

4. An important exception comes in the recent work of Jessica Rosenfeld, which I will discuss later in this chapter.

linearity and interruptivity, causal contiguity and affective likeness—to meditate on the possibility of literary protrepsis.

But in that meditation there will emerge a powerful and multilayered critique of the optimism of the Boethian project: the *Troilus* shows that, at every level, the drive for ethical renewal is vexed, and that the outcome of protreptic writing and reading is far from sure or straightforward. Through the poem's reevaluations of Boethian literary form and function, we see emerge a new canniness about the possibility of literary work as a vehicle of ethical transformation: when the poem holds out the possibility of a lasting ethical renewal through the experience of reading, it quickly withdraws that possibility, or suggests that any performed or imagined ethical renewal is a shimmering possibility founded at least as much upon the violation of the notional principles of Boethian consolation as upon their validation.

TEACHING TRANSFORMATION: CULTIVATING PROTREPTIC READING IN A VERNACULAR AUDIENCE

To explain how this poem teaches, experiments with, and violates the Boethian paradigm of ethically transformative writing and reading, we need first to examine the overt thematic gestures that the poem makes directly toward Boethian literary theories and practices of protreptic literature. These gestures toward Boethian literary theory and practice emerge in the poem's thematization of how language reshapes the psyche in the lives of Troilus and Criseyde. By devising and deploying this thematization, the poem quickens its audience's awareness of Boethian literary theory as a presence throughout. The lives of Troilus and Criseyde familiarize readers with that theory, honing their sensitivity for recognizing techniques of literary transformation that emerge more subtly in formal and stylistic choices that appear in the poem. In particular, the poem hones its audience's sensitivity to Boethian literary theory and practice by thematizing song (what happens in Boethian meters) and dialogue (what happens in Boethian proses) as the dual verbal modes that produce psychological change in Troilus and Criseyde.[5] These two interlocking modes—song and dialogue—constitute a diegetic version of the literary dialectics that com-

---

5. The presence of song and dialogue in the story does not originate with Chaucer: Boccaccio deployed them in *Il filostrato* as well; but Boccaccio does not deploy his songs and dialogues with the same attention to Boethian thematics and literary theory that characterizes the *Troilus*. For a full treatment of Chaucer's changes to Boccaccio's poem, see Boitani, *Chaucer and the Italian Trecento*; Wallace, *Chaucer and the Early*

pose the poem's overall reimagination and redeployment of prosimetrum as a vehicle for protrepsis.

The poem begins thematically to weave in the Boethian theory of how song and dialogue work to produce psychological transformation when Pandarus tries to cure Troilus of his sorrow in book 1.[6] In this scene, the poem channels through Pandarus a classic Boethian passage on how song works on the psyche. Pandarus finds Troilus, stupefied by lovelornness, and tries to rouse him from his emotional lethargy.

> [He] cryde, "Awake!" ful wonderlich and sharpe;
> "What! Slombrestow as in a litargie?
> Or artow lik an asse to the harpe,
> That hereth sown whan men the strynges plye,
> But in his mynde of that no melodie
> May sinken hym to gladen, for that he
> So dul ys of his bestialite?"[7]

This passage reenacts the initial scene from the *Consolation*, when Philosophy makes her first diagnosis of Boece's spiritual ailment. In Chaucer's translation, she says, "He is fallen in to a litargie." Philosophy then sings Boece a song, after which she asks, "Felest thou . . . thise thinges and entren thei ought in thi corage? Art thou like an asse to the harpe?" In asking this question, Philosophy reveals that song's purpose is to pierce into the human heart ("corage," from *cor, cordis*), thereby overcoming the "litargie" into which Boethius has fallen.[8] Parroting Philosophy's theory of song, in the *Troilus* Pandarus casts song as an agent of psychological healing, which works by sensual penetration: unless one is as dull as a donkey, one "hereth sown" as it "sinks" into one's ears, and one is transformed by that sinking in of songful sensation. By echoing the *Consolation*'s metapoetic metaphors, Pandarus begins the process of familiarizing readers with Boethian literary theory in the *Troilus*, making it available thematically before the poem's strategic reinvention of Boethian prosimetrum and redeployment of protrepsis are fully under way.

Writings of Boccaccio; R. Edwards, *Chaucer and Boccaccio*; Boitani, *Genius to Improve an Invention*; Ginsberg, *Chaucer's Italian Tradition*.

6. On Pandarus's Philosophy-like qualities, see Camargo, "Consolation of Pandarus," and Gaylord, "Uncle Pandarus as Lady Philosophy."

7. *Troilus*, bk.1, lines 729–35.

8. *Boece*, bk. 1, pr. 4, sentences 1–3.

Immediately after thematizing the power of song to sink into the human psyche, Pandarus thematizes the power of dialogue to heal a wounded soul. He recognizes that one must bare a wound if it is to be treated, and thus metaphorically casts himself as the doctor of his young interlocutor's emotional ills.

> "And therfore wostow what I the biseche?
> Lat be thy wo and tornyng to the grounde;
> For whoso list have helyng of his leche,
> To hym byhoveth first unwre his wownde."[9]

To what he later calls Pandarus's verbal "lechecraft," Troilus responds by insisting that he is not to be "heeled thus."[10] These medical metaphorics derive from the *Consolation*, when Philosophy says Boethius will be "cured and heeled"[11] by her and notes that "tyme is now . . . of medicyne more than of compleynte."[12] Shortly thereafter, Philosophy refers to herself as a "leche," urging her patient to show her his psychological wound if he wishes to be healed.[13] Through this medical metaphor for how talking works to heal the mind, the poem exposes Boethius as a literary-theoretical presence in the story and fleshes out its audience's vernacular sensitivity to the theory and practice of mixed-form literary transformation that pervade the *Consolation*.[14]

The poem hones this sensitivity for Boethian literary philosophy yet further in book 2, when Antigone sings a song to Criseyde.[15] Her song is densely Boethian in its thematic concerns:[16] it introduces the notion of love as "entent,"[17] characterizes a lover as the "fynder and hed"[18] of all

---

9. Bk. 1, lines 855–58.

10. Bk. 4, line 436.

11. Bk. 1, pr. 1.

12. Bk. 1, pr. 2.

13. Bk. 3, pr. 4.

14. The metaphor of dialogue as "medicine" resurfaces in book 4, when Criseyde has been promised to the Greeks in exchange for Antenor, and Pandarus and Troilus engage in a protracted dialogue, intended to console Troilus.

15. For a reading of the role and function of Antigone in the *Troilus* as a naïve figure, in rough parallel with Troilus, see Wetherbee, *Chaucer and the Poets*, 119.

16. For another reading of this song as Boethian, see Gordon, *Double Sorrow*, 100–101.

17. Bk. 2, lines 828, 838, 854.

18. Bk. 2, line 844.

pleasure, and describes a life lived in pursuit of love as one lived "in alle joie and seurte out of drede."[19] Having heard the markedly Boethian song, Criseyde has a predictable response: she "gan therewith to sike," to sigh with induced love.[20]

> . . . every word which that she of hire herde
> She gan to prenten in hire herte faste,
> And ay gan love hir lasse for t'agaste
> Than it dide erst, and synken in her herte,
> That she wex somewhat able to converte.[21]

Evidently, it is only *after* Criseyde hears Antigone's song that she grants her love to Troilus; she needs to hear Antigone's song in order to become permeable to love, before Pandarus's dialogic suit can move her, much as Boethius needed to hear Philosophy's singing before he could be open to her arguments about divine providence and truth.

In a post-Machauldian vaunting of musicality, further bolstering the sense that it is the song itself and not strictly the Boethian thematics that the song contains that induces Criseyde to love Troilus, Criseyde is soon again bombarded by the affect-transforming powers of song. But this time the song is wordless: above her head, she hears a nightingale singing in a tree. Hearing the wordless song launches her into a dream in which she symbolically surrenders her heart to love:

> A nyghtyngale upon a cedre grene,
> Under the chambre wal ther as she lay,
> Ful loude song ayein the moone shene,
> Peraunter in his briddes wise a lay
> Of love that made hire herte fressh and gay,
> That herkned she so longe in good entente,
> Til at the laste the dede slep hire hente.
>
> And as she slep, anonright tho hire mette
> How that an egle, fethered whit as bon,
> Under hire brest his longe clawes sette,

---

19. Bk. 2, line 833. For discussion of "entente" and love in the poem as Boethian, see Patterson, *Chaucer and the Subject of History*, 138–40.

20. Bk. 2, line 884. See also Borthwick, "Antigone's Song as Mirrour."

21. Bk. 2, lines 899–903.

And out hire herte he rente, and that anon,
And dide his herte in-to hire brest to gon—
Of which she nought agroos ne nothyng smerte—
And forth he fleigh with herte left for herte.[22]

Through Criseyde, the *Troilus* asserts the power of song to work affective transformation—here figured physically as the switching out of hearts—and thus to pave the way for a full psychological "conversion." In hearing the wordless—and hence athematic—nightingale's song, Criseyde is lulled into a sleep.[23] In this sleep, the songbird morphs into a bird of prey, showing how the gentle, affect-shifting music of the nightingale becomes a violent and powerful force for psychological change in the eagle. In adding this episode, the poem emphasizes that song—music itself—is a technique for initiating an emotional transformation in those who hear it, thus channeling not only Boethian ideas about the protreptic power of music but also Machauldian valorizations of music from the *Remède*.

Criseyde is not alone in being subjected to song's transformative power: Troilus's own first song, which he sings to himself in book 1, seems to provoke a similar shift of affect in him. In this song, he interrogates the nature of his own emotions, wondering first whence, if love is good, "cometh my waillynge and my pleynte?" His exploration of his strange emotions continues as follows:[24]

"How may of the in me swich quantite,
But if that I consente that it be?

"And if that I consente, I wrongfully
Compleyne, iwis. Thus possed to and fro,

22. Bk. 2, lines 918–31.
23. By calling the nightingale's song "athematic" unto itself, I do not mean to remove it from the larger thematic economies that it plays into in the plot of the poem. As Carolyn Dinshaw and Aranye Fradenburg have suggested, the nightingale's song plays an important role in the coercion and seduction of Criseyde, making her increasingly susceptible to the amatory aggressions of Troilus. In the dream that Criseyde has, after hearing this wordless song, she imagines her own heart being torn out and traded with that of an eagle. In a sense, then, the nightingale's song, though wordless and, as I suggest, thus athematic unto itself, plays into a larger emerging theme of Criseyde's physical and psychological violation. See Dinshaw, *Chaucer's Sexual Poetics*, 82; Fradenburg, *Sacrifice Your Love*, 224 and 224 n. 48.
24. Bk. 1, line 408.

Al sterelees withinne a boot am I
Amydde the see, bitwixen wyndes two,
That in contrarie stonden evere mo.
Allas, what is this wondre maladie?
For hote of cold, for cold of hote, I dye."[25]

Crucially, as Troilus mulls over the nature of love, he thematizes the role of "consent" in producing and securing that love. The theme of consent is a central focus throughout the poem, as Aranye Fradenburg notes, and it is a theme that is added de novo to this particular song, which is otherwise a fairly close rendering of a Petrarchan sonnet.[26] In thematizing and theorizing consent, Troilus arcs toward the Boethian theory of how song works to produce positive psychological change, by producing assent in a hearer, encapsulated in Boethius's response of "Assentior" to Philosophy's early song.[27] This arcing toward Boethian metapoetic theory attains its goal when Troilus grants his full consent to transform himself to love Criseyde:

"O lord, now youres is
My spirit, which that oughte youres be.
Yow thanke I, lord, that han me brought to this.
But wheither goddesse or womman, iwiss,
She be, I not, which that ye do me serve;
But as hire man I wol ay lyue and sterve."[28]

In Troilus's turn toward love, it seems as though the very act of having sung about his love has helped to produce his consent. As in Criseyde's joint conversion to love by Antigone's and then the nightingale's songs, here the act of experiencing song contributes to the affective conversion

25. Bk. 1, lines 412–20.

26. In her analysis, Fradenburg suggests that "consent" is a false and ethically dangerous construct in the *Troilus*, an effect of sentience that makes a subject believe that he or she consents when, in fact, he or she is constrained both by circumstances and by his or her own desires (*Sacrifice Your Love*, 202–3). This reading of "consent" as a delusion born of the nonawareness of one's own entrapment by historicized desire is one to which I shall return presently as an orienting concern in the poem. On the Petrarchan immediate source of Troilus's song, see L. D. Benson, "Explanatory Notes," in *Riverside Chaucer*, 1028 nn. 400–420.

27. Bk. 3, pr. 11, sentence 1.

28. Bk. 1, lines 422–27.

that Troilus experiences, which moves him from being a love-disavowing young rake to a love-struck paramour.

The poem fleshes out its dialectical reworking of prosimetrum, spending as much energy on the nature of transformation by dialogue and argumentation as it does on the nature of lyrical "conversion" to love. In the third book, with song having already worked its debatably "gentle medicine" on Criseyde's and Troilus's hearts, sinking into them and softening them to the possibility of love, the *Troilus* shifts attention to show the power of dialogue to bring about Criseyde's final consent to love Troilus. Pandarus leads her to believe that Troilus suspects her of infidelity, in order to manipulate her into consenting to Troilus's further amatory advances.

> "Now, wherby that I telle yow al this:
> Ye woot youreself, as wel as any wight,
> How that youre love al fully graunted is
> To Troilus, the worthieste knyght,
> Oon of this world, and therto trouthe yplight,
> That, but it were on hym along, ye nolde
> Hym nevere falsen while ye liven sholde."[29]

In this demonstration of his supposed reason for telling her this news, Pandarus pressures Criseyde to recognize that she, as the lover of the superlative knight, is necessarily compelled to be superlatively faithful to him. She has vowed her love to him, and he is worthy of that love; therefore, Criseyde should never want to "falsen" him by falling short of his mark of excellence through any faithlessness on her own part. Pandarus's rationalizations work: Criseyde yields to his argument as the truth, having been drawn into his net of logical necessity.

When it shows Criseyde's surrender to Pandarus's dialogic rationale, the poem marks that surrender as a decidedly Boethian one. Parroting Boethian vocabulary, Criseyde replies to Pandarus's suit as follows:

> "O God," quod she, "so worldly selynesse,
> Which clerkes callen fals felicitee,
> Imedled is with many a bitternesse!
> Ful angwissous than is, God woot," quod she,
> "Condicioun of veyn prosperitee:

29. Bk. 3, lines 778–84.

For either joies comen nought yfeere,
Or elles no wight hath hem alwey here.

"O brotel wele of mannes joie unstable!
With what wight so thow be, or how thow pleye,
Either he woot that thow, joie, art muable,
Or woot it nought; it mot ben oon of tweye.
Now if he woot it nought, how may he seye
That he hath verray joie and selynesse,
That is of ignoraunce ay in derknesse?

"Now if he woot that joie is transitorie,
As every joie of worldly thyng mot flee,
Than every tyme he that hath in memorie,
The drede of lesyng maketh hym that he
May in no perfit selynesse be."[30]

The lexicon Criseyde deploys—including "selynesse," "fals felicitee," "brotel wele," "joie unstable," "joie muable," "transitorie"—programmatically evokes the *Consolation,* and especially Chaucer's vernacularization of it. "Selynesse," appears in the negative form "unselynesse" four times in the *Boece.* "Felicitee" appears twice, "welefulnesse" numerous times. Chaucer's Lady Philosophy describes the joys of the world as "brotel," "moveable," and "transitorie" repeatedly. To a fourteenth-century reader familiar either with Boethius's *Consolation* or with Chaucer's *Boece,* the content of Criseyde's lament would have been obviously Boethian and would have signaled her conversion as an amatory reflection of Boethius's own transformation.

Deepening this passage's affiliation with Boethius, shortly after Criseyde rattles off Boethian philosophical terms and themes, she shifts to a metacritical mode, which confirms the efficacy of dialogue as a technique for eliciting consent. After Pandarus's extensive dialogic tactics, she consents to put herself in his power: "'For I am here al in your governaunce.'"[31] The term "governaunce" appears many times in Chaucer's translation of the *Consolation,* usually denoting the ordering control that God, as *summum bonum,* exerts on the created world. But, in the case of Criseyde's "governaunce," the valence is different, more ominous, since she is subject

---

30. Bk. 3, lines 813–31.
31. Bk. 3, lines 945.

not to the infinitely good intention of God but to the infinitely scheming machinations of Pandarus. What her admission ultimately makes clear is that dialogue is designed to bring one party into agreement with another; it serves, as it does in the *Consolation*, to cultivate assent.

Whether that "assent" is produced nefariously or not, by showing how the dialectical experience of song and dialogue can produce transformation through the double action of producing affective and rational consent, the *Troilus* makes Boethian literary theory available as a recognizable mode of thought within the poem. Through its medical metaphors and its thematization of song and dialogue as agents of psychological change in Criseyde, the poem teaches its audience to read it as Boethian. It cultivates a vernacular Boethian habit of reading—though that habit will be fully gratified only as the poem moves toward its eventual conclusion.[32]

THE MIXED FORM AND FUNCTION OF *TROILUS AND CRISEYDE*: CAUSALITY AND LIKENESS

While thematizing the dialectical power of song and dialogue to provoke psychological transformation in its main characters, the *Troilus* also reinvents the dialectic of prose and meter formally, as a matter of large-scale poetic strategy. In reinventing the prosimetric embodiment of ethical transformation entirely within verse, the poem resonates with Guillaume's *Remède*, but the *Troilus*'s all-verse reinvention of prosimetric protrepsis reengages with Boethian form and function in a unique way—through its particular and programmatic division into a narrative and a narrator. This dialectic of narrative and narrator makes prosimetrum anew and helps to set the stage for the poem's eventual critique of Boethian literary practice and theory.

That Chaucer's narrator constitutes a significant innovation in English literary practice has long been recognized, and for many reasons. First, unlike many medieval narrators, he seems able to change and learn over the course of the narrative.[33] Second, he sympathizes with all the characters

32. In using the term "habit," I am drawing on the work of Pierre Bourdieu, which shows how modes of knowing and interpreting are constructed by cultural situatedness. See *Outline of a Theory of Practice* and *Distinction*. In applying this concept to medieval texts, I owe much to Katharine Breen. Breen analyzes the *habitus* of Latin grammar in vernacular culture to suggest how exposure to Latinate literary culture could shape and inform a vernacular readership's ability to understand Middle English writings (*Imagining an English Reading Public*, 43–80).

33. McAlpine, *Genre of Troilus and Criseyde*, 124.

in his story and urges his readers to feel empathy for them.[34] Third, he is sometimes distant from his tale and sometimes nearly a participant in it.[35] Each of these observations is important in its own right, but I will suggest in this chapter that they operate together, thereby making manifest Chaucer's deliberate response to Boethius's theory and practice of philosophic literature. In the *Troilus*, the division of the poem into narrative and narrator revisits and strategically reinvents Boethian prose and Boethian meter, respectively. The narrative contains the story of Troilus and Criseyde's love affair, as well as the Trojan history against which their affair plays out. The linear, continuous narrative of that story replicates a specific aesthetic function of the prose in the *Consolation*. The narrator, by contrast, appears largely in the interstitial tissue of the poem—the proems to the books, the frequent editorializing comments that puncture the poem's narrative surface—all of which are monologic and lyrical, and none of which connect to each other in a linear way. These narratorial incursions and interventions reimagine and reinvent the function of Boethian meters.

NARRATIVE CAUSALITY AND PSEUDOPROSE

Lee Patterson argues that the *Troilus*'s representation of history—as something inescapable, constraining, and cruel—is, in origin, Boethian.[36] This argument gets very close to how Boethius matters to Chaucer's overall plan, but it is important to remember that, for Boethius, it is not "history"

---

34. Spearing, "Ricardian 'I,'" 13. For a range of perspectives on the narrator, his relation to the characters, his relation to the author, and his uniqueness in Middle English literature, see R. Jordan, "Narrator in Chaucer's *Troilus*"; Huppe, "Unlikely Narrator"; Salter, "Troilus and Criseyde"; Waswo, "Narrator of *Troilus and Criseyde*." As Lee Patterson puts it, focusing on how the narrator mediates between the characters and the reader, "For the characters, their narrator go-between, and the poem's audience all come to share the desire to suppress the historical consciousness" (*Chaucer and the Subject of History*, 107).

35. Bloomfield, "Distance and Predestination in *Troilus and Criseyde*". See also R. Jordan, "Narrator in Chaucer's *Troilus*."

36. "In Boethius's view a repetitive cycle of meaningless acts of rise and fall, history is significant only in terms of its impact on the inner spiritual lives of those caught in its web" (*Chaucer and the Subject of History*, 87). According to Patterson, this condemnatory and despairing attitude toward human history makes Boethius long for "a utopian world in which origin and end are simultaneously possessed—a world, that is, from which the embarrassment of history has been entirely banished" (153).

per se into which human life is woven, but *causality*, of which human social and political history is merely one manifestation. It is equally important to recall that in the *Consolation*, causality properly understood is not an occasion for lament. Quite the contrary, the *Consolation* construes causality, when properly understood, as a source of tremendous comfort and consolation.

Making a pun on "fortune," meaning both chance and wealth, Philosophy explains that chance is a false construct, born only of the limitations of human vision.

> Ryght as a man dalf the erthe bycause of tylyinge of the feld, and founde ther a gobet of golde bydolven; thanne wenen folk that it is byfalle by fortunous bytydynge. But forsothe it nis nat of naught, for it hath his propre causes, of whiche causes the cours unforseyn and unwar semeth to han maked hap. For yif the tiliere of the feeld ne dulve nat in the erthe, and yif the hidere of the golde ne hadde hyd the golde in thilke place, the golde ne hadde nat ben founde.[37]

The perception of chance as a real force in human life is false, born only of humanity's inability to perceive the causal circumstances that culminate in a particular result: we find a "fortune" and believe that finding "fortunate" because we are unaware of the circumstances by which the fortune was placed in the earth in the first place. "Fortune" is a dangerous cognitive bias that results from believing that one's own inability to *perceive* causality necessarily means that no causality exists. Recognizing that one is bound up in historical causality, although painful at times, should make one recognize fortune's impotence, since that causal netting emanates from God, and reminds human beings of their ordained and ordered place in the universe. Thus, human subjection to causality, although constraining and often agonizing, is meant to bring Boethius comfort, not despair. This is why Philosophy goes on from the treasure example to explain that the order of causation governs all life, "by an uneschuable byndinge togidre, whiche that descendeth fro the welle of purveaunce that ordeyneth alle thingis in hir places and in hir tymes."[38] Just because we cannot see causality does not mean that "the welle of purveaunce" is not there. Someone, above us, is always watching, always designing, always plotting.

By making plain and available the interwoven nets of historical causal-

---

37. Bk. 5, pr. 1, sentences 70–80.
38. Bk. 5, pr. 1, sentences 93–96.

ity, the Trojan narrative of the *Troilus* is designed to bring a specific kind of consolation to the *Troilus* narrator—though certainly not to the characters Troilus and Criseyde, who so rarely perceive the full causal systems into which their lives are woven. The narrator, as witness to and creator of his own narrative, can see that everything happens through causation, not chance. He is aware of the reason for Calkas's initial treachery, and of the eventual demise of the Trojans:

> So whan this Calkas knew by calkulynge,
> and ek by answer of this Appollo,
> That Grekes sholden swich a peple brynge,
> Thorugh which that Troie moste ben fordo . . .[39]

The narrator makes clear that he is also specifically aware of the fate to which Troilus will ultimately succumb, as he reveals in the first stanza of the poem: "how his aventures fellen / fro wo to wele, and after out of joie."[40] He knows the futility of Troilus's love, its destined end in disappointment and abandonment, far before Troilus does. The narrator also has access to Pandarus's and Troilus's secret schemes to seduce Criseyde: when they connive to dupe her in book 2, the narrator witnesses their connivances; later, when they scheme to get her into bed with Troilus, the narrator again sees their subterfuges. He knows, far before Criseyde does, what Pandarus and Troilus intend for her; he knows that she is being manipulated, even when she does not. He knows all this, and he reminds his readers of that foreknowledge incessantly.

The effect of the narrator's incessant foregrounding of his omniscient vantage on his story is to show that he has unrestricted access to causality in his narrative—he can see *why* things happen in a way that none of his characters can.[41] For Criseyde in love and for the Trojans in war, full causality is as irretrievable as it is ineluctable; hence, in large part, her ready subsumption under the coercive "governaunces" of others. For the narrator, however, who witnesses the lives of the characters and who re-

---

39. Bk. 1, lines 71–74.

40. Bk. 1, lines 3–4.

41. Bloomfield analyzes the narrative's careful emplotment as the aesthetic correlative of Boethian predestination, noting that the narrator knows in advance the inevitable and tragic outcome of his narrative. Through this vantage, Bloomfield suggests, the narrator has a perspective akin to that of God: he is all-seeing and all-knowing ("Distance and Predestination in *Troilus and Criseyde*").

minds his readers that he has read the story of Troilus and Criseyde before and is only now repackaging it for us, causality is accessible everywhere, because he already knows how things will turn out in the end, and why. The lesson, both cognitive and aesthetic, that the narrator's vantage on causality conveys is one ultimately taken by Boethius himself: that the universe is governed by an inscrutable and inevitable order of causation, whether the people on the ground perceive it or not. Through his obsessive foregrounding of his unimpeded vantage point on causality, the narrator presents an aesthetic reflex of the idea that logical order governs human life, whether the people actually living those lives can perceive it or not. This aestheticizing of causality in carefully constructed order reproduces a cardinal function of Boethian proses, namely, to make linear order sense-perceptible through writing that is artificed to emphasize the relations of causality and contiguity among argumentative propositions.[42]

By suggesting that the narrator's pellucid perspective on the causality of the narrative could be motivated by the poem's drive to reinvestigate the ethically transformative dynamics of the *Consolation*, my analysis re-textures Carolyn Dinshaw's reading of the authoritarianness of the narrator's vantage. Dinshaw suggests that "such a concept of an omniscient poet can itself be seen as part of a patriarchal literary project: with its concern to authorize, legitimate, and, finally, delimit meanings, the concept of an author as all-controlling locus of meaning promotes patriarchal values of final authority, fidelity, and legitimacy."[43] Boethian literary practice and theory, which animate the *Troilus*, can certainly be construed as a patriarchal and authoritarian tradition, because they presuppose a *telos* toward which a narrator must arc—a *telos* that is understood to be the divine *summum bonum* of consolation. Boethius himself is quite concerned to limit and control meaning, and to show that there exists exactly one legitimate path toward spiritual renewal—a path toward God. But, as we will see, the "patriarchal," "authoritarian," meaning-delimiting power of the Boethian paradigm is sharply critiqued in the *Troilus*. In the end, the *Troilus*'s aestheticization of causality toward the creation of a protreptic

---

42. Focusing on Boethius's demystifying attitude toward the concept of chance, Eileen Sweeney suggests that "Boethius does not reject providence or even the view that there is some sense in which change is a result of a limited perspective rather than real randomness. Rather he rejects a providence that necessitates everything on moral grounds" (*Logic, Theology and Poetry*, 19–20).

43. *Chaucer's Sexual Poetics*, 37.

narrative undercuts itself, eroding the possibility of literary transformation even at its moment of seeming vindication.

NARRATOR AND LIKENESS: MODELING TRANSFORMATION, MAKING PROTREPSIS

But before the final critique of Boethian patriarchalism, the authoritarianism of the causality dynamic in the poem is first augmented by its close association with another important aspect of the poem's meditation on how ethical transformation might inhere in aesthetic form: its lyrical interruptions, which work in a strategic dialectic with the causality of the main narrative. These lyrical interruptions come in the narrator's intermittent commentaries on his causally emplotted narrative. These commentaries arise in the proems to many of the books of the *Troilus* and in the final palinode. These passages are all monologic, spoken by a single voice like Boethius's meters, and are thus markedly different from the poem's main polyvocal narrative. These monologic excursuses are also conspicuously affective.[44] Chaucer cultivates his narrator's affect-shaping role from the very beginning of the poem:

> The double sorwe of Troilus to tellen,
> That was the kyng Priamus sone of Troye,
> In lovynge, how his aventures fellen
> Fro wo to wele, and after out of joie,
> My purpos is, er that I parte fro ye.
> Thesiphone, thow help me for t'endite
> Thise woful vers, that wepen as I write.[45]

Here, the narrator's use of terms such as "sorwe," "joie," and "wepen" bespeak his investment not just in the facts of his story but in its affective trajectory, its arc from "wo" to "wele" and back again. He intimates, in

---

44. Bloomfield registers an affect-shaping role of the narrator, though he admits it as an exception to the narrator's larger predestination function, saying that certain of the commentaries seem simply to "emphasize the tragic end of the tale" and "the pity of it all" ("Distance and Predestination in *Troilus and Criseyde*," 21). He parses the narrator's shepherding of affect, then, as a departure from the tactical Boethianness of the poem, rather than, as I will show, a fuller realization of it.

45. Bk. 1, lines 1–7.

fact, that mercy, pity, and empathy are at the core of his response to the *Troilus* at the end, when he expresses understanding of Criseyde:

> Ne me list this sely womman chyde
> Forther than the storye wol devyse.
> Hire name, allas, is publysshed so wide
> That for hire gilt it oughte ynough suffise.
> And if I myghte excuse hire any wise,
> For she so sory was for hire untrouthe,
> Iwis, I wolde excuse hire yet for routhe.[46]

It is because of Criseyde's own "sorriness" that the narrator feels inclined to pardon her; he feels sorry for her because she herself feels sorry. He feels, or acts as though he feels, empathy for her.

Not only does he express his own empathy, but he also urges it on his readers, by transforming his intention to "excuse hire" into a normative recommendation, couched in modal verbal constructions: "for hire gilt it *oughte* ynough suffise." In book 3, the narrator again expresses his empathy for Criseyde as normative, by asserting that her intentions were always good and that she did the best she could do, given her circumstances: "Considered alle thynges as they stoode / No wonder is, syn she did al for goode."[47] Again in book 4, the narrator urges pity in his audience, especially for Criseyde, who risks the condemnation of all who hear of her treachery:

> Allas! That they sholde evere cause fynde
> To speke hire harm! And if they on hire lye,
> Iwis, hemself sholde han the vilanye.[48]

Through the narrator's modeling of empathy for Criseyde (in his "Allas!") and through his condemnation of those who would speak ill of her (in his "hemself sholde han the vilanye"), he urges his audience not to condemn her but to feel sorry for her. He does so by claiming that a normative reaction to her plight exists.[49]

---

46. Bk. 5, lines 1093–99.
47. Bk. 3, lines 923–24.
48. Bk. 4, lines 19–21.
49. Lee Patterson also sees Chaucer's revisions to Boccaccio's poem as designed to amplify the audience's empathy with Criseyde (*Chaucer and the Subject of History*, 107).

Equally programmatically, the narrator shepherds readers toward empathy with Troilus. In the final stanza of book 4, he guides the audience's affect, emphasizing Troilus's suffering by comparing it with the "torment down in helle," and insisting that that torment is beyond human ken:

For mannes hed ymagynen ne kan,
N'entendement considere, ne tonge telle
The cruele peynes of this sorwful man,
That passen every torment down in helle.[50]

The narrator's affective excursuses are thus not pure lamentation, but affect-shepherding moments, when he pushes his audience toward an affective alignment with his heroine and with his hero. Indeed, the narrator's impulse to interrupt his narrative in order to provide affective guideposts, rules for empathy, to his readers is one of the organizing principles of the poem. It works as, in effect, a complementary form of authoritarianism to what we see in the narrator's disclosing of full causality to his readers: through his affect-shepherding, he governs and delimits how his readers can encounter his poem.

Taken as a whole, the narrator's manipulative cultivation of empathy not only indicates the poem's will to exert authoritarian emotional control over its subjects but also points toward a larger identificatory drive in the poem, one that operates not within the narrative but at the perimeter of that narrative. That is, the poem is designed not simply to force readers to identify with Troilus and Criseyde but also—and more importantly—to induce them to identify with the *Troilus* narrator himself. Readers are urged, in particular, to identify with the narrator because he is, as they are, a past *reader* of the poem, as well as its present redactor.

The poem deploys several poetic forms that facilitate identification between narrator and reader. The first is the frame of the poem, which foregrounds the narrator's status as sometime reader of the poem. Not as overt as the *Canterbury Tales*, the *Troilus*'s framing is simply this: a man, the narrator of the *Troilus*, has read the poem before, ostensibly in the translation of one "Lollius."[51] He has found this poem so powerful that he has decided to translate it into English. By itself, this revelation that an author is translating a work he found moving in another language is not remarkable—medieval literature is rife with similar instances. But what

50. Bk. 4, lines 1695–98.
51. Bk. 1, line 394.

makes the *Troilus* narrator's situating and framing of his poetic translation so unusual is the number of times he refers back to the preexisting
writtenness of his source poems. He reminds his readers, again and again,
that his primary relationship to his poem was as a *reader*, and he now only
secondarily acts as a translator who labors under constraint to follow the
sources he himself has already encountered as an audience.[52] Of course, as
Chaucerians well know, the narrator's protestations of constraint do not
end up meaning that the poem is, in fact, all that closely derived from any
single source; where Chaucer wishes to take liberties with his sources, he
certainly takes them.[53] But the conceit of the frame remains intact and
insistent: the narrator of the poem is also a longtime and devout *reader*
of the poem, who has already been moved and shaped by its contents. The
frame of the poem, then, carefully aligns the narrator's relation to the
poem with the reader's.

A second form that sculpts likeness between the narrator and his
imagined readership is direct, apostrophic exhortation to that readership.
As the narrator puts forth his suit for pity early on in the poem:

> But ye loveres, that bathen in gladnesse,
> If any drope of pyte in yow be,
> Remembreth yow on passed hevynesse
> That ye han felt, and on the adversite
> Of othere folk.[54]

The narrator wants to remind his readers of "hevynesse" in a very particular way: he seeks to cultivate empathic affect in them by having them
recall their *own* "passed" woes—heavinesses *"ye* han felt." He wants, that
is, the readers to recognize resonances and echoes between their own emotional experiences and those of his characters. Reading the poem becomes
an exercise in cultivating a sense of emotional understanding between

---

52. For passages that foreground the narrator's status as reader-turned-writer, labor-
ing under some degree of constraint and some degree of inability to follow his sources,
see bk. 1, lines 141–47, 239–45, 260–66, 393–99; bk. 2, lines 8–14, 48–49; bk. 3, lines 447–
48, 491–504, 1195–97, 1324–30, 1408–9, 1814–17; bk. 4, lines 12–14, 799–805, 1415–21;
bk. 5, lines 834–40, 1037–53, 1086–90, 1562, 1653–55, 1751–78. The narrator, at one point,
projects this sense of writing-under-constraint onto Troilus, at the moment at which
he completes his letter to Criseyde and exclaims, "I nevere did thing with more peyne /
Than writen this, to which ye me constreyne" (bk. 2, lines 1231–32).

53. See Lewis, "What Chaucer Really Did to *Il filostrato*."

54. Bk. 1, lines 22–26.

one's own "passed hevynesses" and the joys and sorrows felt by Troilus and Criseyde. It becomes an exercise in getting a reader to feel an affective likeness to the main characters in the poem. But this exercise is first modeled, implicitly, by the narrator himself: in his own reading of the tragedy of *Troilus and Criseyde*, he has felt pity for his characters. Now, when he transmits that tragedy to his readers, they are meant to feel his characters' sorrows along with him.[55] Indeed, his usage of the apostrophic "ye" creates a dyadic relationship between him and his readers, almost creating his poem as an epistolary address to a group of friends, a missive intended to draw an audience into alignment with his own perspective. Readers are meant, as I have discussed, on one level to identify with Troilus and Criseyde; more lastingly, they are meant to identify with the *Troilus* narrator and his own ongoing empathic reading of their lives. They are meant to become good readers, by the *Troilus* narrator's own standards.

A third formal maneuver that helps the narrator sculpt likeness between himself and his readers comes in his famous metonymic and anthropomorphic address to his pen, at the opening of the penultimate book of his poem:

And now my penne, allas, with which I write,
Quaketh for drede of that I moste endite.

For how Criseyde Troilus forsook—
Or at the leeste, how that she was unkynde—

55. In suggesting a protreptic purpose behind the poem's cultivation of "pity," I part ways with the long-standing tradition of reading the *Troilus* primarily as a romance, in which the cultivation of "pity" is more a trope of courtliness and gentility than a serious philosophical drive. For an older but still very influential reading of the *Troilus* as a romance, see Young, "Chaucer's 'Troilus and Criseyde' as Romance"; on romance values in the poem, see Gaylord, "Gentilesse in Chaucer's *Troilus*." For a treatment of how the romance gestures of the poem create a certain courtly dynamic between the narrator and his readers, see Knopp, "Narrator and His Audience in Chaucer's *Troilus and Criseyde*." The generic classification of the *Troilus* as a romance is certainly warranted, and the attribution of a courtly motive to the pity mandate is certainly part of what is happening in the poem—indeed, elsewhere in his writings, Chaucer associates "pity" with courtly behavior that has no relationship with ethical protrepsis, as in his characterization of the Prioress in the *Canterbury Tales*. But the presence of courtliness in the vocabulary and tone of the *Troilus* does not remotely mean that "pity" can or should have only one meaning or cultural significance, and to focus overly on the romance valences, to the elision of the serious philosophical ones, blunts the literary-historical significance of Chaucer's work.

Moot hennesforth ben matere of my book,
As writen folk thorugh which it is in mynde.[56]

The anthropomorphic "quaking pen" externalizes the narrator's own emotions at what he must relate. Through this metonymic and anthropomorphic externalization of emotion, the narrator thematizes the pity as something contagious, something anyone—even an inanimate pen—would
feel at Troilus and Criseyde's plight. But crucially, this particular poetic
choice—to animate the inanimate pen—works in two ways. First, it depicts the pen as alive and as preemptively reacting to the impending tragedy of the main characters of the poem. But second, it simply narrates how
a pen, if held in the quaking hand of a writer, would be likely to tremble.
In this more literal reading, the "pen" serves as a reminder that the narrator-poet holds in his hand the power to affect his audience with "drede."
Reading this work of poetic fiction is meant to produce a contagious quaking, transmitted from the narrator to his pen via his hand, and from his
pen to the reader. In that contagious quaking, readers are urged to feel the
force of the narrator's own emotions; they are urged to feel a kinship with
him.

The poem amplifies this kinship between narrator and reader through
a fourth formal maneuver: it introduces the first-person plural into the
narrator's empathic outbursts, as when he laments the cruelty of fortune:

But O Fortune, executrice of wierdes,
O influences of thise hevenes hye!
Soth is, that under God ye ben oure hierdes,
Though to us bestes ben the causez wrie.[57]

In this introduction of the first-person plural, readers are made to understand that it is not only Troilus and Criseyde who are trapped by fortune,
but also the narrator and all his readers. "We" are all "bestes," unwilling
subjects of the "hevenes hye." With his "though to us bestes," the *Troilus* narrator cinches himself together with his readers. He thus pushes the
Troilus toward protrepsis, suggesting that his own lessons, born of his engagement with this story, are exportable to a readership, since he and they
are alike in beastliness and in their entrapment in fortune, fate, and the
indifferent motions of the heavens.

56. Bk. 4, lines 13–18.
57. Bk. 3, lines 617–20.

Anchoring the Boethianness of this moment, as W. A. Davenport notes, this passage neatly paraphrases the fifth meter of the fifth book of the *Consolation*.[58] And indeed, the narrator often anchors and amplifies the Boethianness of his own empathy and of his cultivation of a parallel empathy in his readers by deploying Boethian terms and concepts in his affect-shepherding excursuses. This recurrent pattern of alluding to or paraphrasing well-known Boethian passages constitutes the fifth formal means by which the poem creates a feeling of likeness between narrator and reader. When readers encounter vernacularized passages of Boethian wisdom spewing forth from the narrator, their own readerly skill sets are gratified; they realize that they, like the narrator, are steeped in Boethian thought as they navigate the poem. They are made to feel aware of the shared Boethian interpretive habit that joins them to their narrator.

Boethian allusions ring out loudly again in the proem to book 4, which forecasts the coming doom of Troilus's relationship with Criseyde. In this case, the narrator's descriptions of Fortune paraphrase those from the first two books of the *Consolation*.

> But al to litel, weylaway the whyle,
> Lasteth swich joie, ythonked be Fortune,
> That semeth trewest whan she wol bygyle
> And kan to fooles so hire song entune
> That she hem hent and blent, traitour comune!
> And whan a wight is from hire whiel ythrowe,
> Than laugheth she, and maketh hym the mowe.[59]

Here, the narrator deploys gleeful affective terms, such as "joie" and "laugheth," only to explode them with phrases such as "weylaway the whyle" and "traitour comune," which urge the audience to feel sorrow over the brevity of human joy, disdain for the treacheries of fortune, and empathy for the inescapability of Troilus's fate.[60] He couples this affective discourse with decidedly Boethian descriptions of Fortune: her cruel laughter and mockery, and her use of the "whiel" to throw men down, her changefulness and cruelty in making the "mowe" at the very people

---

58. *Complaint and Narrative*, 12.

59. Bk. 4, lines 1–7.

60. In Gordon's phrasing, the narrator makes a series of "appeals to the fellow-feeling that anyone must have who has ever waited, alternating between hope and doubt, for something or someone desperately longed for" (*Double Sorrow*, 132).

whose lives she has overthrown. Thus the narrator uses thematic allusions drawn from the *Consolation* to mark this passage as Boethian, urging readers to understand that it is specifically a Boethian literary theory and formal practice that are at issue in the *Troilus*.

What the narrator is actually doing in the "wheel of Fortune" passage, however, is yet more pointed than a reference to Boethius and his literary world. The narrator is making a distinction between how Troilus and Criseyde fail to perceive the "hidden causes" in their lives and how he has, through his own narrative, consistently and programmatically made causality plain to himself and to his readers. Thus, what he ends up doing in this dual evocation of Boethian theories of causality is to affirm literary reading as one's best access to causality, and also one's best access to empathy with other people. Troilus and Criseyde, who are living their lives, cannot see causality; readers, helped by the emotional shepherding of the tireless narrator, can see causality perfectly clearly in the story and can find their emotional bearings through the narrator's guidance. Readers are urged to feel kinship with the narrator, to share in his perspective, attitudes, and feelings. Readers are urged, that is, to take the narrator as their Boethian guide through the stormy lives of Troilus and Criseyde. The "compassion" or "pity" or "empathy" that scholars have long discerned as a motivating force behind the *Troilus* is not simply an emotion of pity for the characters: it is an aesthetic experience of *likeness* between oneself and the narrator.

That experience becomes the foundation for an implicit defense of literary experience as a means of accessing likeness and causality that far outstrips what can be achieved in the real world of occulted causes and secret allegiances. In its yoking together of reader with narrator, and its deploying of formal devices and literary dialectics to create the yoke, the poem reveals that it is, on some level, *about* the possibility of literary protrepsis, that it is *about* the viability of pinning ethical transformation to aesthetic form. It is concerned with whether the dialectic of the proselike, relentlessly causal narrative with the narrator's songful and likeness-oriented excursuses will be able to work any kind of ethical transformation. The denouement of these metapoetic concerns comes at the very end of the work.

TRANSFORMATION IN THE *TROILUS*: TRAGEDY AND THE VEXED REMAKING OF BOETHIUS

Troilus's postmortem ascent through the heavenly spheres is well established as a revisiting of Boethius's transformative ascent from despair to understanding.[61] Troilus's ascent, though, is not the main Boethian event of the end of the poem. Instead, it prepares the reader for the more complete and seemingly "philosophical" transcendence that the narrator undergoes, much as the "litargie" and "leche" passages preform a sensitivity to Boethian song and dialogue, and much as the narrator's third proem preforms a sensitivity to Troilus's song. Shortly after Troilus's ascent, the *Troilus* ends as follows:

> With al myn herte of mercy evere I preye,
> And to the lord right thus I speke and seye:
>
> Thow oon, and two, and thre, eterne on lyve,
> That regnest ay in thre, and two, and oon,
> Uncircumscript, and al maist circumscrive,
> Us from visible and invisible foon
> Defende, and to thy mercy, everichon,
> So make us, Jesus, for thi mercy, digne,
> For love of mayde and moder thyn benigne.
> Amen.[62]

Showing the narrator to be so altered by the narrative he tells, of course, draws him into parallel with the narrating Boethius: the narrator, like the narrating Boethius, is changed and edified by his experience of telling his tale.[63] Thus, in the end, the poem seems to be as much about the narrator, and about his experience of being transformed by reading and rewriting the story of Troilus and Criseyde, as it is about the main characters themselves.

But the narrator's seeming transformation to higher consciousness would have been baffling to a medieval reader steeped in Boethian thematics. From within a Boethian philosophical frame of reference, the narrator's putative turn from worldly tragedy to divine contemplation in the palinode seems anything but warranted. He has not been engaged in a

---

61. See Steadman, *Disembodied Laughter*, 1–20, 66–83, and Bloomfield, "Distance and Predestination in *Troilus and Criseyde*," 26.

62. Bk. 5, lines 1861–70. This passage translates a Dantean passage; see Kean, "Chaucer, an Englishman Elusively Italianate," 390.

63. Gordon also compares the narrator to Boethius. She says of the end of the poem, "the narrator becomes a kind of 'Boethius,' whose unseeing eye is brought gradually to a clearer vision as the story proceeds to its inevitable end" (*Double Sorrow*, 61).

conversation with Philosophy, has not heard her comforting explanations
of divine order, nor has he heard her beautiful illustrations of cosmic har-
monics. Although there are lengthy Boethian passages stitched into the
Troilus, they are invariably stitched in with the needle of irony: to be sure,
Troilus is, in a manner of speaking, healed from his desperate love of Criseyde by the "medicine" of dialogue, but it is critical to bear in mind that
Pandarus's offered dialogic tonics are actually quite toxic, urging Troilus
into the love affair that will be his eventual undoing. Although Criseyde,
like a good Boethian subject, is coaxed into love by the experience of song,
she finds no salvific, philosophical transformation in exchange for her
openness to the affective power of song. True, Troilus attacks the problems
of free will and fate in book 4 of the *Troilus*, much as Boethius does in
books 4 and 5 of the *Consolation*, but whereas Boethius eventually gleans
comfort and understanding from this attack, Troilus only works himself
into a deeper state of befuddlement and benightedness.[64] To be sure, Troilus praises the orderliness and harmony of the universe, but that praise,
because it is based on sexual love rather than spiritual love, ultimately
proves fragile and disappointing. Even the narrator himself seems unable
to get beyond the idea of Fortune's rampant tyranny in the world—an idea
Boethius himself must dispense with quite early on in his own protreptic
narrative. The poem is crafted in order first to evoke and then to *destabilize* Boethian thematics. And yet, somehow, the narrator seems to attain
transformative understanding in the end anyway. He seems, in the end, to
free himself from the wheel of Fortune and to find his way to a contemplation of God.

Jessica Rosenfeld suggests that the seeming transcendences of the *Troilus* stem from commentaries on Boethius that circulated in the late Middle Ages and that recognized the possibility of a worldly kind of transcendence, one that did not necessarily mandate the radical abdication of ties
to mundane aspects of life, including and particularly romantic love or
friendship.[65] This is a persuasive account for the transformation and transcendence (however abortive, in the end) of Troilus himself, but I would
suggest that the irony of the *narrator's* seeming transformation at the end
ultimately has its roots elsewhere. Namely, it has its roots in a metapoetic
squabble that Chaucer is having with Boethius over the nature and purpose of tragedy.

Perhaps the pinnacle of the narrator's ironic revision of the *Consola-*

---

64. Bk. 4, lines 954–1078.
65. Rosenfeld, *Ethics and Enjoyment*, 12, 144–45.

tion is that he has been engaged in the one form of poetic activity that Philosophy herself pointedly shuns as deleterious to the health of the soul: tragic poetry. In her first appearance, Philosophy realizes that Boethius is enmeshed in self-pity, surrounded by the poetic muses, what she further calls the "scenicas meretriculas" or, as Chaucer puts it "commune strompettis of swich a place that men clepene the theatre."[66] These "theatrical" strumpet muses are recognizably the muses of tragedy. Before she even attempts to heal Boethius, as discussed in chapter 1, Philosophy first violently casts out these tragic muses, saying they pierce into him with venomous spines and damage his ability to profit from her teachings. This banishment of tragedy from philosophy's consolation would be familiar to any medieval person who had read Boethius, and would have made the final turn of the *Troilus*, which the narrator explicitly calls, at that very moment, a "tragedy," a mind-boggling shock.

But shock is precisely the point. The narrator finishes with a renewed conviction in God's eternity—in that "oon, and two, and thre eterne on lyve"[67]—and a turn toward prayer. He finishes, that is, in a state of consolation and contemplation. This ending echoes the protreptic end of the *Consolation* itself, but with a literary-theoretical twist. The poem demonstrates that Philosophy's twin consolation can inhere as readily in tragic fiction as in philosophical allegory.[68] Chaucer uses Boethius as a literary-theoretical provocation, not just for representing his narrator's transformation and modeling one for a reader, but also for defending the ethical utility of tragic fiction against the likes of Boethius himself. [69]

More specifically, the *Troilus* demonstrates that its stylistic reinvention of prosimetrum, with its creation of the aesthetics of causality and likeness, can produce ethical transformation on its own. The narrator, ap-

---

66. Boethius, *Philosophiae consolatio*, bk. I, pr. 1, sentence 8; *Boece*, bk. I, pr. 1, sentences 49–50.

67. Bk. 5, line 1863.

68. Thomas Stillinger, too, recognizes the cultivation of empathy as a fundamental part of Chaucer's design, saying, at the end of his book, "He writes a book in which it is possible to identify with Troilus or with Criseyde or with the narrator who identifies (in different ways) with both" (*Song of Troilus*, 216).

69. Here, I disagree with McAlpine's reading, which examines the *Troilus*'s generic affiliations with Boethius, reading the *Consolation* as an antitragedy (a demonstration of Boethius's ascent from despair to joy and thus a reversal of the Senecan tragic paradigm by which a man goes from joy to despair) and the *Troilus* as a response to it that reaffirms Boethius's condemnation of tragedy (*Genre of Troilus and Criseyde*, 17–19, 30, 52–85, 89, 90, 120).

parently, does not need to learn the specific *thematics* of Philosophy's lessons, because the aesthetics—the forms and styles and, specifically, the
oscillation between causality and likeness—are sufficient to teach him.
The poem works, then, as a defense of the power not just of tragic poetry
but specifically of the *aesthetics* of tragic poetry to ignite transformative
understanding in a reader. It is a work of vernacular literary theory, put
into practice.

In suggesting this, I want to push even beyond the boundaries of literary theory in Boethius's *Consolation*, to look to a literary theorist whose
theories of how literary experience could be transformative for an audience seem to inform Chaucer's "litel tragedy." It is well known that Aristotle, in his *Poetics*, identifies "fear and pity" as the two primary feelings
that tragedy should inspire in its audience, toward the eventual realization of purgative and psychologically salutary catharsis.[70] It is equally well
known, at least among Chaucerians, that when the *Troilus* narrator calls
his work a "litel tragedy," he is drawing upon the Senecan definition—
filtered, in fact, through Boethius—in which a great hero falls from joy to
sorrow.[71] Indeed, so obvious and ever-present seem these Senecan notions
of tragedy in the *Troilus*, in Chaucer's other works, and, indeed, in the
Middle Ages writ large that it borders on unsayable that any other under-

---

70. Aristotle, *Poetics* 6.64 (1449b 23–28). Howell Chickering approaches this idea as
well, noting that "Troilus' suffering increases our sympathy . . . while at the same time
[the poem] also invite[s] a critical detachment from, and conceptualization of, Troilus's
situation because these very same sonorities and figures of speech are set inside our
ironic foreknowledge of the narrative" ("Poetry of Suffering," 243). Chickering's characterization of the tension between sympathy and foreknowledge coincides with my own
characterization of the fundamental working of the narrator: he shepherds the readers'
emotions while forcing them to register the supervening order and momentum of the
main narrative, presenting to them all the causal linkages in it.

71. Analyses of Chaucer's notion of tragedy as "Senecan," based on the fall of a
great man from joy to sorrow, are numerous. See, for instance, L. D. Benson, introduction to *Canterbury Tales*, in *Riverside Chaucer*, 17–18; Brewer, "Comedy and Tragedy
in *Troilus and Criseyde*"; Windeatt, "Classical and Medieval Elements in Chaucer's
Troilus"; M. Nolan, *John Lydgate and the Making of Public Culture*, 127, 136; for a corrective of the version of Senecanism that Chaucer seems to have known, focusing not
so much on the idea that wicked or deserving great men get punished by fortune but
instead on the idea that innocent people are stricken with fortune, and for a discussion
especially of the notion of an undeserved and *unforeseen* collapse in fortunes, see Kelly,
Chaucerian Tragedy, 52, 55. Kelly notes that Chaucer seems to derive this idea of an
"unwar stroke" of misfortune from Nicholas Trevet's commentary on Boethius (54–69).

standing of "the tragic" might animate and motivate the *Troilus* narrator's not-so-"litel" experiment with transformative fiction. Nevertheless, that is precisely what I want to suggest, augmenting an argument made by Henry Ansgar Kelly.[72]

In deploying a narrative/narrator dialectic that renders causality and likeness sense-perceptible in form and literary structure, the *Troilus* performs exactly what Aristotle identifies as the transformative two-step of cathartic, tragic fiction.[73] First, by relentlessly highlighting the causal nexus of history into which Troilus and Criseyde are woven and by insistently telegraphing forward to the inevitably sorrowful end they both will meet, the *Troilus* narrator creates a dynamic of fear—anticipatory dread—both in himself and in his audience. Then, by devising his system of likenesses between Troilus and himself, between Criseyde and Antigone, between his emotions and his readers' emotions, between his emotions and those of his characters, and between Boethius's *Consolation* and his own *Troilus*, the *Troilus* narrator sets up a formal structure designed to cultivate what he calls "pity" throughout his poem. The narrator, then, deploys his protreptic as an Aristotelian defense of tragedy against Boethius's Platonic condemnation of it as unsalutary.

Admittedly, there is no evidence that Chaucer ever encountered Aristotle's *Poetics* directly. There is, in point of fact, no Middle English version of the *Poetics*. But there were commentaries on Aristotle's works in circulation during Chaucer's lifetime, which could have informed his sense of tragedy.[74] Averroes composed commentaries on the *Poetics*, highlighting Aristotle's belief in the ethical efficacy and necessity of "pity and

72. Kelly suggests that with its focus both on "general lessons of caution and resignation" and on the cultivation of readerly "sympathy," Chaucer's *Troilus* stands up well to the Aristotelian standards for tragedy, whether he designed it deliberately to do so or not (ibid., 141).

73. Kelly notes this as well, and further notes that Chaucer alone seems to have seen this empathy cultivation as a part of medieval tragedy. In the Middle Ages, he says, "[t]here was no generic demand for the sort of empathetic sorrow for the disasters of others that both Aristotle and Chaucer required of tragedy" (*Ideas and Forms of Tragedy*, 221).

74. Jessica Rosenfeld shows that Boethian literary works of the late Middle Ages are, themselves, pervasively shot through with Aristotelianizing commentaries and ideas, particularly about ethics, so applying this particular Aristotelian notion to a poem suffused with Boethian echoes does not seem much of a stretch for a medieval author (*Ethics of Enjoyment*, 1–13, 32–38).

fear" in tragic poetry, and this commentary was known and distributed in the medieval west.[75] Avicenna, too, focuses on the "pity and fear" mandate in Aristotle's *Poetics,* and his commentaries have a significant presence in late medieval literary culture.[76] William of Aragon and Nicholas Trevet—the latter having unquestionably informed Chaucer's translation of the *Consolation*—both compose Aristotelianizing commentaries on Boethius.[77] My analysis of the narrative/narrator dialectic in this chapter suggests that Chaucer's exposure to such Aristotelianizing readings of Boethius might have urged him to devise his *Troilus,* through the intermediate Boethian agent of the *Troilus* narrator, precisely as a versified Aristotelian commentary on the ethical utility of tragedy.

Not concerned only with the ethical utility of tragedy writ large, the *Troilus* is concerned particularly with how protrepsis can be worked through such a tragedy—with how reading can prove central to an ethical transformation. It is, after all, a story of how a book that the *Troilus* narrator has read already, in his own life, and that he now renarrates for his readership has proven transformative for him. That experience of reading, retelling, and attempting to convey transcendent understanding constitutes him not only as an author but also as a subject of a protreptic experience. The foregrounding of the narrator's status as reader thus constitutes his *Troilus* as a sly and decidedly tragic protreptic and the narrator himself as the hero of that protreptic story.

But even unto the very end of the poem, the narrator's transformation seems vexed, since a metapoetic unrest manifests at the moment of his seeming transcendence into the beyond of divine contemplation. When the narrator turns from his fictive world to the comforts of divine contemplation, he enacts his own withdrawal from tragic poetry. The very moment, then, in which the narrator takes full possession of his ethical transformation and offers up his poem as a protreptic work for his readers is when he outgrows the fictional world he has created. He has seen the truth and ineluctability of ordered causality, has felt the harmonious likeness between himself and his characters, and has cultivated a sense of likeness between himself and his readership. He has seen and felt the power of tragic fiction to produce ethical renewal through aesthetic ac-

---

75. See Minnis and Scott, *Medieval Literary Theory,* 284–85 and 304–5, for a treatment of different editions of Hermann the German's edition of *Averroes' Middle Commentary,* which addresses the "pity and fear" element of Aristotle's poetic teachings.

76. Ibid., 286–87.

77. Ibid., 315–21, 326; Rosenfeld, *Ethics and Enjoyment,* 46, 141–44.

tion. But as soon as he has internalized these transformative forms, he transcends them. His defense of tragic poetry thus seems tinged with loss; it reads at once as an affirmation of the possibility of protrepsis through tragic catharsis and as an abdication of authorship and a disavowal of fictive literature. In the *Troilus* narrator, the *Troilus* incarnates the possibility that tragic poetry can be protreptic, when constructed of a mixed style whose functionality replicates that of Boethian prosimetrum. But even at the same time that it asserts its own literary power, the poem is bent on transcending and truncating the very fictive form that it has endorsed as transformative. Tragic fiction is a mode, however powerful in its capacity to inspire "drede" and "pite," that is to be moved through, to arrive at something better and higher: the contemplation of that "oon, and two, and thre eterne on lyve."

CHAPTER FOUR

Prosimetrum and the *Canterbury* Philosophy of Literature

D espite its ostensible final turn away from fictive worlds, the *Troilus* is neither Chaucer's last nor even his most concerted effort to practice or theorize ethical transformation as a function of the mixed form. Containing the prose *Tale of Melibee*, the prose *Parson's Tale*, and the prose *Retractions*, the mostly metrical *Canterbury Tales* is Chaucer's only formally prosimetric work. Though it does not alternate prose with meter as regularly as do other prosimetra, the form of the *Tales* is designed as a pointed gesture toward prosimetrum, and toward Boethian prosimetrum in particular. That gesture underpins the work's larger literary-theoretical ambition to explore how and whether aesthetic experience can be ethically transformative. Like Boethius's prosimetrum, the *Tales* not only practices both prose and meter but also explicitly theorizes the difference between them as opposed methods of producing learning in an audience. Through this practice and theory of prosimetrum, Chaucer aligns his vernacular fictive work with Boethian protreptic, though to an end that might have been unrecognizable to Boethius himself.

Like the stylistic and structural experimentation in the *Boece* and in the *Troilus*, the formal experimentation with literature's transformative power in the *Canterbury Tales* originates in a particular problem of fourteenth-century vernacular literary philosophy. But whereas the *Boece* is stylistically infused with a drive to render meaning aesthetically available through syntax and semantics, and whereas the *Troilus* is animated by a drive to reconsider the specific protreptic power of tragedy, the *Canterbury Tales* starts with two more basic questions of literary philosophy. The first is how and whether composing, reading, or hearing literature can constitute a good use of time. The second is how aesthetic form and style might contribute to literature's ability or failure to make the most of time.

Throughout the Middle Ages, the question of literature's ability to make good use of time vexes and animates penitential writings and sermons, which accuse fictive literature, variously figured as "jestes," "rhymes," and "lesynges," of proving harmful to the soul by proving an ill use of time, often leading to greater "sins of the tavern," such as gluttony, sloth, and lechery.[1] Toward the end of the fourteenth century, it is not just penitential writers or sermonists but also contemporary fictive writers, including William Langland, who increasingly associate the wasting of words with the wasting of time.[2] The *Canterbury Tales* refracts these ethical charges through a Boethian formal and functional lens, to meditate on the possibility that fictive literature can not just constitute a good use of time but also offer a path to ethical transformation for a narrator and audience.[3]

WHAT'S THE USE OF LITERATURE? THE MAN OF LAW'S CRUX AND THE *THOPAS-MELIBEE* CRISIS

The first step in this process of literary justification comes at the beginning of the *Man of Law's Tale*, when the Host notes the lateness of the hour and demands a narrative contribution from the Man of Law:

1. Circa 1275, the *Cursor mundi* asserts a link between wastefulness in general and lechery, which includes lying, troth breaking, dice playing, gaming, visiting harlots, gambling, "rimes unright," "gest of jogolour," and fornication. It argues that each of these lecherous activities "wastes bodi and als catel."*Cursor mundi*, line 27934ff. A few generations later, Dan Michel's 1340 *Ayenbite of Inwit* rails against tavern sins in particular as wastes of time, noting that all modes of "outrageous" behavior that destroy a person's spiritual goods "wasteth and dispendeth in folyes and in outrages . . . the guodes that ne byeth naght his, ac byeth his lhordes guodes, hwer-of him behouveth straitliche yelde rekeninge and scele." *Dan Michel's Ayenbite of Inwyt*, 18. Dan Michel accuses people of wasting their time who spend all their time at chess, in carols, in rhyming, in sitting idly eating too much meat and drinking too heavily, in follies like songs and other "fole gemenes." In such "lighthoods," he insists, not only do they waste their bodies and money but more immediately, they "wasteth hare time" (207). Between 1275 and 1340, the penitential focus came increasingly to indict the wasting of time, in particular, as a sinful consequence of indulging in carols, games, songs, and other "lighthoods." "Thus wasteth the wrecche his time and his wyttes and his guodes and wretheth God and harmeth his bodi and more his zaule" (52).

2. See Burrow, "Wasting Time."

3. Katherine Heinrichs has already pointed in this direction by suggesting how Chaucer's addition of the pilgrimage frame narrative to his largely Boccaccian basic narrative structure reflects a Boethian structural impulse (*Myths of Love*, 105).

Leseth no tyme, as ferforth as ye may.
Lordynges, the tyme wasteth nyght and day,
And steleth from us, what pryvely slepynge,
And what thurgh necligence in oure wakynge,
As dooth the streem that turneth nevere agayn,
Descendynge fro the montaigne into playn . . .
Lat us nat mowlen thus in ydelnesse.[4]

The Host uses traditional arguments about the use of time, drawn from
the penitential tradition: the idea underlying his claim is that a person
has only a certain fixed amount of time to live and thus should use that
limited time to the best possible end. Because time flows in only one
direction—forward, like the stream that flows inexorably down from the
mountain into the plain—one must be extremely careful to use that time
wisely, since that flow cannot be reversed or recovered for any reason.[5]
Normally, in penitential writings, these cautions would be followed by an
insistence that one must make good use of that time primarily in prayer
and in good works. But the Host marshals this penitential rhetoric only
to undercut its religious valences. He tells the Man of Law, "Sire man of
lawe . . . so have ye blis, / Telle us a tale anon, as forward is."[6] In his request to resume tale-telling lies the decidedly unpenitential idea that tale-
telling itself—far from imperiling the soul—is what constitutes a good use
of time. Because time is always slipping by, the pilgrims must persevere in
their narratives. In his view, silence is a form of "necligence" and "ydelnesse," the latter being a synonym for the sin of sloth to which Chaucer
will return in later tales. By asserting silence as a form of idleness, Harry
Bailley inverts the logic of penitential manuals that condemn storytelling as a waste of time, suggesting, on the contrary, that *not* telling tales
wastes time. By thus evoking and inverting the association between tale-
telling and time-wasting, the *Canterbury Tales* creates its own autoch-
thonous literary-theoretical problem, the idea that fictive storytelling can
and, indeed, must be a good use of time.
  Having created this literary-theoretical challenge, however, the *Tales*

4. Chaucer, introduction to *Man of Law's Tale*, fragment 2, lines 19–24, 32.
5. Cf. "& this [God] doth for he wil not reuerse the ordre or the ordinel cours in
the cause of His creacion. For tyme is maad for man, and not man for tyme." *Cloud of
Unknowing*, chap. 4, p. 20, lines 9–11.
6. Fragment 2, lines 33–34.

cannot rest easy in the idea that storytelling must make the most of time. An interpretive crux immediately follows Bailley's urging, in which the Man of Law positions himself in relation to literary work as, at once, an eager consumer and an unwilling producer. First he laments a contemporary glut of verse in English—attributing that glut to none other than Chaucer himself:

> But nathelees, certeyn,
> I kan right now no thrifty tale seyn
> That Chaucer, thogh he kan but lewedly
> On metres and on rymyng craftily,
> Hath seyd hem in swich Englissh as he kan
> Of olde tyme, as knoweth many a man;
> And if he have noght seyd hem, leve brother,
> In o book, he hath seyd hem in another.[7]

"Chaucer," in the Man of Law's view, has overstuffed the world with verse, though he knows only "lewedly" about metered rhyming. Second, in response to this glut of "lewedly" metered verse, and the implicitly too-daunting prospect of rhyming "learnedly" to make a good use of time, the Man of Law bows out, promising a tale in prose rather than verse: "I speke in prose, and lat [Chaucer] rymes make."[8] In this seeming disavowal of "ryme," he not only refuses to try his hand at poetry but also implicitly nominates prose, rather than verse, as the ready answer to the Host's mandate to make the most of time.

I say "seeming" because, after this promise of prose, the Man of Law produces the versified, stanzaic, rime royal story of Custance—not at all what medieval readers would automatically understand as "prose." In response to this puzzling disjuncture between promise and product, some scholars have suggested that the word "prose" may be a scribal error, while others have argued that it may indicate Chaucer's original intention to give the prose and highly legalistic *Tale of Melibee* to the Man of Law.[9] Alfred David suggests that the Man of Law's confusing gesture toward prose and his subsequent adoption of poetry evinces Chaucer's anxieties about the ethical validity of poetry.[10] Martin Stevens has found evidence

---

7. Fragment 2, lines 45–52.

8. Fragment 2, line 96.

9. Alfred David notes this possibility ("Man of Law vs. Chaucer," 217).

10. Ibid., 224.

that the word "prose" in late Middle English could denote the rime royal form, which, in point of fact, is the verse form of the Man of Law's story.[11] He suggests that the Man's tale is a "prose" tale after all but suggests further that "prose," in this case, was simply a label for a particular type of rhymed verse. This is an intriguing possibility, but the fact remains that the Man of Law specifically dissociates himself from rhyming, leaving all the "rymes" to Chaucer, when, after all, rime royal is very clearly a rhymed form. There is an ineradicable slippage between Chaucer's "rhyming," of which the Man of Law ostensibly wants no part, and the form of his tale, which unquestionably rhymes.

The tale never resolves whether it should be seen in some way as a prose work or simply as a poem; instead, it leaves a tension hanging in the air between the two forms. Then, oddly, once that tension is created and the ambiguously "prose" tale is told, the very distinction between prose and verse quickly appears to be beside the point. Taking as authentic and sincere the Host's response to the Man of Law in the epilogue to the *Man of Law's Tale*, in which he calls the tale "thrifty . . . for the nones!,"[12] urges the conclusion that whether classified as "prose," "rhyme," or somewhere in between the two, the Man's tale has proven a good use of time—at least in Harry Bailley's estimation. The question of what the Man of Law's tale does, exactly, that constitutes a good use of time remains unclear. But the audience of the *Tales* is now attuned to the idea that time's good usage is a primary metapoetic concern for the poem.

Having raised but not resolved the issue of how literary experience— whether in prose or verse—can constitute a good use of time, the *Tales* recurs to it between the tales of *Sir Thopas* and *Melibee*, both of which are told by the Chaucer pilgrim himself. These tales, constituting Chaucer's only direct "performance" in the *Tales*, have been read as his attempt to show his literary mastery of two distinct genres: the insular romance and didactic allegory.[13] Rather than reading *Sir Thopas* and *Melibee* as Chaucer's pointed performance of these two genres, however, I read them as two sides of a single literary topos: prosimetrum as a formal vehicle for meditations on the possibility of ethically transformative writing. This

---

11. Stevens, "Royal Stanza in Early English Literature," 62–76. See also A. S. G. Edwards, "'I speke in prose.'"

12. Fragment 2, line 1165.

13. Patterson reads the two tales as, respectively, insular romance and didactic literature. ("'What man artow?'").

miniature prosimetrum is designed, first, to wrestle with the question of how literature can make use of time and, second, to align the Chaucer pilgrim, however ironically, with the tradition of mixed-form protrepsis.

Like the *Consolation*, the *Remède*, and *Troilus and Criseyde*, *Thopas* thematizes the affective powers of song as a way of grounding its meditation on how aesthetic experience can produce psychological transformation.

> The briddes synge, it is no nay,
> The sparhauk and the papejay,
> That joye it was to heere;
> The thrustelcok made eek hir lay,
> The wodedowve upon the spray
> She sang ful loude and cleere.
>
> Sire Thopas fil in love-longynge,
> Al whan he herde the thrustel synge,
> And pryked as he were wood.[14]

Listening to the lays of the hawks, popinjays, thrushes, and doves makes Thopas fall into "love-longynge," much as song affects Troilus and Criseyde by "converting" them to love of each other. This reengagement with the idea that song transforms affect, however, is ironic—far more ironic than is Criseyde's helpless fall into love-longing upon hearing Antigone's song or when she overhears the birdsong from the trees above her. In *Thopas*, song's power to influence affect is exaggerated to the point of absurdity: not one bird, as in Criseyde's transformation in the *Troilus*, but a veritable menagerie of birds unleashes its affect-transforming might on the unsuspecting Thopas. Surrounded by the cacophony of birds, it seems inevitable that Thopas should have an emotional reaction: bombarded by sound and melody, he feels love, but he feels it unto the point of madness— he "pryke[s] as he were wood." What the *Troilus* undertook as a serious demonstration of song's affective power, *Thopas* undertakes as a ludicrous parody of how song influences the human psyche. Chaucer shows how song can reform affect to create love, but he also demystifies that "love": Thopas's love is a maddened "prykyng"—a pun on sexual love and hunting—rather than the spiritual love of the *Consolation* or, for that matter,

14. Fragment 7, lines 766–74.

the elegant courtly love of the *Remède*. Chaucer has begun to turn his eponymous double's performance into a critique of the putative power of song to effect salvific transformation in its hearers.

This critique takes a more fixed shape in the form of *Thopas*'s "drasty" rhyme. Although the prologue to *Thopas* is in rime royal, the tale itself diverges from that verse form and into tail-rhyme stanzas, typical of popular medieval romance. The stanzas are six lines long, and most follow the rhyme scheme *aabaab*, but several instead follow the rhyme scheme *aabccb*, and a few tack on sets of variably rhymed four-line groupings at the end. In addition to the irregularity in number of lines per stanza and in rhyme scheme, the lines within stanzas have variable numbers of stresses per line, although they usually follow a 4-4-3 4-4-3 pattern. In direct apposition with the highly regular and metrically meticulous form of the rime royal prologue, this form seems disorderly, excessively wrought, and inconsistent.

On one level, the irregularity of the verse serves to embody the Chaucer pilgrim's irregularity of ideation as he tells his tale. His narrative of Thopas meanders from topic to topic, aimlessly and indiscriminately listing Thopas's clothes, his appearance, the foods he eats, the flowers and trees he sees, and the armor he wears, while weaving in the fact that Thopas, along the way, is bewitched by love for an Elf-queen. The story is every bit as lurching, indecisive, meandering, and irregular as its metrical form, so that the latter becomes the formal correlate of the former.

But the metrical irregularity and narrative digressiveness of *Thopas* are more than inertly correlated with each other; they combine to make *Thopas* a particular kind of poetic experiment. When the Chaucer pilgrim departs from his main narrative about Thopas's love-longing, he swerves into highly aesthetic, sensory description. He tells of Thopas's face "Whit . . . as payndemayn / His lippes rede as rose,"[15] "His heer, his berd was lyk saffroun / That to his girdle raughte adoun,"[16] "The lycorys and the cetewale"[17] that blossom at his feet, the "softe gras"[18] on which he hunts, "the sweete wyn / And mede eek in a mazelyn, / And roial spicerye / Of gyngebreed that was ful fyn / And lycorys, and eek comyn / With sugre that is trye"[19] that he eats and drinks, and the "fyn hawberk . . . And over

---

15. Fragment 7, lines 725–26.
16. Fragment 7, lines 730–31.
17. Fragment 7, lines 761.
18. Fragment 7, lines 779.
19. Fragment 7, lines 851–56.

that his cote-armour / As whit as is a lilye-flour."[20] The narrative's digressions are relentlessly aesthetic, so much so that they create a sensory maelstrom within the tale. As they accumulate, these discrete sense impressions refuse to grant primacy or even autonomy to the story itself, so that a reader is utterly and perhaps unpleasantly lost in sensory overload. Through this sensory inundation, the story becomes, in effect, about sensation itself. With this in mind, the irregular form of the verse begins to seem more innately motivated: in a tale that takes aesthetic experience as its theme, a verse form that, because of its refusal of regularity, makes a reader constantly aware of it as constructed, various, and disjointed and refuses to allow a reader to settle into a patterned expectation of sounds and rhythms seems entirely appropriate. The Chaucer pilgrim produces an aria on aesthetic overload, a poem designed to show how overly wrought verse creates sensory experience.

But the success of this experiment in overworked sensation is quickly challenged as having any ethical utility by how the pilgrim audience responds to it. Not long into *Thopas*, the Host interrupts, making comments that amplify the tale's ironic relevance to a transformative practice and theory of song by denying the very affect-transforming sensory pleasure that is so overdetermined in the tale itself. First the Host critiques *Thopas* for aesthetic failures: its rhymes make him "wery" and make his "eres aken."[21] In failing to please the senses or to engage the mind, *Thopas* is cast as an antithesis to Boethian song; even though it is versified, it conspicuously fails to do what meter is theorized to do by Boethius, his commentators, Dante, Guillaume, and Chaucer himself at points in the *Troilus*: namely, to provide sweet and educative delight. Boethius's work emphasizes that song should bring a hearer into a state of heightened attention, should draw him out of his weary "litargye," and should be sensually sweet, bringing rectitude and fortification to a hearer's ears. As Chaucer's *Boece* puts it, "whan the swetnesse of here dite hadde thurw perced me, that was desyrous of herknynge, and I astoned hadde yit streyghte myn eres."[22] In being diametrically opposite to this description of sweetly healing song, the Host's critique casts the Chaucer pilgrim as an inept and bumbling Boethius.

As he goes on, the Host specifies the Chaucer pilgrim's shortcomings further: his second complaint is that the "drasty rymyng" of *Thopas* does

20. Fragment 7, lines 863, 866–67.
21. Fragment 7, lines 921, 923
22. *Boece*, bk. 3, pr. 1, sentences 1–4.

"noght elles but despendest tyme."[23] In this complaint, the Host adopts not only the position of his contemporary sermonists and penitential manual writers but also a literary-theoretical position akin to that of Philosophy in the beginning of the *Consolation*. When she finds Boethius lamenting his fate in song, she reminds him that song should be "fructifying" rather than "venomous"; it should bring profit to the soul rather than do harm.[24] She insists not that he abandon song altogether, as I have emphasized, but that he abandon deleterious song. Following hard upon the heels of the Chaucer pilgrim's unsalutary singing, the Host's insistence that the elvish songster turn to some matter of "murthe or som doctryne" captures the essence of Philosophy's goal: to turn her interlocutor toward productive learning, by either music or argument, and away from fruitless song of any kind.[25] Appropriately, the Chaucer pilgrim meets the Host's complaint with the same maneuver Philosophy uses against Boethius's initial lamentations to the muses of tragedy. He turns to prose.

The specific prose tale that the Chaucer pilgrim tells accentuates its affiliation with the proses of the *Consolation* and deepens this miniature prosimetrum's thematization of Boethian literary theory and practice, much as the *Troilus*'s thematizations of song and dialogue worked to create a vernacular sensitivity to Boethian metapoetics. The *Tale of Melibee* is based on Albertano of Brescia's story of Prudence, filtered through the French translation by Renaud de Louens. Both of these sources for *Melibee* fall recognizably within the Boethian tradition and would have read as Boethian consolations to Chaucer and his contemporary readers for several reasons.[26] First, *Melibee* and its sources tell how a rational and comforting female personification helps a despondent man find comfort in his hour of despair; the basic narrative conceit thus echoes the *Consolation* quite closely.[27] Second, throughout her conversation with Melibee, Prudence, like Philosophy, emphatically and repetitively uses "causes and resouns" to reinforce her argument, gradually bringing him to understand that he must abandon his passionate anger and sorrow in favor of mea-

23. Fragment 7, lines 930–31

24. As she says in the *Boece*, bad song "wolden fedyn and noryssen hym with sweete venym" and bring "nothyng fructifyenge nor profitable," but would instead "destroyen the corn plentyvous of fruytes of resoun." Bk. 1, pr. 1, sentences 52–53, 56–57.

25. Fragment 7, line 935.

26. Kreuzer, "Note on Chaucer's *Tale of Melibee*"; Foster, "Has Anyone Here Read *Melibee*?," 403.

27. For a comparison of the sources of *Melibee* with *Melibee* itself, see Bornstein, "Chaucer's *Tale of Melibee* as an Example of the 'Style Clergial.'"

sured reason.[28] Third, the process of ethical reeducation is long and tortu-
ous, with many setbacks. Lee Patterson calls these setbacks "devastating
failures,"[29] but when viewed in the context of the Boethian paradigm of
transformative fiction, in which setbacks are a natural part of reeducation, Melibee's repeated failures to grasp Prudence's wisdom seem generi-
cally warranted and didactically inevitable: before a person can conquer
his own ignorance, he must face it in all its particulars. He must see his
own unreasonableness before seeing his teacher's argumentative reason;
he must see his own internal disorder before seeing his teacher's logical
order. This process of failure is essential to the process of healing. Eventually, just as Boethius conquers his setbacks to internalize the consolation
of Philosophy, Melibee internalizes Prudence's lessons:

> Whanne Melibee hadde herd the grete skiles and resouns of dame Pru-
> dence, and hire wise informaciouns and techynges, his herte gan en-
> clyne to the wil of his wif, considerynge hir trewe entente, and con-
> formed hym anon and assented fully to werken after hir conseil.[30]

Thus, fourth, as in the *Boece*, the *Remède*, and the *Troilus*, dialogic argumentation in *Melibee* gradually but ineluctably produces "full assent"
in its audience—here, in Melibee himself. Moreover, like the end of the
Boece and of the *Troilus*, the end of *Melibee* gestures toward the promise of salvation: God "wole foryeven us oure giltes and bryngen us to the
blisse that nevere hath ende."[31] The tale, though derived from Albertano
and Renaud, is chosen as a complement to *Thopas* because of its generic
affinities with Boethius's *Consolation*; its position opposite the metrical
mock-Boethian *Thopas* cements the Boethian affinities it already contains.[32] The psychological transformation that *Melibee* both narrates and
offers to its audience is a reordering of passionate emotions by reason, by
logical order, and by dialogue. It offers the salvific consolation of causality
that is borne by Boethian prose.

Melibee devises a formal correlate for its orderly logic and gradual

28. Fragment 7, line 1054.
29. "'What man artow?,'" 158.
30. Fragment 7, lines 1869–71.
31. Fragment 7, lines 1886–87.
32. C. David Benson observes that Prudence's rhetorical and philosophical sophis-
tication create echoes with Philosophy (*Chaucer's Drama of Style*, 42). More recently,
Amanda Walling has also noted the resonances between this tale and the allegorical
faceoff between Boethius and Philosophy ("In Hir Tellyng Difference," 173).

piecing back together of Melibee's fractured psyche, just as *Thopas* devises a formal correlate for the sensory overload that it describes. In *Melibee*, that correlate is twofold. The first part is *cursus*. As Margaret Schlauch has shown, *Melibee* is heavily laden with *cursus* endings, so that over one-third of the final cola end with Latinate *cursus* patternings: *planus*, *tardus*, and *velox*.[33] If we also include in the count of *cursus* endings the ones that Schlauch sees as adaptations of the Latinate stress patterns into English, then nearly two-thirds of *Melibee*'s cola are cadenced: indeed, at the beginning of *Melibee*, Schlauch finds more densely clustered cadencing than appears in the *Boece*.[34] As he did in the prose *Boece*, Chaucer here takes aesthetic syntax as an opportunity for making ideation sensible, feelable, and persuasive.[35] The second part of *Melibee*'s formal rendering of its conceptual logic is its extraordinarily sequential, carefully laid out, logical argument, which unfolds in the conversation between Prudence and Melibee. Just as in Boethius's *Consolation*, Prudence offers a series of propositions to Melibee, the truth of which he gradually and grudgingly recognizes, before moving on to newer, higher logical and affective problems.[36] In its combined strategies of making meaning—via cadencing—sensible at the level of the clause and of making larger-scale argumentative structures perceptible through the back-and-forth Socratic dialogue between Prudence and Melibee and their gradual production of "full assent" in Melibee, the design of *Melibee* reproduces the prose effects of the *Boece*. It aestheticizes causality and thereby brings Melibee himself back to reason from his impassioned anger.

Despite the cadencing and aestheticization of causality that animate the tale, however, *Melibee*'s Boethian message of rationalism sails over the head of Harry Bailley, the *Tales*' primary advocate of using tale-telling to make good use of time and the outright condemner of *Thopas*. Rather than understanding *Melibee* as a tale about the value of wise counsel, Bailley takes away from this ethical tale merely an image of the perfect woman that he does not possess—namely, Prudence herself.

---

33. "Chaucer's Prose Rhythms," 583. See also Robinson, *Chaucer's Prosody*, 78–79.

34. "Chaucer's Prose Rhythms," 583–85.

35. Arvind Thomas has recently suggested that *Melibee* is deeply rhetorically and structurally indebted to the *ars dictaminis* tradition. In his view, the multiclausal, multigenre, and highly directed nature of *Melibee* bodies forth Chaucer's effort to situate this work within a recognizably academic, persuasive framework. See "What's Myrie about the Parson's Tale," 419–38, esp. 428 and 431.

36. See, for instance, fragment 7, lines 1222–35, 1466–24, 1526–39, 1713–25, 1836–71.

Whan ended was my tale of Melibee,
And of Prudence and hire benignytee,
Oure Hooste seyde, "As I am feithful man,
And by that precious corpus Madrian,
I hadde levere than a barel ale
That Goodelief, my wyf, hadde herd this tale!"[37]

Epitomizing his ethical tone-deafness, Bailley longs for Prudence because he understands her as "benign"—harmless and kind—rather than focusing on her real value in the tale, which consists in her learnedness, her sage counsel, and her ability to help her interlocutor grow and change. Thus, even though the Host approves *Melibee* as a good use of his time, the tale itself is evidently a failure, since it provokes no more rational learning in him than *Thopas* provokes sensory pleasure. *Melibee* fails to fulfill the goal of aesthetic prose, just as *Thopas* fails to achieve the aesthetic efficacy of transformative song.

Given this twin failure, the *Thopas-Melibee* link enacts a crisis of literature's ethical efficacy as a crisis of literary form: it enacts an unresolved contest between prose, here offered as a didactic form, and meter, offered as an aesthetic one. Ultimately, neither form seems clearly to be a good use of time: by missing its central ethical messages, the Host's support of *Melibee* reaffirms the difficulty of using literature—even didactic literature composed in prose—to make good, ethically beneficial use of time. The *Thopas-Melibee* coupling is thus a mixed-form antiprotreptic, able neither to provide sensual pleasure nor to impart rational understanding to a reader. Whereas the *Troilus* affirmed the power of song and dialogue to transform Troilus and Criseyde en route to its reinvention of prosimetrum, the prosimetric junction of *Thopas* and *Melibee* carefully evokes how song and dialogue *should* work, only to demonstrate each form's particular susceptibility to failure, each form's potential for failing either to penetrate into or rationally reorder the psyche of its audience, no matter how carefully tailored each form may be to its contents.

Since these two tales are told by none other than the Chaucer pilgrim, their status as an antiprotreptic has great significance. The putative coincidence of author, narrator, and main character in the Chaucer pilgrim affiliates the *Canterbury Tales* even more directly than the *Troilus* with the more overtly autobiographical mixed-form works I discussed in my first chapter, including the *Consolation, De planctu*, the *Vita nuova*, and the

37. Fragment 7, lines 1889–94.

Remède de Fortune. But Harry Bailley's reaction to the two tales that the narrator-author-protagonist tells ominously suggests that Chaucer's fiction cannot prove a successful work of protrepsis, because its narrator can produce neither aesthetic pleasure nor ethical learning for his audience. Through the failure of this dyad of prose and meter to provoke ethical learning and ethical renewal in its audience, the *Canterbury Tales* both evokes and radically undercuts the Boethian, Dantean, and Machauldian fantasies of ethical transformation by aesthetic action.

The *Thopas-Melibee* passage is not, however, the final word on mixed-form protrepsis in the *Canterbury Tales*. The *Tales* deploys another dyadic formal contest that assays and, eventually, reasserts the protreptic possibility that inheres in the experience of literary narration. The eighth fragment's *Second Nun's Tale* and *Canon's Yeoman's Tale* compose the next ethically transformative and mixed-form dyad. Like Boethius's *Consolation*, both of these tales thematically center on the idea of transformative learning, or what the tales themselves call "conversion"—reproducing the critical vocabulary that the *Troilus* devises for describing the transformations of Troilus and Criseyde from lovelessness to love-boundness. The Second Nun's "lyf of Seinte Cecile" focuses on spiritual conversion through religious devotion and prayer, while the Yeoman's story focuses on material conversion through alchemy.[38] In its twin enactment of conversion, this fragment again posits a relationship between literature and the use of time, but does so differently than the *Thopas-Melibee* conjunction. Rather than pitting a prose tale against a tale in verse, this fragment allows each of two decidedly versified tales to use its own distinctive poetic form to render time sense-perceptible as a tool of ethical transformation. Each tale does so, furthermore, in a way that links them with Boethius's *Consolation*. The *Second Nun's Tale* aestheticizes time in the syntactically bounded rime royal form, which I will call, in keeping with the Second Nun's own idiom, "bisy rhyme." The *Yeoman's Tale*, by contrast, engages with temporality in the overflowing lines of what I will call, in keeping with the Yeoman's time-bending aesthetic, "verse alchemic."

38. Fragment 8, line 554. These two tales create a pointed literary dialectic. See Grennen, "Saint Cecilia's 'Chemical Wedding,'" "Canon's Yeoman and the Cosmic Furnace," and "Chaucer's Characterization of the Canon and His Yeoman"; Rosenberg, "Contrary Tales"; Olson, "Chaucer, Dante, and the Structure of Fragment VIII"; and Campbell, "Canon's Yeoman as Imperfect Paradigm."

THE SENSE OF TIME IN THE *CONSOLATION*

To see how this fragment constitutes a reworking of transformative pro-simetrum, I will first return to the *Consolation* itself, in Chaucer's translation of it. The final book of the *Boece* most explicitly articulates Philosophy's ideas about temporality, though it begins with her exploring the nature of happenstance and fortune—what Chaucer calls "hap" and "fortunous betydynge."[39] She argues, "hap is bytydynge ibrought forthe by foolisshe moevynge and by no knyttynge of causes," thus foregrounding a radical incompatibility between causation and chance.[40] Philosophy then launches into a lengthy demystification of the idea of fortune, in which she reveals that the human experience of "hap" is merely the lack of awareness of the causes that underlie all events and circumstances. Everything, she claims, "hath his propre causes, of whiche causes the cours unforseyn and unwar semeth to han makid hap."[41] The experience of "hap" is an artifact of the imperfect awareness of causality that humanity possesses. If man could understand or perceive all the causes in the universe, she suggests, he would neither believe in nor experience fortune. Man cannot, however, perceive all causality. The only being who has perfect awareness of all causality is God.

This does not mean, however, that human beings are constrained to live as though bound by fortune; quite the contrary, it means that human beings must find a way to trust utterly in God's perfect awareness of all events, in his superhuman vision. This is a tall order—to have absolute faith in what one cannot see oneself—but there is a tool that makes man's imperfect knowledge of causation easier to bear and shores him up against the vagaries of seemingly "fortunous" events. That tool is time. Despite the limits of human vision, man can grasp the phantasmatic nature of fortune simply by observing time's ordered passage. Philosophy registers this order of temporality by recourse to a grammatical metaphor: "For alle thing that lyveth in tyme, it is present and procedith fro preteritz into futures."[42] No present time emerges ex nihilo; the present arises from the past, and the future arises from the present. This inevitable order of time thus embodies the inevitable truth of causation, the truth that noth-

---

39. Bk. 5, pr. 1, sentences 69, 73.
40. Bk. 5, pr. 1, sentences 33–34.
41. Bk. 5, pr. 1, sentences 74–75.
42. Bk. 5, pr. 6, sentences 17–19.

ing really "happens" in the created world without a necessitating cause
coming before it in time. Humans cannot always perceive causality, but
they can always perceive time, and in that perception they can find consolation, since they find a steady, sense-perceptible manifestation of God's
providence.

Since human beings, as part of the created world, exist within this
causal temporality, their lives, too, are governed by its order; because we
live in time, we experience the succession of past into present and thence
into future.[43] Seen from this perspective, to live in time is to live outside
the "fortunous betydynges" of hap and instead to live within the order of
necessary, successive, orderly moments. Moreover, to live in the order of
time is to live within the order of divine providence, from which temporal
order proceeds. Indeed, in Philosophy's argument, time itself is a manifestation of divine vision: "lat the unfoldynge of temporal ordenaunce, assembled and oonyd in the lokynge of the devyne thought, be cleped purvey-
aunce."[44] By calling divine providence "the unfolding of temporal order,"
Philosophy implicitly casts time as an epiphenomenon of providence, as
the readiest and steadiest demonstration of the ever-present divine order
and divine knowing of causes. She offers her philosophic charge, in effect,
the consolation of temporality.

But how could temporality be "consoling" to Boethius? After all, Philosophy contrasts the experience of being locked into temporality with
the experience of divine eternity and construes temporality as a debased
and adulterated condition, a divergence from the divine origin, into which
humanity has regrettably fallen. By contrast, God's eternity is construed
as the highest, noblest, and best state of being.[45] According to Boethius,
God's eternity enables him to be just, steady, and loving toward mankind,
because it allows him to see the past, present, and future and to know the
intents of the good and the deeds of the wicked.

> Manet etiam spectator desuper cunctorum praescius deus uisionisque
> eius praesens semper aeternitas cum nostrorum actuum futura quali-
> tate concurrit bonis praemia malis supplicia dispensans. Nec frustra
> sunt in deo positae spes precesque, quae cum rectae sunt inefficaces

---

43. Bk. 5, pr. 6, sentence 17.

44. Bk. 4, pr. 6, sentences 73–75.

45. Indeed, As Elisabeth Andersen has noted, Boethius is one of the most important
resources for theorizing the eternity of God throughout the Middle Ages (*Voices of
Mechthild of Magdeburg*, 220, 224).

esse non possunt. Auersamini igitur uitia, colite uirtutes, ad rectas spes animum subleuate, humiles preces in excelsa porrigite. Magna uobis est, si dissimulare non uultis, necessitas indicta probitatis, cum ante oculos agitis iudicis cuncta cernentis.[46]

[For God always remains the constant, foreknowing watcher, and his eternally present vision runs forth with the future quality of our actions, dispensing boons to the good, punishments to the bad. Not in vain are hopes and prayers placed in God; when these are rightful, they cannot but be efficacious. Avoid therefore vices, collect virtues, lift up your soul to righteous hopes, give your humble prayers on high. If you do not choose to lie, a great charge of probity is yours, for you act before the eyes of an all-seeing judge.]

For Boethius, God's eternity signals the certainty of salvation for the good and of punishment for the wicked. His eternity is, implicitly, the source of his unfailing justice. Because God's justice is necessary to Philosophy's consoling message that fortune is a false construct, his eternal knowing becomes a source of comfort for Boethius. If God's eternity is the sine qua non of philosophical comfort, how is it possible for Philosophy also to offer "the consolation of temporality"?

Though it is thus unquestionably true that eternity is construed in the *Consolation* as a perfect state and as a source of consolation to Boethian readers, and though it is also true that temporality and eternity are made to contrast in Boethius's argument, those truths are not incompatible with the idea that Boethius makes the experience of time a proxy for eternity, a sign and sample of eternity though, to be sure, without its definitive and enduring satisfactions. For him, temporality is humanity's consolation in view of its imperfect ability to perceive divine causality. People cannot see all causation, but they *can* see that past, present, and future have a steady, definite, necessary, and causal relationship with each other. Thus the lived experience of time enables people to understand—albeit by analogy—the supervening truth of the divine plan and its providential management of all causality. Time's status as an epiphenomenal manifestation of divine providence explains why, given Boethius's attention to the debasement of time and time-bound humanity's distance from divine unchangingness, he nevertheless gives so much attention to the precise nature of living within time.

46. Bk. 5, pr. 6, sentences 45–48.

Chaucer's translation grasps this lesson and amplifies it, adding a gloss just after Philosophy's assertion that time proceeds from preterite to present to future, "that is to seyn, fro tyme passed into tyme comynge."[47] By unpacking Boethius's grammatical metaphorics, the gloss simplifies Philosophy's explanation. The simplification bespeaks both Chaucer's awareness of the centrality of time to Philosophy's consolation and his deep investment in conveying that notion as clearly as possible. Later, lest his readers should fail to understand the specific sensation of temporality, and the way in which it ties into consolation, Chaucer adds another gloss, in which he specifies that time moves "by successioun" from past to present and into future.[48] The addition of the term "successioun" indicates how humanity experiences time: in a series or sequence of moments that follow each other in order. Chaucer's gloss thus strengthens Philosophy's implicit claim that man should take comfort in time, by reminding his readers that time is sense-perceptible in its sequentiality; he takes an abstract idea and reminds his readers how it is perceptible by the senses.

In its specification of how time feels, though, Chaucer's *Boece* does not depart from its source. Instead, it expands upon a tremendously important sensory rendering of comfort that appears in the *Consolation* itself. Boethius, throughout his work, carefully embodies the consoling feeling of temporality in his prosimetric writing. He does so, on the one hand, in the proses, since, as I have argued, protreptic proses are designed to aestheticize causality. But since Philosophy specifically demonstrates that causality has an aesthetic correlate in temporality, and since causal succession makes sense only in the context of temporal "successioun," the causally emplotted proses necessarily also embody the linear order of temporality itself.[49]

On the other hand, Boethius embodies temporality in a different way through his meters. To get at the particular aesthetic embodiment of time that the meters offer, it is useful first to revisit Philosophy's use of the term "penetrate" to describe how song works on Boethius's mind, suggesting that song has a capacity to pierce into a person's consciousness. This

47. Bk. 5, pr. 6, sentences 19–20.

48. Bk. 5, pr. 6, sentence 92.

49. Paul Strohm demonstrates that Chaucer is pervasively interested in rendering the experience of temporality through narrative form: "In his constant experimentation with narrative form, Chaucer shows himself to be urgently concerned with matters of temporality in narrative" (*Social Chaucer*, 110–44, esp. 112).

thematization of poetic penetration reflects the narrative functioning of the meters in the overall structure of the text. The meters are independent lyrical interludes that pierce into the supervening and continuous order of prose exposition to create a series of disconnected excursuses from the main narrative. They do not link up with each other, as the successive proses do, but instead stand outside of time, spoken in a narratively disembodied voice that seems sometimes to be Boethius's own voice and sometimes seems to be the voice of Philosophy. Often, the meters seem to address the reader and the diegetic Boethius at once, using proverbial or gnomic discourse. In the *Boece*, a typical passage reads, "Whoso it be that is cleer of vertue, sad and wel ordynat of lyvyng, that hath put underfote the proude wierdes, and loketh upryght upon either fortune, he may holden hys chere undesconfited."[50] This meter and its sentiment are not integral to the narrative flow of the conversation between Philosophy and her tutee; instead, the meter operates as a sapiential interjection, an interruption to the temporal narrative from the beyond-time of gnomic utterance. Meter, then, bodies forth a different temporality, perhaps better called a supratemporality, that hovers outside of the orderly, logical, and temporal causality of the prose narration.

When they occur, these supratemporal meters perforate and violate the causal and temporal order of the proses. But that perforation and violation do not vitiate the rational truths that the proses contain, nor do they undercut the feeling of sequential order, temporality, and hence causality that the proses embody. Quite the contrary, by their violation of temporal order, the meters make the continuous temporal order of the prose narrative all the more perceptible, because when the narrative resumes its linear temporal flow, Boethius and, through him, the reader are brought back to a consciousness of the supervening order of time as something continuous and successive.

The *Consolation*'s stylistic and formal toggling between continuity and interruption proves a constructive provocation for the eighth fragment of the *Canterbury Tales*. The *Second Nun's Tale*, though composed in verse, embodies continuity, linearity, and the orderly succession of time; the *Canon's Yeoman's Tale*, by contrast, creates ruptures in time and divagations from continuous, linear order. Taken together, these two verse tales enact a meditation on the nature of being in time, and they do so by making temporality sensible—aesthetically available through the

50. Bk. 1, m. 4, lines 1–5.

forms of literary language—in a way that discursive analysis cannot. Each tale's sensible renderings of time will prove central to the *Tales'* supervening meditations on the utility of literary reading and on the possibility of protrepsis.

"BISY RHYME": THE SECOND NUN
AND DIVINELY ORDERED TIME

The Nun thematizes time at the very beginning of her performance and names it as the driving concern for her entire narrative, when she condemns "ydelnesse" and urges her audience to avoid this vice of wasting time by embracing "leveful bisynesse."[51] She then links her own narrative work to this idea of "bisynesse":

> I have heer doon my feithful bisynesse
> After the legende in translacioun
> Right of thy glorious lif and passioun,
> Thou with thy gerland wroght with rose and lilie—
> Thee meene I, mayde and martyr, Seint Cecilie.[52]

For the Nun, translation is justifiable work and cannot be confused with "ydelnesse"; it is a mode of using time "faithfully" in verbal "bisynesse." By labeling her verbal work "bisynesse," the Nun asserts that it, unlike *Thopas*, will not simply "dispend time."

Her assertion reflects the verbal "bisynesse" of Saint Cecile herself: almost all of Cecile's actions are speech acts. She is never engaged in domestic chores, tending to the sick, or performing any other nondiscursive activity. When she works, she speaks, preaches, teaches, interrogates, or responds. All Cecile does, throughout the story, is talk: "She nevere cessed . . . Of hir preyere."[53] Even in her final hours, when her head dangles from her partially severed neck, Cecile manages to teach, preach, and order the construction of a church:

---

51. Fragment 8, lines 2, 5. The Nun's prologic aria on idleness is unprecedented in any single source, seeming instead to weave together the *Legenda Aurea*, passages from Dante's *Paradiso*, and a number of proverbial and commonplace sources. See L. D. Benson, *Riverside Chaucer*, 942.

52. Fragment 8, lines 24–28.

53. Fragment 8, lines 124–25.

Thre dayes lyved she in this torment,
And nevere cessed hem the feith to teche
That she hadde fostred; hem she gan to preche

. . .

And seyde, "I axed this of hevene kyng,
To han respit thre dayes and namo,
To recomende to yow, er that I go,
Thise soules, lo, and that I myghte do werche
Heere of myn hous perpetuelly a cherche."[54]

A busy saint indeed, but busy in words rather than in bodily acts. Even her church will be built by her words rather than by her hands.[55]

In this insistence that Cecile is a verbal saint, the tale offers a theory of how words work on the soul. Cecile's verbal "bisynesse" performs "conversion" many times over: once she herself is converted, she easily converts her husband, brother-in-law, and numerous bystanders to Christianity simply by talking with them.[56] This "bisynesse" recalls both Prudence and Philosophy, since they, too, are women whose primary mode of action is verbal and who use language to produce transformative learning in their audiences. Like theirs, Cecile's is a world in which language is efficacious, in which words can *do* things to people, can produce salvific transformation of both self and other. Cecile is a living text, a walking, talking protreptic, whose own conversion to faith proves likewise salvific for those around her.

Cecile's verbal "bisynesse" informs the Second Nun's faith and verbal habits, much as Philosophy's verbal economy in her prose dialogue infiltrates and animates Boethius's mind and speech. Through this shaping of author by heroine, the Nun becomes a new version of Cecile herself—just as the authorial Boethius is a version of the character Boethius, or as the *Troilus* narrator is a version of Troilus. When, early on in her tale, the Nun says, "Thee meene I, mayde and martyr, Seint Cecilie," there is a

54. Fragment 8, lines 537–39, 542–46.

55. Kolve reads her deathbed bequests as proof of the tale's emphasis on a Christian family and of Cecilia's love for her Christian children ("Chaucer's *Second Nun's Tale* and the Iconography of Saint Cecilia," 157–58).

56. Kolve sees her marriage to Valerian as inaugurating a metaphor by which Cecile produces new "fruit" for the Christian church; to me, the marriage seems far less immediately involved in her augmentation of the Christian community than does her effective use of rhetoric (ibid., 152).

secondary paronomastic meaning, in addition to "I intend to talk about you, maid and martyr, Saint Cecile."[57] That secondary meaning is that the Nun herself "means"—signifies or reembodies—Saint Cecile herself. The inversion of "thee" and "I," so that the "I" is positioned closer to the word "mayde," which could apply equally to the Nun and to Saint Cecile, further sets up the protreptic conversions that will take place in the Nun's tale by grammatically rendering the ethical porosity between reader (the Nun) and protagonist (Cecile).

The stanzaic verse form the Nun chooses for her "bisy" tale is intimately linked both to her alignment of herself with Cecile and with her attempt to work conversions in her audience by a logic of protreptic identification with narrator and heroine. The Nun's chosen form is the rime royal stanza of the *Troilus*. As in the *Troilus*, the vast majority of stanzas in the Nun's story are end-stopped, most with the ends of grammatically and ideationally complete sentences.[58] The Nun's metrical precision then extends deeper into the structure of her verse, in that most of her grammatical clauses are enfolded seamlessly into lines of verse. When she records Cecile's counsel to her husband, she asserts,

Cecile answerde anon-right in this wise:
"If that yow list, the angel shul ye see,

57. Fragment 8, line 28.
58. The exception to this rule appears in two main cases. First, syntax overflows meter when Cecile describes moral and/or physical excesses. When she describes the effects of "ydelnesse," for instance, claiming it makes a person want "Oonly to slepe, and for to ete and drynke // And to devouren al that othere swynke" (fragment 8, lines 20–21), her syntax overflows her metrical boundaries, coursing from one stanza into the next. This overflow is atypical for Cecile, but it is pointed: it sensibly reinforces the idea of idleness as a sin of excess. Second, syntax overflows in instances of heightened irascible emotion in Cecile's interlocutors. In a moment of fury against Cecile's unflappable faith, her main persecutor Almachius exclaims, "'Do wey thy booldnesse,' seyde Almachius tho, / 'And sacrifice to oure goddes er thou go! / I recche nat what wrong that thou me profre, / For I kan suffer it as a philosophre; // But thilke wronges may I nat endure / That thou spekest of our goddes heere,' quod he." Fragment 8, lines 487–92. As though he simply cannot contain his irritation at Cecile's spiritual effrontery, Almachius's sentences refuse to sit comfortably within his stanzas, so that stanzaic overflow renders aesthetically available the disorder and chaos of his mind. Apart from these instances of pointed overflow, the Nun enfolds her syntax neatly into her stanzas, allowing units of rhythm and meter to reinforce units of thought and meaning. Thus, the rime royal practice in this poem closely resembles that of the *Troilus*.

So that ye trowe on Crist and yow baptize.
Gooth forth to Via Apia," quod shee,
"That fro this toun ne stant but miles three,
And to the povre folkes that ther dwelle,
Sey hem right thus, as that I shal yow telle."[59]

Throughout this passage, the Nun fits her clauses neatly into metrical lines and her sentences neatly into stanzas. Shortly thereafter, when Valerian is christened, the Nun reports the episode with a similar attention to the correlation between metrical boundaries and ideational ones:

Whan this was rad, thanne seyde this olde man,
"Leevestow this thyng or no? Sey ye or nay."
"I leeve al this thyng," quod Valerian,
"For sother thyng than this, I dar wel sey,
Under the hevene no wight thynke may."
Tho vanysshed this olde man, he nyste where,
And Pope Urban hym cristned right there.[60]

In measuring her syntax neatly into five-stress lines, and thence into seven-line stanzas, the Nun accentuates the syntactic and ideational boundaries of her writing through the rhythm of her verse. The Nun's seamless enfolding of ideation into metrical units works like rime royal in the *Troilus* and alliterative *cursus* in the *Boece*: it renders ideation aesthetically, thus allowing readers to sense the coming end of a unit of thought. The Nun's conditioning of a reader to sense the boundaries of syntax and ideation contributes to a feeling of naturalness, order, and efficiency in her story. The metrical and syntactic architecture of her "bisy rhyme" is thus designed to reinforce its ethical effect, to make its lessons seem familiar and predictable, so that "sother thyng than this . . . no wight thynke may."[61] Thus, the aesthetic sentence reaches a further evolution here: the rhythmically bounded units of ideation become aesthetic units of efficacious spiritual persuasion.

The Nun's avoidance of metrical overflow and of enjambment reflects, on a local scale, the global efficiency of her narration: the chronological linearity of her tale's plot lays out its causal logic, and it permits precious

59. Fragment 8, lines 169–75.
60. Fragment 8, lines 211–17.
61. Fragment 8, lines 215, 214.

few divagations. The tale begins with Cecile's birth and childhood.[62] From there, it tells of her betrothal, her marriage, her refusal to consent to sex, and her conversion of her husband to Christianity.[63] Once he is converted, he requests that his brother also be converted; the next episode of the story deals with that second conversion.[64] These successful conversions meet with opposition from the Roman judge of the town, and an elaborate persecution of the three Christians results, ending in their deaths and in Cecile's consecration of a church.[65] The plot of the story is streamlined, orderly, and sequential: each episode is clearly caused by the preceding one and leads naturally to the one that follows. There are no lurches or spasms in the Nun's speech, no recursions or regressions;[66] there is no excess, no superfluity, no meandering ideation in her tale, nor any in her verse. Instead, her "bisy rhyme" actualizes time as linear and orderly. Since "bisy rhyme" is a poetics of efficiency, sufficiency, and precision, it is the formal antithesis of idleness, displaying at the level of form her inaugural ethical lesson: to avoid wasting time.[67]

The Nun's temporally ordered poetics manifest the power of literature to make the most of time, contributing to the larger metacritical concerns in earlier sections of the *Tales*. Her rhyme, though it makes a narrative rather than a strictly logical "argument," functions much like Boethius's prose, claiming psychological renewal as a function of the sense of order and temporality and as the product of a series of rational, dialogic encounters— in this case, with Cecile. That psychological renewal is framed as religious conversion in the tale, and that conversion is dual. First, the addressees of Cecile's efficient poetics within the tale (her husband and brother-in-law) are converted and saved; second, the Nun, who has implicitly already read and internalized the Nun's protreptic tale before narrating it in the present moment of the *Canterbury Tales*, has evidently been transformed as well, into the efficient poet and user of time that she is. The Nun is, implicitly, already Cecile's protreptic convert to "bisynesse."

62. Fragment 8, lines 120–24.
63. Fragment 8, lines 125–34.
64. Fragment 8, lines 235–357.
65. Fragment 8, lines 358–553.
66. For a different reading of temporality in the Nun's performance, see Jankowski, "Chaucer's Second Nun's Tale and the Apocalyptic Imagination," 133.
67. It is thus a far more pointedly aesthetic achievement than some critics would suggest. Kolve, for instance, called the tale "a saint's life Englished, no more, no less" ("Chaucer's Second Nun's Tale and the Iconography of Saint Cecilia," 139).

Thus, in the *Second Nun's Tale*, the Nun has doubly addressed the aesthetic and ethical breach of the *Thopas-Melibee* conjunction. First, she has composed a tale that programmatically uses language and narration to make an efficient use of time, both within and without the narrative surface of the tale. Second, she has done so by reengaging with the rime royal verse form that Chaucer deployed in the *Troilus*, to reproduce the aesthetic of order in which the ethical effect of chronological and causal prose dialogue inheres. In so doing, she deploys a form of poetic composition that is utterly opposite, in both style and effect, to the "drasty rymyng" of *Thopas*.

The Nun's performance of efficient, proselike rime royal retrospectively also addresses the very first metapoetic crux in the *Tales*: it reverse-engineers an explanation for the formal crux at the beginning of the Man of Law's performance. Martin Stevens's observation that rime royal is "prose" is exactly right, though in a manner somewhat different from what his argument suggests. The Man of Law's rhyme, like Cecile's, is "prose" in that it is designed to make the most of time—to be, in Bailley's own words "a thrifty tale for the nones." Indeed this form's narrative efficiency, metrical order, and temporal tidiness account for why rime royal has become, in the *Canterbury Tales*, Chaucer's preferred form for expressing what Barbara Nolan calls "the theme of Christian transcendence" within his fictive works.[68]

BOOTE OF HIS BALE: VERSE ALCHEMIC AND THE YEOMAN'S TRANSFORMATION

The Nun's bounded stanzas, efficient verse, and linear, causal narrative stand in pointed formal opposition to the tale that follows, the Canon's Yeoman's, in which overflow, intrusions, and recursions are the rule. But the Yeoman's decidedly inefficient tale nevertheless bodies forth a verbal theory and a practice that answer to the charge that poetry wastes time as loudly as the Second Nun's do, though they answer in a fundamentally different way. The Yeoman's verse affirms the possibility of working transformation through an alternate mode of expression, a mode unavailable in

68. B. Nolan, "Chaucer's Tales of Transcendence," 23. In Nolan's view, this "transcendent" thematic that Chaucer articulates through rime royal also animates the *Man of Law's Tale*, *Clerk's Tale*, and *Prioress's Tale*—all four of the *Canterbury Tales* that appear in the form.

the Nun's "bisy rhyme" but readily available in "verse alchemic"—a mode nonlinear, noncausal, and decidedly disorderly.

Just as the Nun's verse style originates in her Christian theory of time—that is, in her ethical adherence to "bisynesse" as a salvific use of time that protects the soul against the sin of "ydelnesse"—the Yeoman's style originates in his adherence to the alchemical theory of time. According to alchemists, all elements exist in a natural state of gradual improvement over time. Lead tends naturally toward gold—just very slowly. It is the office of an alchemist to hurry that process along, but to hurry it so quickly that time collapses and the future becomes the present.[69] Alchemists thus recognize natural time as linear and orderly, as does Boethius, but see alchemical time as nonlinear and disorderly, a time in which present and future can coincide. Alchemical time is the antithesis of the linear and causal order of the Nun's story or of Boethian prose: it denies the necessary and gradual succession of past into present, present into future, and, thus, denies causality itself.

Chaucer thematizes the alchemical theory of time from the very beginning of the Yeoman's performance and shows it to be part and parcel of the Yeoman's consciousness. When the Yeoman and his patron first appear, they intrude upon the other pilgrims suddenly, arriving at such a clip that they and their horses are sweat-drenched with the effort.[70] This overhasty entry into and interruption of the tale-telling contest metonymically forewarn readers of the temporal aberrances that will characterize the plot of the tale as well as the Yeoman's very manner of speaking.[71] His first claim, "faste have I priked," ushers in a practice of verbal haste.[72] He will repeat "faste" (in the sense of "quick" or "quickly") eight more times during his tale.[73] The temporality of alchemy suffuses the Yeoman's essential character and manner of speaking, much as the Nun's "bisy" shunning of "ydelnesse" suffuses her efficient poetics.

An acute narrative manifestation of the Yeoman's alchemical speech arises in his tendency to forecast endings. He makes the prophetic proclamation "O sely preest! O sely innocent! / With coveitise anon thou shalt

---

69. See Patterson, "Perpetual Motion," 50–51 n. 72.

70. Fragment 8, lines 561–63.

71. Historically, the Yeoman's verbal tics and the strange divagations of his tale have been construed as evidence of a complex manuscript history. See Baum, "Canon's Yeoman's Tale."

72. Fragment 8, lines 584.

73. Fragment 8, lines 682, 863, 1105, 1146, 1192, 1235, 1260, 1423.

be blent!," though the denouement it describes comes almost three hundred lines later.[74] His eagerness to get ahead of himself narratively also appears in his attempt to conclude his tale before it is at its end. Four hundred lines before the end of his tale, he declares, in an apostrophe to the aforementioned "sely preest,"

> Wherfore, to go to the conclusion
> That refereth to thy confusion
> Unhappy man, anon I wol me hye.[75]

In this lurching insistence, the Yeoman not only advertises his conclusion but also promises to hurry there—which he decidedly does not do. Toward the end he says again, "Thanne conclude I thus" ten full lines before his tale ends.[76] Whereas the Nun conveys temporality as an ordered sequence of moments, the Yeoman seems always eager—yet unable—to skip ahead to the end. In addition to forecasting his ending, the Yeoman constantly advertises what he shortly will narrate, betraying his inability to remain in the present of his narrative: he says "I wol" to preface what he is about to say four times in the *Prologue* and seven times in the *pars prima* of the story. Narratively, the Yeoman is unable to stop himself from superimposing the future on the present.[77] The Yeoman's verbal style and tale point toward his alchemical inability to grasp—let alone take comfort in—time's linear progression as an epiphenomenal indication of divine providence and eternal love.

By logical extension, his verbal style points toward his inability to work within the natural causal orders that God has established, according to Boethius, for the benefit of mankind. This inability to understand causality preys not just upon the Yeoman but also upon all the alchemists he represents in his prologue and tale, suffusing their very manner of speaking. One of his alchemists says, "And though this thyng mysshaped have as now, / Another tyme it may be well ynow."[78] By asserting that the alchemy will work at "another" time, this alchemist manifests an-

---

74. Fragment 8, lines 1076–77.

75. Fragment 8, lines 1082–84.

76. Fragment 8, line 1472.

77. This focus on the future has been noted in criticism and read as symptomatic of Chaucer's pervasive awareness of the pressures of modernity. Lee Patterson reads the Yeoman's performance as perhaps Chaucer's last and clearest articulation of the crisis of modernity ("Perpetual Motion").

78. Fragment 8, lines 944–45.

other bias of the alchemical theory of time: value does not accumulate "in tyme," "through tyme," or "over tyme" but simply at another time. This assertion implicitly construes time as modular—consisting of individual, unconnected instants—rather than gradual and causal. This construction solidifies when the alchemist compares himself to a merchant:

> A marchant, pardee, may not ay endure,
> Trusteth me wel, in his prosperitee.
> Sometyme his good is drowned in the see,
> And somtyme comth it sauf unto the londe.[79]

The key word here is the unprepossessing "sometyme." Alchemy will "sometimes" bear fruit, and "sometimes" will not, regardless of what might happen in or through time—regardless, that is, of causality. The accumulation of material fortunes, as far as these alchemists can see, depends not on gradual accumulation but on futurity itself. "Us moste putte oure good in aventure," the canon asserts, encoding the idea of futurity ("aventure," from *adventura*, "about to happen") in his very lexis of fortune.[80] It is no wonder the Yeoman constantly seeks to skip to the end: his narrative world is peopled by men who maniacally hope to avoid the linear progression of time, who hope to shortchange causality in the interest of quick profit.

This alchemical hope comprises a challenge to Boethian notions of time. Hoping for a "futur temps," a "sometyme," or "another tyme" of sudden fortune is hoping for the impossible, because, according to Boethius, time must pass in an ordered fashion from past through present to future. Time, like everything else in God's ordered universe, must be caused. Again, as Chaucer puts it in the *Boece*: "For alle thing that lyveth in tyme, it is present and procedith fro preteritz into futures." By hoping ever to race into the future, alchemists disavow the governing and comforting order of causality that time embodies. If Boethius's philosophy of consolation is correct, alchemists should be constitutionally unable to receive

79. Fragment 8, lines 947–50.

80. Fragment 8, line 946. The *Middle English Dictionary* does not cite the meaning of "future" as a possible meaning of *aventure* in English, but this particular story encourages us to read that sense hovering in the margins, particularly since *aventura* signifies "future" in Italian, a language with which Chaucer was quite familiar, given his extensive translations from Boccaccio and his borrowings from Dante.

consolation, unable to grasp the comforting nature of divine providence. This tale, however, will call this privileging of causal linearity into question, suggesting that literary transformation can arise within noncausal, nonsequential alchemical time.

The first formal device the Yeoman's tale deploys to make this suggestion is frantic, ecstatic listing. Pointedly, the Yeoman introduces his lists with a disavowal of order:

> Though I by ordre hem nat reherce kan,
> By cause that I am a lewed man,
> Yet wol I telle hem as they come to mynde,
> Thogh I ne kan nat sette hem in hir kynde.[81]

By calling attention to his inability to tell the ingredients "in order," the Yeoman performs the familiar rhetorical trope of *occupatio*. But his hand-waving disavowal of order has a second, far deeper significance: in saying he "kan" not rehearse the ingredients, rather than that he simply will not, or does not have time to, the Yeoman labels his utterance as one incapable of linearity, sequence, and order, and he labels himself as a narrator incapable of mustering normative causality as an element of storytelling. Appropriately, his list is a jumble:

> As boole armonyak, verdegrees, boras,
> And sondry vessels maad of erthe and glas,
> Oure urynales and oure descensories,
> Violes, crosletz, and sublymatories,
> Cucurbites and alambikes eek,
> And othere swiche, deere ynough a leek—
> Nat nedeth it for to reherce hem alle—
> Watres rubifiyng, and boles galle,
> Arsenyk, sal armonyak, and brymstoon;
> And herbes koude I telle eek many oon,
> As egremoyne, valerian, and lunarie,
> And othere swiche, if that me liste tarie
> . . .
> Oure fourneys eek of calcinacioun,
> And of watres albificacioun;

81. Fragment 8, lines 786–89.

Unslekked lym, chalk, and gleyre of an ey,
Poudres diverse, asshes, donge, pisse, and cley,
Cered pokkets, sal peter, vitriole,
And diverse fires maad of wode and cole;
Sal tartre, alkaly, and sal preparat,
And combust materes and coagulat;
Cley maad with hors of mannes heer, and oille
Of tartre, alum glas, berme, wort, and argoille,
Resalgar, and oure materes enbibyng,
And eek of oure materes encorporyng,
And of oure silver citrinacioun,
Oure cementyng and fermentacioun,
Oure yngottes, testes, and many mo.[82]

The Yeoman's frantic listing aesthetically underscores his inability and his unwillingness to bound language efficiently or to structure linguistic sequences. His verse is designed to frustrate order and is thus utterly unlike the Nun's "bisy rhyme." Whereas her narrative is hypotactic, linear, and orderly, his is relentlessly paratactic, diffuse, and chaotic. Where hers is carefully emplotted, his is an assemblage of discrete objects, thrown together into confusion. Instead of a poetics of efficiency, the Yeoman's verse alchemic is a verbal practice in excess of time—metrical time—itself.

Coupled with the Yeoman's literary technique of making alchemy aesthetically available as a practice in narrative disorder and excessive, logorrheic listing, his use of enjambment is his technique for bending time and showing causality itself to be a construct, subject to fractures and transmogrifications—showing causality to be subject to alchemical transformation. Enjambment creates a temporary doubling of meaning, which depends on the brief pause between the moment at which the reader grasps the first meaning at the end of the first line and the moment at which she understands the second, more complete meaning after the second line. Frequently, the Yeoman's enjambed lines thematize what they perform formally: nonlinear time, as when the Yeoman explains the psychology of seeking the philosopher's stone.

Swich supposyng and hope is sharp and hard;
I warne yow wel, it is to seken evere.

82. Fragment 8, lines 790–801, 804–18.

That futur temps hath maad men to dissevere,
In trust therof, from al that evere they hadde.[83]

With modern punctuation, these lines are not particularly complex. Without modern punctuation, they create a doubling of meaning: reading through line 874 produces the warning that to practice alchemy "is to seek forever that future time," to seek, that is, futurity itself. Of course, the rest of line 875 disposes of this enjambed reading by completing the grammar of the phrase and demonstrating that "That future temps" is the subject of the verb "hath maad" rather than the object of the verb "to seek." But, for a moment, across two enjambed lines appears the alchemical glimmer of two meanings alive at once.[84] Thus, these lines embody in form the very refusal of temporal order that they describe in content. Later, another aestheticization of alchemical time occurs when the Yeoman describes the nearness of alchemists to the devil:

Though that the feend noght in oure sighte hym shewe,
I trowe he with us be, that ilke shrewe!
In helle, where that he is lord and sire,
Nis ther moore wo, ne moore rancour ne ire.[85]

In this example, line 917 could be read as end-stopped, suggesting that the devil is in the real world alongside alchemists: "I trowe he with us be, that ilke shrewe." The next two lines would then mean, "In hell, where he is lord and sire, there is no more woe, rancor, or ire than there is in the here and now." A second reading could move through the enjambment at 917, which suggests that the devil and the alchemists are all in hell already: "I trowe he with us be, that ilke shrewe, in hell, where he is lord and sire." In this reading, alchemists, by practicing alchemy, already live in hell, so that a hellish afterlife coincides with their actual lived experience, and the damned future *is* the damned present. Even though the unfolding grammar

83. Fragment 8, lines 873–76.
84. Judith Herz notes the "Protean" character of the Yeoman's use of language ("Canon's Yeoman's Prologue and Tale"). Donald Dickson, similarly, argues that the "real drama" of the Yeoman's performance lies in his own "sliding" character, which seems at times to condemn and at times to idolize alchemists and their art ("'Sliding' Yeoman").
85. Fragment 8, lines 916–19.

of the sentence eventually disposes of this second meaning, the enjambment creates an ambiguity that makes two readings temporarily available.
Through its enjambments, the Yeoman's tale shows time to be recursive
and breakable, rather than linear and continuous. It shows poetic time to
be not quite causal but, quite literally, accidental: a haphazard falling and
disordered tumbling toward the future. In other words, the Yeoman's versified time is alchemical—a time that produces a conversion of meaning
between lines of verse. Like listing, enjambment ruptures the experience
of order, causality, and linearity normally inherent in narrative—the very
experience the Second Nun's verbal style strove to create and promote to
an organizing principle of her protreptic narrative.

Thus, the Yeoman's performance becomes an aesthetic exercise *against*
the order that constitutes the fundamental motive behind the Nun's "bisy
rhyme" and behind Boethian prose. There is no need, no narrative necessity, to rehearse all of the alchemical ingredients in their proper order: as
he says himself, "Nat nedeth it for to reherce hem alle." The Yeoman's
choice to make his lists anyway, in spite of their narrative superfluity and
chaos, suggests that something other than narrative need motivates his
poetry. His poetry, I would suggest, serves primarily to reinvent the particular temporal sensibility of Boethian meters in Middle English rhymed
couplets. The Yeoman's interruption of the Canterbury pilgrimage enacts
the same kind of rupture that Boethius produces whenever he introduces
a meter into the supervening temporal order of his prose dialogue. Once
they interrupt the linear prose narrative, Boethius's meters mandate a
temporality of reading that differs from that of his proses: they are recursive and analogical rather than linear and logical. To make sense of them,
one must navigate repetitions of sound, returns to specific themes, and
echoes of imagery and meter. The Yeoman's verse alchemic reproduces the
metrical recursions through enjambment; through listing, with its refusal
of "ordre" and its reliance on collocation, verse alchemic mimics the nonlogical nonlinearity of Boethius's meters.

All of these formal and effectual consonances with Boethian meters
serve to set up the end of the Yeoman's performance, when he makes his
final turn to God.

> Thanne conclude I thus, sith that God of hevene
> Ne wil nat that the philosophres nevene
> How that a man shal come unto this stoon,
> I rede, as for the beste, lete it goon.

For whoso maketh God his adversarie,
As for to werken any thyng in contrarie
Of his wil, certes, never shal he thryve,
Thogh that he multiplie terme of his lyve.
And there a poynt, for ended is my tale.
God sende every trewe man boote of his bale![86]

At the end, like the narrator of the *Troilus* and like Boethius, the Yeoman realizes that only God can bring "boote" of human "bales." Indeed, Bruce Grenberg argues that the Yeoman thematizes the opposition between worldly wealth and the search for God that also preoccupied Boece, and thus reads the end of the tale as Boethian.[87] The Yeoman has abandoned his quest for the "philosopher's stone," having attained a transformative understanding, and he hopes that his readers—at least "every trewe man"—may do the same. He has created, or hopes to have created, a protreptic that, like the Nun's, originates in his own experience of life and language and might model spiritual salvation for readers. But he has done so through decidedly different formal and discursive means from those found in the Second Nun's performance. His ethical renewal suggests that verse alchemic, complete with its ability to manipulate time, violate causality, and create recursive aesthetic pleasure, is as apt a vehicle for ethical transformation as "bisy rhyme" was for the Nun, and as prosimetrum was for Boethius himself.

Fragment 8 is distinguished by an interest in temporal order and its relation to literary transformation, a twin "conversion" theme that it carries through at the level of form. The fragment plays with time by using two verse modes, each of which reproduces one half of prosimetrum: a bounded, causally ordered, and linear "bisy" rime royal in the *Second Nun's Tale*, which reproduces the aesthetic effects of the proses of Boethius's *Consolation* as well as of Chaucer's own *Boece*, and the overflowing rhymed couplets of verse alchemic in the *Canon's Yeoman's Tale*, which reproduce the effects of Boethian meter. In linking these tales, Chaucer revisits and recreates prosimetrum, now refiguring it stylistically—as a poetry of order paired with a poetry of disorder, narrative with antinarrative, temporal linearity and causality with recursion and likeness. In this fragment, then, Chaucer recreates a verse dyad that answers to the literary

---

86. Fragment 8, lines 1472–81.
87. Grenberg, "Canon's Yeoman's Tale."

theory and practice found in the *Consolation*. The dyad also answers to
the *Canterbury Tales'* own repeated privileging of prose over meter as an
ethically transformative use of literary time: through the Yeoman and the
Nun, Chaucer provides two very different demonstrations of how verse
can make use of and indeed embody time in order to represent and model
conversion. Together, "bisy rhyme" and "verse alchemic," which immediately follow the fragment containing the Chaucer pilgrim's own abortive prosimetric performance, redeem poetic form—in two very different
versions—as a vehicle of protrepsis, which takes effect precisely by aestheticizing temporality.

But the eighth fragment crucially differs from the *Consolation*, in both
its idea of protrepsis and its practice of the mixed form. Fragment 8 seg-
regates the effects of "prose" and "meter" and distributes them between
two narrators; the Nun is consoled by "bisy rhyme," while the Yeoman
is transmuted by "verse alchemic." There is no suggestion that the Nun's
faith profited from the Yeoman's verse; conversely, the Yeoman had not
even heard the Nun's "bisy rhyme" before launching into his own tale.
Therefore, while the conversion fragment's mixed poetic styles evoke protreptic prosimetrum, each tale by itself suggests that its particular form—
whether "bisy" or "alchemic"—can produce "conversion" on its own.
Boethius's necessary toggling back and forth between prose's argumentative order and metrical beauty and likeness seems otiose for each of these
pilgrims.

By designing two diametrically opposed modes of using time through
verse, Chaucer enacts a two-pronged defense of poetry as a legitimate
mode of transformation unto itself. In validating poetry in this way, this
dyad denies the Man of Law's and Harry Bailley's implied approbations of
prose as a more naturally effective mode of using time than verse. Tele-
scoping out from those two instances, the eighth fragment gives the lie to
the broader sociocultural tendency to read poetry as unethical or as ethically dangerous, by demonstrating the power of poetic sense experience to
provoke salvific learning, to provoke turns toward God rather than toward
the tavern. Thus, it constitutes a vernacular defense of poetry as not only
an aesthetically rich mode but as a mode capable on its own of being ethically salvific. In that sense, fragment 8 carries on the literary experiment
that began in the *Troilus* and is in dialogue with the prosimetra of Dante's
Vita nuova and Guillaume's *Remède de Fortune*, in which the aesthetically wrought and formally intricate poetry is where the transformative
action really happens.

THE CONCLUSION OF THE *TALES*:
TRANSFORMATIVE METAPOETICS

The end of Chaucer's motley fiction deploys yet another prosimetric contest, though this time it is one in which poetry seems the decided loser. The final three performances in the narrative—the Manciple's poem, the Parson's prose, and the prose of Chaucer himself in the *Retractions*—seem to reinscribe poetry within a logic of wasted time and to undercut any theory of its protreptic efficacy that the eighth fragment might have successfully practiced.[88] Like the beginning of the Man of Law's fragment, the Manciple-Parson fragment begins with the Host's worrying over the passing of time and over the absence of a good story. Both of these worries get focused on the Cook, who, because of his excessive drunkenness, has fallen "al bihynde" the other pilgrims—thereby registering how his gluttonous ways place him both spatially and temporally in the rear of the pilgrim fellowship and how his tardiness holds up the tale-telling competition.[89] To the Host's worrying about the slowness of the Cook and the resultant stalling of both the pilgrimage and the tale-telling competition, the Manciple responds by deriding the Cook for his drunkenness. This derision causes the Cook to become angry and fall from his horse. Seeing the reactive disarray into which the pilgrimage threatens to fall, the Host urges the Manciple to make peace with the Cook, which he does, ironi-

---

88. In pointing up their shared critique of poetry as a technique of transformation, I mean to suggest that the *Manciple's Prologue* and *Tale* and the *Parson's Prologue* and *Tale* are meaningfully joined together. Although it is traditional among textual scholars of the *Tales* to separate the *Manciple's Tale* from the *Parson's Prologue*, both because they are in separate fragments and because, within the chronology of the *Tales* overall, the former seems to take place in the morning, while the latter begins in the afternoon, this division between the two pilgrims seems to me unnecessary and even misleading on three counts. First, the assertion that the Manciple speaks in the morning has to do with the Host's insistence that the Cook, who will be the brunt of the Manciple's harsh humor in the *Prologue*, sleeps "by the morrow." (fragment 11, line 16) This phrase "by the morrow" could as easily be translated "through the morning" as "during the morning"; the former rendering is entirely compatible with the afternoon as the moment of speech. Second, the first line of the *Parson's Prologue* makes explicit reference to the Manciple's performance, indicating that Chaucer intended the two to be read together and perceived as constitutively related to each other. Third, the poetic values articulated and practiced in each performance are intimately linked and signify fully only when read in conjunction.

89. Fragment 9, line 7.

cally, by plying the Cook with yet more liquor. To this, the Host responds
in a manner that sets up the poetic crisis to follow:

> "For that wol turne rancour and disese
> T'acord and love, and many a wrong apese.
> O Bacus, yblessed be thy name,
> That so kanst turnen ernest into game!
> Worshipe and thank be to thy deitee!"[90]

On one level, this assertion, by raising the proverbial glass to Bacchus, recognizes the power of wine to make peace in a community. But, on a second
level, the Host introduces a metapoetic problem, which will continue to play
out over the course of the Manciple's story: the need to rely on Bacchanalian
modes of persuasion when Apollonian modes are no longer efficacious.[91]

"Phebus" Apollo appears in the first line of the Manciple's actual tale
and is both the hero and the victim of the Manciple's narrative.[92] Through
the Manciple, Chaucer situates his "Phebus" quickly in a Boethian aesthetic and ethical universe. Phoebus has a wife, from whom he wants and
expects sexual fidelity; but, as the Manciple notes, by recourse to the second meter of Boethius's book 3, "Quantas rerum flectat," no one can constrain a free being:

> Taak any bryd, and put it in a cage,
> And do al thy entente and thy corage
> To fostre it tendrely with mete and drynke
> Of alle deyntees that thou canst bithynke,
> And keep it al so clenly as thou may,
> Although this cage of gold be never to gay,
> Yet hath this brid, by twenty thousand foold,
> Levere in a forest that is rude and coold
> Good ete wormes and swich wrecchednesse.
> For evere this brid wol doon his bisynesse
> To escape out of his cage, yif he may.
> His libertee this brid desireth ay.[93]

90. Fragment 9, lines 97–101.
91. For a much later but similarly ecstatic yet horrified affirmation of the power of
Bacchanalian song, see Nietzsche, *The Birth of Tragedy*.
92. Fragment 9, lines 104.
93. Fragment 9, lines 163–74.

The Manciple uses this rendering of the first section of Boethius's meter not only to make a point about the futility of trying to "destreyne a thyng" but also to situate Phoebus and his imminent poetic disaster within a Boethian frame of reference.[94] As the Manciple goes on, he introduces an analogy for the caged birds: a cat, who, like the bird, will return to his nature and shred a mouse whenever he sees it, no matter how well fed and tended he may be. This comparison with the housecat refigures at a reduced, domesticated scale the "Carthaginian lions" passage from the same meter in the *Consolation*: the Manciple, like Boethius, uses his poem to introduce a series of what he calls "alle this ensaumples," thereby causing his audience to meditate upon the likeness between them, namely, the futility of trying to constrain something in unfreedom.[95] By using "alle this ensaumples" in specific, the Manciple allusively evokes Boethian literary theory and practice.

But he evokes Boethius only to contradict his literary theory immediately thereafter, through a programmatic figural defrocking of Phoebus himself. Throughout the *Consolation*, Phoebus is associated with poetic healing, relief, and recovery of one's reason. It is Phoebus's penetrating rays that bring light back to Boethius's eyes—in Chaucer's translation, "thanne schyneth Phebus ischaken with sodeyn lyght and smyteth with his beemes in mervelynge eien."[96] For Boethius, Phoebus is the poetic healer, the musician qua savior who chases the dark clouds of misunderstanding from both mind and heart. In the Manciple's story, by pointed contrast, Phoebus is a profoundly flawed character, a victim of his own passions, who cannot see what is right and what is wrong or distinguish what is true from what is false. When he learns of his wife's infidelity, he is categorically unable to save himself from suffering. Instead, in Phoebus's reaction to the crow's disclosure of his wife's infidelity, we see Phoebus abandon Apollonian poetic logic altogether and fall back instead on one of the mainstays of Bacchanalianism: violent aggression and cacophony. He murders his wife and strips the crow of his beautiful song—a Chaucerian addition, not present in his Ovidian source—and replaces it with a shrill caw.[97]

Most damaging of all to the idea that Phoebus might embody a salvific poetics, a poetics of healing harmony, in a passage Chaucer also adds de novo to his Ovidian source, Phoebus is shown to be unable to hold back even from destroying his own musical instruments:

94. Fragment 9, line 161.
95. Fragment 9, line 187.
96. Bk 1, m. 3, lines 15–17.
97. *Riverside Chaucer*, 954, note to lines 295–96.

> For sorwe of which he brak his mynstralcie,
> Bothe harpe, and lute, and gyterne, and sautrie;
> And eek he brak his arwes and his bowe.[98]

Having evoked Boethius, a believer in and advocate for the specific power of Apollonian musical healing, the Manciple depicts a Phoebus not only emotionally frail and vulnerable to deceit but also, and more distressingly, utterly lacking in self-awareness and subject instead to the whims of passion. Through Phoebus's violent inability to control his passions or to resort to his own healing music as a way out of his suffering, Boethius's vision of a salvific and songful poetics is completely and specifically undermined. This undermining of Boethian poetic optimism is what the crow calls attention to when he tells Phoebus that he is being cuckolded:

> "By God," quod he, "I synge not amys.
> Phebus," quod he, "for al thy worthynesse,
> For al thy beautee and thy gentilnesse,
> For al thy song and al thy mynstralcye,
> For al thy waityng, blered is thyn ye."[99]

In the *Consolation*, Phoebus clears the blindness from one's eyes. In the Manciple's version, Phoebus's own eyes are "blered," despite his aesthetic gorgeousness. Phoebus, Boethius's divine embodiment of salvific song, becomes song's undoing.

With that undoing in the story comes the undoing of poetry in the Manciple's performance overall. At the end of the tale, in lockstep with Phoebus's deterioration from a would-be Apollonian hero to a deranged Bacchanalian antihero, the Manciple's own poetic practice and narrative control deteriorate: he switches from a carefully emplotted, linear narrative to a panicked cascade of concatenated sententiae. He urges his audience—figured as "his sone"—repeatedly to avoid speaking rashly, to "Beth war, and taketh kep what that ye seye," "to kepen his tonge weel," to "keep wel thy tonge," and "to restreyne and kepe wel thy tonge."[100]

---

98. Fragment 9, lines 267–69.

99. Fragment 9, lines 248–52.

100. Fragment 9, lines 310, 315, 319, 333. Much of this section of Chaucer's poem derives from Albertano of Brescia's *Tractatus loquendi et tacendi*. See *Riverside Chaucer*, 954, notes to lines 325–28, 332–33, 338, 355–56.

My sone, beth war, and be noon auctour newe
of tidynges, wheither they been false or trewe.
Whereso thou come, amonges hye or lowe,
Kepe wel thy tonge, and thenk upon the crowe.[101]

This ironically prolix overemphasis on reticence formally underscores the
larger crisis of poetics in the tale: in a post-Apollonian world, there can be
no true narrative progress or poetic healing, but only terrified repetition
leading to silence. With Phoebus shown to be self-blind, subject to his
passions, destructive of himself, his art, and those he loves, the Manciple
urges his audience to stay silent, taking the crow as witness to the folly
that is trying to speak truth through song. So soon after its affirmation
in the *Second Nun's Tale* and the *Canon's Yeoman's Tale*, poetry's power
to provoke generative "conversion" has once again come under fire. This
tale's transformation, embodied in the crow, entails mute subordination,
not philosophical transcendence. Simultaneously, the protrepsis that the
Manciple recommends to his readers is one of paranoid silence, not spiritual renewal. Harry Bailley's earlier insistence, in the introduction to
the *Man of Law's Tale*, that silence constitutes negligent time-wasting
is inverted, as the Manciple shows that songfulness and truth are eventually replaced by mute submission to arbitrary authority and that the
exemplary world of ethical meaning-making can degenerate rapidly into
hollow aphorism. The tale ends up being a dark, metapoetic exemplum,
expressing in exemplary discourse poetry's self-destructiveness and susceptibility to formal unraveling. The Manciple's story brings with it a
critique of the possibility that poetry could do any kind of salvific ethical
work.[102]

---

101. Fragment 9, lines 359–62.

102. In this critique of poetic ethics, the Manciple's exemplum stands as a fascinat-
ing instance of what J. Allan Mitchell has shown to be the richly diverse and often
quite serious ethical discourse that takes place in medieval texts within the space of
exemplary narrative. Borrowing Mitchell's phrasing, if we "read for the moral" in the
Manciple's poem, we find ourselves learning, paradoxically, *not* to rely on poetry for
our ethical bulwarking in life (*Ethics and Exemplary Narrative*, 13–14). Indeed, if, as
Mitchell puts it, "[e]xemplary narratives too are capable of refining the moral sensibility" (141), the Manciple's exemplum seems clearly designed to refine a reader's sensibilities away from poetry as an ethical resource. Mitchell himself reads the Manciple's
performance as "an exemplum showing the destructive results of haste or recklessness"
(138–39).

Poetry's power to work ethical transformation seems yet more dubious in the versified *Parson's Prologue,* in the tenth and final fragment of the *Tales.* This verse prologue is, however, quickly followed by his long, sermonic piece, which he composes, pointedly, in prose. In combination, these two elements of the Parson's performance create another miniature prosimetric contest in the *Tales,* after which the prose form decisively wins, forcefully and permanently ejecting poetry from the *Canterbury Tales.* This ejection retroactively highlights the banishment of the lyric from Phoebus's home and creates an intertale prosimetrum with the Manciple's performance as well as the intratale one within the Parson's own performance. Thus the Parson's sermon creates a prosimetric juncture on two levels—between his own prologue and tale and between the Manciple's verse tale and his prose one. On both levels, the Parson's prose discourse rejects poetry as a technology for didactic work, further undermining the eighth fragment's redemption of poetry as an ethically salvific use of time.

The Parson's rejection of poetry occurs, like the Manciple's, both on the level of form and on the level of thematics. Thematically, the Parson's prologue explicitly reawakens the problem of using poetry to make a good use of time. It does so when the Chaucer pilgrim calculates the hour by examining the length of his shadow. The particular phrasing he uses, however, to describe the length of that shadow is a pun, encoding a description of an alexandrine line of verse:

> My shadwe was at thilke tyme, as there,
> Of swiche feet as my lengthe parted were
> In sixe feet equal of proporcioun.[103]

After the Chaucer-pilgrim evokes poetics by using the phrase "six feet of equal proportion" to note the passage of time, the Parson picks up the Host's narrative mandate to tell a tale. But when he does so, he immediately shuts down the poetic energy of the passage, shifting pointedly from verse to prose and calling attention to that shift as both ethically and aesthetically motivated:

> I kan nat geeste 'rum, ram, ruf,' by lettre,
> Ne, God woot, rym holde I but litel bettre;

---

103. Fragment 10, lines 7–9.

And therfore, if yow list—I wol nat glose—
I wol yow telle a myrie tale in prose.[104]

By saying he "kan nat geeste 'rum, ram, ruf,' by lettre," nor can he "rym
. . . but litel bettre," the Parson makes a double-voiced assault on poetry.
On the one hand, he seems to disavow competency at poetry; he "kan nat"
achieve its formal intricacies. But, on the other hand, he could mean that
he, as a parson, under obligation to keep truth for the Christian public, is
ethically unable to compose verse, which, as Wycliffite writers and historiographers of his period point out, is more susceptible to falsehood and deceit
than prose. Since the Parson "wol nat glose," he "kan nat" tell "geeste" or
"rym," but must instead speak in prose. Thus, at the end of the tale-telling
competition, the Parson both affirms the catastrophic conclusion of the
Manciple's Tale and recurs to the Chaucer pilgrim's own metapoetic principle from the *Thopas-Melibee* conjunction, suggesting that prose makes
a better and more ethically defensible use of time than does "geeste" or
"rym." If Phoebus's lyre is smashed, the Parson seems to say, so much the
better: far more worthy speaking, with less glosing and in a more "myrie"
manner, can be accomplished in prose than it could in songful verse.[105]
   When he moves from his versified prologue to his prose sermon, the
Parson reengages with the Manciple's overt warnings against rash speech
through his condemnation of "ydel wordes," and he does so with consequences for the overall shape and impact of the *Canterbury Tales* as a concerted project of formal experimentation and vernacular literary theory.

> Now cometh ydel wordes, that is withouten profit of hym that speketh
> tho wordes, and eek of hym that herkneth tho wordes. Or elles ydel
> wordes been tho that been nedelees, or withouten entente of natureel
> profit. / And al be it that ydel wordes been somtyme venial synne, yet
> sholde men douten hem, for we shul yeve rekenynge of hem bifore God.
> / Now comth janglynge, that may nat been withoute synne . . . After
> this comth the synne of japeres, that been the develes apes; for they
> maken folk to laughe at hire japerie as folk doon at the gawdes of an
> ape . . . Looke how that vertuouse wordes and hooly conforten hem

104. Fragment 10, lines 43–46.
105. For a detailed reading of how in particular we might construe Chaucer's meaning in having the Parson call his tale "myrie," see again Thomas, "What's Myrie about
the Parson's Tale."

that travaillen in the service of crist, right so conforten the vileyns
wordes and knakkes of japeris hem that travaillen in the service of the
devel.[106]

As far as the Parson is concerned, any "jangling" or speaking "withouten
profit of hym that speketh tho wordes, and eek of hym that herkneth tho
wordes" is idelness, a sinful activity for which "we shul yeve rekenynge . . .
bifore God." The only kind of speech the Parson seems to allow as potentially useful is "vertuouse wordes and hooly" that "conforten hem
that travaillen in the service of crist." All other speech, and, by implica-
tion, the entire foregoing Canterbury tale-telling contest, is "in the service of the devel."

The Parson embodies his decrying of "jangling" or "ydel speche" in his
simple and unornamented prose style. Throughout his tale, he avoids both
alliteration and *cursus*, the two formal ornaments that Chaucer deploys
in his more aesthetic prose. As far as the Parson is concerned, straightforward, unartificed prose discourse is the didactic order of the day and
the only possible formal answer to a mandate to make the most of time
through tale-telling. The Host's notion that *fictive* tale-telling could prove
a good use of time by producing aesthetic pleasure is shown for what, in
the Parson's view, it is: pure fantasy. Together, the Parson's denunciation
of poetic form in his prologue, his "myrie tale's" enunciated condemnation of "ydel" fictions, and his avoidance of prose ornamentation read as a
metapoetic principle that exiles poetry from the Canterbury project.

Indeed, the Parson's puritanical mandates colonize the end of the
Tales: from the *Parson's Tale*, we turn at last to the prose *Retractions*, in
which Chaucer admits to feeling guilty that his poetic works, including
sections of the *Canterbury Tales*, "sownen unto synne."[107] The *Retractions*
has long puzzled Chaucerians because their sullen and morose depiction
of Chaucer seems discontinuous with the ironic, playful Chaucer of the
rest of the *Canterbury Tales* and *Troilus and Criseyde*. But there is a reading of the *Retractions* that reveals a Chaucer whose ironic, playful, and
experimental sensibility remains intact from the early *Boece* to the end
of the *Tales*. The *Retractions* should indeed be read in light of the *Parson's
Tale*, but even more in the light of the *Consolation of Philosophy*, as a final
Boethian turn in a long career of imitating, responding to, and challenging
the idea of literary transformation in both form and content.

106. Fragment 10, lines 647–49, 651–52.
107. Fragment 10, line 1085.

Retroactively, the *Retractions* casts the entire *Tales*—including the verse-canceling performances by the Manciple and Parson—as a vernacular response to Boethius, staging the ethical transformation of the narrating Chaucer through his experience of witnessing the tales of all the foregoing pilgrims. In this passage, the distance between the authorial Chaucer and the narrating Chaucer pilgrim protagonist has collapsed: with no obvious break from the Canterbury narrative, readers are suddenly told that their narrator—the Chaucer pilgrim—is the same Chaucer who wrote the *Legend of Good Women, Troilus and Criseyde,* and, of course, "the translacion of *Boece de Consolacione.*"[108] The collapse of author and narrator draws the *Tales* into an ever-closer literary kinship with the *Consolation*: at the very end, we realize that we have been reading a fictional, mixed-form work in which the narrating author Geoffrey Chaucer has also been a main character, whose literary sensibilities had to be formed and reformed over the course of his literary-philosophical transformation, and who finishes that process of literary transformation by transcending fiction and turning his attention to prayer. We realize, that is, that we have been reading a fiction of narratorial transformation, a protreptic where the ethical transformation in question is from elvish rhymester to a supposedly serious poet who composes ethically weighty literary projects.

Once he has collapsed the Chaucer pilgrim narrator and character into his own authorial identity and has confessed his sinful works, the author-narrator-protagonist Chaucer disavows almost his entire corpus, excepting works of obvious "moralitee and devocioun" like the *Boece.*[109] In so doing, Chaucer responds at once to the hard-lined antipoetic manifesto of the Parson and also to Boethian mandates: at the very end of the *Consolation,* Boethius exhorts his audience,

> Withstond thanne and eschue thou vices; worschipe and love thou virtues; areise thi corage to ryghtful hopes; yilde thou humble preieres an heyhe. Gret necessite of prowesse and vertu is encharged and comaunded to yow, yif ye nil nat dissimulen; syn that ye worken and don . . . byforn the eyen of the juge that seeth and demeth alle thinges.[110]

With Boethius's final words in mind, the *Retractions* reads as though written as a response to their injunction, filtered through the rigid lens

---

108. Fragment 10, line 1087.
109. Fragment 10, lines 1085–87.
110. Bk. V, pr. 6, lines 302–10.

of the Parson. First, Chaucer lists his works, acknowledging and revoking those that "sownen unto synne." He then prays to God, Jesus and Mary, "bisekynge hem that they from hennes forth unto my lyves ende sende me grace of verray penitence, confessioun and satisfaccioun to doon in this present lyf . . . so that I may been oon of hem at the day of doom that shulle be saved."[111] The *Retractions* is crafted to reveal Chaucer—as narrator, author, and even protagonist of the *Tales*—as, at last, a good student of Boethian literary practice and theory, as well as a good student of his own pilgrims' many tales. Not just in local pockets, but also in overarching structure, the *Canterbury Tales* is Chaucer's most thorough reengagement with prosimetrum as a possible vehicle of protrepsis. Rather than constituting a "dismantling" of the *Canterbury Tales* project, the last entries into the work—fragments 8, 9, and 10—constitute Chaucer's revelation of the formal topos that has given shape and structure to the whole literary experiment.[112] The *Tales* has offered a mixed-form protreptic, designed to meditate on the possibility that literature could work ethical renewal in either a narrator or audience. In the *Canterbury Tales* Chaucer shows the mixed form's availability as a foundation on which to build metapoetic explorations of literary experience, culminating with a transformation of its narrator into a vernacular author of a work of literary philosophy.[113]

111. Fragment 10, lines 1089, 1091.

112. The "dismantling" reading is James Dean's, who sees the *Manciple's Tale* as a dark moment in the *Tales*, pivotal in anchoring what he calls Chaucer's "dismantling" of the Canterbury project in his last series of tales (*The Second Nun, Canon's Yeoman, Manciple, Parson,* and *Retractions*) ("Dismantling the Canterbury Book," 752–54). Donald Howard and Traugott Lawler also see these last four pieces as a coherent set piece that is designed to close the entire poem (Howard, *Idea of the Canterbury Tales*, 305; Lawler, *One and the Many*, 145–46).

113. C. David Benson has also noted the influence of Boethius on the work: "General precedent for the stylistic experiments of the *Canterbury Tales* is provided by Chaucer's favorite philosophical work, Boethius's *Consolation of Philosophy*. Its alternation of prose exposition and soaring poetry (later imitated, though hardly matched, in such works as Alain de Lille's *De Planctu*) may have suggested something of what different kinds of artistries within the same work could accomplish" (*Chaucer's Drama of Style*, 23).

In a similar vein, Anne Payne has suggested that Chaucer's poem is a deliberate response to the genre of Menippean satire, to which Chaucer was exposed precisely by his readings of Boethius's *Consolation*. Payne, however, focuses primarily on Menippean structures within individual tales—the Knight and the Pardoner, for instance—rather than on how Boethian form might influence the overall construction of the *Tales* as a

But this reproduction of Boethius's final consolation is revisionist and thorny in one very consequential way: taken as a whole, the *Canterbury Tales*, although it stages its author-narrator's own eventual turn toward God, does not seek to produce any particular lesson for his readership. It does not have a unified didactic goal or message that emerges for a reader gradually and progressively as he or she approaches the end of the work. It does not point clearly or decisively toward a particular vision of divine truth or transcendent contemplation. In this lack of didactic specificity, Chaucer's reengagement with prosimetric practice and transformative theory marks a pronounced departure from Boethius, who uses prose and meter as vehicles for a carefully sculpted and specific demonstration of divine order. Boethius is not interested in literature's transformative potential per se; he is interested in literature's power to work a particular process of learning, to take its narrator and audience from despair to an awareness of God's supremely ordered goodness. He is interested not just in any consolation but specifically in Philosophy's consolation—a consolation born of the feeling of prose and meter, but also of the specific lessons that those forms carry when wielded by Philosophy. Instead of being concerned with *what* particular lesson a narrator might learn from a literary work, Chaucer is concerned with *how and whether* one can learn from literature, with how literary techniques, juxtapositions, and formal interactions can produce transformation in a narrator or model one for an audience. Through their modeling of learning and change through the Nun, the Yeoman, and the narrating Chaucer pilgrim, the *Tales* suggests that the specific lessons of fictive literature are not as important as is an indwelling in the dialectics of meaning and feeling, narration and interruption, linearity and recursion, dialogue and monologue, and prose and meter. Paradoxically, through the *Retractions*, the *Canterbury Tales* offers itself, finally, as a metapoetic defense of literature as an aesthetic mode of doing ethical work, though it leaves the precise quiddity of that work titillatingly underdetermined. The Chaucer pilgrim of *Thopas-Melibee* may have transformed into Chaucer, author of the *Boece*, but we as readers are left walking among ethical penumbras.

---

unified but multiplicitous literary production. Payne suggests that Chaucer used Boethius as a crib for making Menippean satire as a means of destabilizing authority, so that "no answer or position, no matter how authoritative it may seem, can ever provide certainty" (*Chaucer and Menippean Satire*, 219).

CHAPTER FIVE

Political Protrepsis: Usk and Gower

Chaucer's troping and reinventing of the mixed-form protreptic and its metapoetic investments become critical to the ambitions of the works of Thomas Usk and John Gower, the former being a devotee of Chaucerian poetry and the latter being Chaucer's friend and the explicitly designated audience of the *Troilus*.[1] At the beginnings of their stories, Usk and Gower both represent their narrators, following the trope of the protreptic protagonist that exists in the *Consolation, De planctu, Vita nuova,* and *Remède,* as incomplete, imperfect, psychologically vulnerable, and in need of ethical reeducation. As in the poems of Dante and Guillaume, the narrators of Usk's and Gower's poems are enthralled by unhealthy love. As in the *Vita nuova* and the *Remède de Fortune,* these two narrators need a new infusion of rational learning in order to rectify their will and understanding, to bring them to a higher state of self-awareness and philosophical wholeness. For both of these Middle English authors, however, that self-awareness is eventually shown to be inextricably linked to a political agenda: Usk and Gower, as will become clear, use their narrator's psychological incompleteness, his need to learn a better way of feeling and thinking, as a springboard for launching a sociopolitical critique. The protreptic frame that each author devises functions not simply as a justification for fiction but also eventually as a mask—a genre-based persona—behind which each author can pursue potentially incendiary political ends without seeming ever fully to leave the realm of imaginative, literary narration.

---

1. *Troilus,* bk. 5, line 1856.

THE TESTAMENT OF LOVE: THOMAS USK AND THE PEARL OF PROSE

In the late 1380s, Thomas Usk composes his autobiographical fiction, the *Testament of Love*, which retrospectively narrates a lengthy prose dialogue between Usk himself and the unflappably rational Lady Love.[2] This dialogue is intended to and supposedly does heal the author-narrator-protagonist Usk of his obsessive love of one "Margarite," teaching him instead to love with measure. The *Testament* theorizes this amatory transformation as the culmination of a process of self-remembering,[3] much as Philosophy theorizes Boethius's transformation in the *Consolation*.[4] The *Testament* also claims that during Usk's rational healing by love, the "lynes of [his] understondynge wyttes" are "revolved," that is, his rational powers and cognitive faculties are turned back toward his essential self—a self from which he has until now been alienated.[5] In identifying his gradual comprehension of consoling ideas as an experience of self-remembering and of returning to one's natural state, the *Testament* offers itself as a new vernacular work in the tradition of the *Consolation of Philosophy*.[6]

In addition to evoking Boethius's theory of how protreptic learning takes place cognitively, the *Testament* also evokes Boethian theories of how the process of ethical transformation feels—sensorily—to the transformee. Early on, we learn that Love's lessons come in two types: harsh and sweet, painful and delightful, much like the bittersweet lessons of

2. Julia Boffey has shown that this genre of writing, the testament, popular in the late English Middle Ages, is often used by authors because of its simultaneous resonances in legal, spiritual, and literary registers ("Lydgate, Henryson, and the Literary Testament," 46, 56). As we will see, all of these elements—with the "legal" construed more nearly as "apologia" or "self-justification"—are present in Usk's *Testament*.

3. At the end of his *Testament*, he says, "And anon al these thynges that this lady said, I remembred me by myself." Usk, *Testament of Love*, bk. 3, chap. 8, lines 5–6.

4. She famously observes, upon seeing Boethius's initial derangement, that he has, as the *Boece* puts it, "a litil foryeten hymselve" (*Boece*, bk I, pr. 2, sentences 21–22), and that the goal of the philosophical healing process will be to remind him of his true and essential nature—a nature that naturally would incline toward virtuous will and rightful love.

5. Bk. 3, chap. 8, line 6.

6. Paul Strohm has demonstrated the organizing and pervasive linkages, in both thematics and genre, between the *Testament* and the *Consolation* ("Politics and Poetics").

Philosophy, which consist in part of the "sweet drafts" of music and in part of the "harsh tonics" of prose.[7] Much as Philosophy realizes she cannot simply bludgeon Boethius with the blunt force of her prose argumentation, and thus repeatedly switches to the sweetly penetrative delights of song, Love recognizes that she cannot launch into the heaviest logic too early but that she must first help Usk "light out of" his "hevy charge,"[8] so she begins "deliciously [to] comforte [him] with sugred wordes."[9] Evidently, like Boethius, Usk needs a spoonful of sugar to make the medicine go down.

Shortly thereafter, the *Testament* reveals that the sweetness of Love's discourse inheres in its form and thereby pushes its theory of the forms of transformative writing closer to what exists in the *Consolation*. At the end of book 1, Usk asks Love for a respite in her strenuous teachings: "'Ah, peace,' quod I, 'and speke no more of this. Myne herte breaketh, nowe thou touchest any suche wordes.'"[10] To this plea for gentleness, Love replies, "A, wel . . . thanne lette us syngen. Thou herest no more of these thynges at this tyme."[11] Usk's claim that Love's words were too hard for him to handle results in her turn not just to "sugred" words but specifically to song. Love thus mimes the didactic and aesthetic tactics of Philosophy, in which sweet and gentle song makes the bitter stuff of rational argument easier to swallow.

Immediately thereafter, however, the *Testament* unsettles its relation to the *Consolation*. Upon reading Love's proffer of song, a reader is primed to expect a poetic interlude, such as typify the formal oscillations of the *Consolation of Philosophy*. But no verse ever comes. As soon as Love has offered to "syngen" as a reprieve from heavier words and thereby has gestured toward the literary practice and theory of the *Consolation*, the first book concludes, and no metrical writing appears in the next book.[12] In this bait-and-switch maneuver of gesturing toward song but refusing to repre-

---

7. Cf: Boethius, *Philosophiae consolatio*, bk. 4, pr. 6.

8. Cf: Boethius, *Philosophiae consolatio*, bk. 1, pr. 3 and 4, and Usk, *Testament*, bk. 1, chap. 3, line 8.

9. Bk. 1, chap. 4, lines 29–30.

10. Bk. 1, chap. 10, lines 111–12.

11. Bk. 1, chap. 10, lines 113–14.

12. Although they often overlook the bizarre evocation and then disavowal of song and meter that Usk's writing enacts, critics have noted that the "songs" of Love are Boethian in content. David Carlson points out the shaping effect of Boethius's "Felix nimium prior aetas" (bk. 2, m. 5) and "O qui perpetua mundum ratione gubernas" (bk. 3, m. 9) in Usk's work ("Chaucer's Boethius and Usk's *Testament*," 59).

sent it in versified form, the *Testament* evokes Boethian literary theory but blocks its realization in practice; it evokes prosimetrum as a technique of protrepsis but refuses actually to deliver it in form.

The combined gesture toward and refusal of Boethian song gains a linguistic specificity in the second book, when Lady Love again moves to "comfort" Usk and moves to do so by singing to him in Latin. Once again, however, the *Testament* blocks the appearance of song in form. Usk, in introducing Love's song to his readership, admits his limitations as a writer and translator and says he will convert Love's Latin song into English prose:

> this comfortable lady ganne synge a wonder mater of enditynge in Latyn. But trewly, the noble colours in rethorik-wyse knytte were so craftely that my connyng wol not stretche to remember; but the sentence, I trowe, somdele have I in mynde.[13]

It is again through song that "this comfortable lady" brings sweet learning into Usk's mind. But ostensibly because the lady sings in highly wrought Latin, Usk translates that song into English—and, significantly, into prose. In this move, the *Testament* takes the twin form of Boethius's work and reconceives it as an implicit twinning of Latin and English, in which Latin is associated with poetry, and thus with difficulty, while English is associated with prose, and thus with naturalness and ease.[14] Leave the learned Latin and the difficult poetry to Lady Love and to Boethius, the *Testament* seems to say; Usk will pursue his own agenda in English prose, because prose and the English vernacular are clearer, easier to glean "sentence," or meaning, from. Prose translation is equal to the task of conveying Love's lessons, so formal song can be infinitely deferred.

Given the emergent trends in prose practice and theory in the English Middle Ages, it is easy to surmise why the authorial Usk might feel keen to defer the poetic in his work. Usk writes, after all, shortly after Chaucer has composed his *Boece*, at the same time that the Wycliffites produce their prose translations of the Bible and Trevisa translates the *Polychronicon*, when prose is coming to be prized for its supposedly unique access to truth and clarity, while poetry is increasingly seen, among vernacular literary theorists, as prone to lying and deceit. Indeed, along these same

13. Bk. 2, chap. 2, lines 1–4.

14. For a discussion of vernacularity per se in the *Testament*, see the introduction to Usk's Prologue, in Wogan-Browne, *Idea of the Vernacular*, 28–29.

literary-theoretical lines, the *Testament*'s commitment to prose and to clarity first appears long before Love's aborted Latin songs, in the prologue, which discusses how literature works on men's minds.

> Many men there ben that with eeres openly sprad so moche swalowen the delyciousness of jestes and of ryme by queynt knyttyng coloures, that of the goodnesse or of the badnesse of the sentence take they lytel hede or els none.[15]

Like the Parson at the end of the *Canterbury Tales*, the narrating Usk claims that artful literature—especially poetic forms like "jestes" and "ryme"—by dint of their aesthetic "deliciousness," can have a deleterious effect on hearers, deafening them to the "goodness" or "badness" of the "sentence," or meaning, of a work. Like the contemporary prose theory articulated by Wycliffite Bible translators and vernacular historiographers, the *Testament* treats poetic artistry as ethically dangerous, because it can blur a work's meaning. As a result, like Wycliffite prose, Trevisan historiography, and Chaucer's *Boece*—the lattermost of which Usk read with great care[16]—Usk's *Testament* manifests a commitment to prose as a literary technique for conveying ideation accurately.[17]

The incompatibility of poetic form with fidelity to meaning that the *Testament* perceives and thematizes not only mandates an avoidance of metrical composition but also necessitates the stylistic choices that Usk expressly avows. He claims, first, that he is unable to produce ornamented "endytyng" and, second, that "rude wordes and boystous percen the herte of the herer to the inrest poynte and planten there the sentence of things."[18] Since simpler language, composed in prose rather than in verse, full of

---

15. Bk. 1, Prologue, lines 1–4.

16. David Carlson notes Usk's eagerness to affiliate himself specifically with Chaucer, much more than with any other contemporary author. Further, Carlson demonstrates that Usk derived much of his Boethian material from Chaucer's translation ("Chaucer's Boethius and Usk's *Testament*," 33–35).

17. For tables that compare Usk's writing with those of Chaucer's *Boece* and *Troilus* and Boethius's *Consolation*, line by line, see *Testament of Love*, ed. Shawver, 27–31. Indeed, so closely linked have Usk and Chaucer's corpuses traditionally been considered that for many years the *Testament* was believed to have been written by Chaucer himself. For the reasons why this was believed to be a Chaucerian work, see Bonner, "Genesis of the Chaucer Apocrypha," 466.

18. Bk. 1, Prologue, lines 5, 6–8.

"rude" or unlearned language rather than poetic diction, enables meaning to pierce into the mind of a hearer more readily than does the more ornamented stuff of meter and rhyme, Usk explains, he will write not just in prose but specifically in "rude" prose. Usk thereby converts a traditional modesty topos—that the writer is incapable of artful writing—into a not-so-modest claim for his work's lofty ethical value: although he *cannot* write poetry, it is, as it turns out, ethically for the best that he not even try. He makes this twinned ethical avowal and aesthetic disavowal more explicit when he goes on to praise his own "rude" and "boystous" book for its ease of comprehension and for its rendering "sentence" or meaning more available than would be possible in more artful writing.[19] His prose style, Usk reveals, is "so drawe togyder to maken the catchers therof ben the more redy to hent sentence."[20] His prose, unornamented ("rude") but carefully organized ideationally ("so drawe togyder"), will allow meaning to "percen" deep into the ears of his audience. In theorizing how simple, prose discourse "pierces" into a hearer, Usk both evokes and derogates Boethius's valorization of poetry as the best vehicle for the very same didactic function: the "penetration" of ideas into the mind. Whereas the sensation of song is what pierces or penetrates for Boethius, "sentence"—pure and simple meaning—is what penetrates for Usk. Aesthetic underachievement, though not pretty, works protreptic learning better, the *Testament* suggests, than a more artful form.

But there is a serious problem with the *Testament*'s dogged commitment to prose. Despite its banishment of "song" to the outer reaches of the work and Usk's concomitant protestations of stylistic naïveté, the *Testament* cultivates a sustained formal complexity in its putatively natural, "rude" prose. In fact, the extreme and perhaps excessive ornateness of the *Testament*'s supposedly plain and "rude" prose style has provoked long-standing controversies in criticism: some critics see Usk as a hack prose stylist, a Euphuist *avant la lettre*, unable to free himself from the impulse to make his writing overly wrought. Others have seen more value

19. Jocelyn Wogan-Browne has also addressed Usk's preference for "plain" and unornamented style, suggesting that this preference bespeaks Usk's desire to compose in the vernacular, as opposed to Latin, and to demonstrate how English, with its "embodiedness" and "immediacy" can achieve in simple style the same communicative function that previous authors—including Boethius—achieve only in Latin ("The Notion of Vernacular Theory," in *Idea of the Vernacular*, 326–27).

20. Bk. 1, Prologue, lines 10–11.

in Usk's style and extrapolated from it a strong bond between his work and Chaucer's.[21] Setting Usk's work into the context of contemporary prose theory and Boethian writing helps resolve the tension between these two critical camps by suggesting that the *Testament*'s intermittent ornateness originates in an overarching and specific literary-theoretical goal. When the *Testament* deploys its most ornate passages of prose writing, it engages with a subtle aspect of Boethian metapoetics, namely, how the mixed form can contribute to a successful literary apologia.[22]

During the 1380s, Thomas Usk repeatedly finds himself on the wrong side of sociopolitical controversies in London. More than once, he finds himself in prison—much like Boethius does in the *Consolation of Philosophy*. When he writes his *Testament of Love*, he does so in part to clear himself of various charges that have been brought against him over the course of his public career.[23] In showing himself gradually to be affectively reformed by the didactic interventions of Lady Love, Usk couches as a fictive, amatory "consolation" what is always also his own political apologia, his defense of himself as a good citizen, a loyal supporter of the English monarchy who should not be condemned for his perhaps questionable political past. In Paul Strohm's formulation, "Usk sought to turn literary

21. George Krapp, although recognizing Usk's work as having played a role in the development of English prose, condemned the *Testament* for its excesses of style and ornament (*Rise of Early English Literary Prose*, 30). Skeat similarly lamented the difficulty and lack of clarity in Usk's style (introduction, xix). For other scholars, Usk's florid prose seems internally consistent with his evident interest in ornamentation and authorial self-fashioning. See, for instance, Hayton, "Many Privy Thinges Wimpled and Folde," and Turner, "'Certaynly his Sayinges Can I Nat Amende.'" Yet others see his richly ornamented prose as consistent with his overall commitment to artistry in bookmaking, since the *Testament* is organized by a supervening acrostic that sequences the episodes in the work itself. Indeed, the *Testament* has come to be regarded as a book of tremendous material craftsmanship, bespeaking the burgeoning of the late medieval urban bookmaking industry (Middleton, "Thomas Usk's 'Perdurable Letters'").

22. Paul Strohm also suggests that Usk may have derived his famously variable levels of stylistic ornamentation, in part, from the mixed form of Boethius's work: "That this dialogue leading to spiritual comfort is interrupted by intermittent visions of exaltation and stretches of unmediated apology is not in itself unusual, since the *consolatio* as shaped by Boethius and others has always been mixed, in its dialogic content and even in elaborate formal variation (as in Boethius's alternation of prose and verse passages)" ("Politics and Poetics," 104).

23. This literary apologia was more a rule than an exception in Usk's writerly life: he performed something similar in his *Appeal*, as Paul Strohm has shown (*Hochon's Arrow*, 145–60).

form to personal account, importing materials of personal and factional apology and complaint into an apparent *consolatio*."[24]

The *Testament* does not invent the generic compatibility of *consolatio* with apology de novo. Quite the contrary, an apologetic agenda suffuses Boethius's own *consolatio* as well. The *Consolation of Philosophy* makes plain its own apologetic thrust early on, when Philosophy asks Boethius why he is in prison.

At cuius criminis arguimur summam quaeres. Senatum dicimur sa-luum esse uoluisse. Modum desideras. Delatorem, ne documenta de-ferret quibus senatum maiestatis reum faceret, impedisse criminamur. Quid igitur, o magistra, censes? Infitiabimur crimen, ne tibi pudor simus? At uolui nec umquam uelle desistam. Fatebimur? Sed impe-diendi delatoris opera cessauit. An optasse illius ordinis salutem nefas uocabo?[25]

[But axestow in somme of what gylt I am accused? Men seyn that I wolde saven the companye of the senatours. And desirestow to here in what manere? I am accused that I schulde han disturbed the accusour to beren lettres, by whiche he scholde han maked the senatours gylty ayens the kynges real maieste. O Maystresse, what demestow of this? Schal I forsake this blame, that Y ne be no schame to the? Certes I have wolde it, (that is to seyne the savacioun of the senat), ne I schal nevere letten to wilne it. And that I confesse and am aknowe; but the entente of the accusour to ben distorbed schal cese. For schal I clepe it thanne a felonye or a synne that I have desired the savacioun of the ordre of the senat?][26]

Here, Boethius addresses Philosophy as a naïve audience to the story of his own recent trials and tribulations, explaining to her how his imprison-ment came to pass, asking her judgment ("O Maystresse, what demestow of this?") and confessing those accusations against him that are warranted,

24. "Politics and Poetics," 84. This apologetic aspect of Usk's writing has also been noted by Shawver. See *Testament of Love*, ed. Shawver, 8–24.

25. Bk. 1, pr. 4, sentences 20–23.

26. Bk. 1, pr. 4, sentences 138–54. I present the *Boece* as a translation of the Latin since Chaucer's translation may well have been Usk's mainstay in composing his own Boethian work. Gary Shawver, in his edition of the *Testament*, has presented compel-ling textual evidence that Usk had encountered Chaucer's *Boece* as well as *Troilus* prior to composing his *Testament*. See *Testament of Love*, ed. Shawver, 27–31.

while always protesting his fundamental innocence. As the passage continues, Boethius both accounts for and justifies himself to Philosophy,
asking all the while for her understanding and clemency. In narrating the
injustices he has suffered and in confessing the errors or decisions he has
indeed made, Boethius's inset narrative constitutes an apologia, a defense
and an explanation of his life and, in particular, of his choices as a public
servant.

Medieval writers other than Usk are well aware of this apologetic aspect of Boethius's work and eager to draw on it in their own works. In his
Convivio, Dante wrestles with and seeks to justify his choice to narrate a
story about himself. This choice, he admits, would be easy to condemn for
its narcissism and hubris. But, he notes, there are two literary exemplars
to look to for instances of justifiable self-narration, instances in which the
act of self-narration is not inevitably tainted with the sin of pride. The
first is Augustine, whom Dante praises for having written about himself
for the purpose of educating other people in the *Confessions*. The other
writer is Boethius, who, in Dante's estimation, wrote about himself in
order to exonerate himself from crimes he had not committed. Boethius
is thus to be pardoned for writing about himself because he wrote in an
apologetic mode.[27] Having made this assertion, Dante commits his own

---

27. "Veramente, al principale intendimento tornando, dico, come è toccato di sopra,
per necessarie cagioni lo parlare di sé è conceduto: e intra l'altre necessarie cagioni due
sono più manifeste. L'una è quando sanza ragionare di sé grande infamia o pericolo non
si può cessare; e allora si concede, per la ragione che de li due sentieri prendere lo men
reo è quasi prendere un buono. E questa necessitate mosse Boezio di se medesimo a
parlare, acciò che sotto pretesto di consolazione escusasse la perpetuale infamia del suo
essilio, mostrando quello essere ingiusto, poi che altro escusatore non si levava. L'altra
è quando, per ragionare di sé, grandissima utilitade ne segue altrui per via di dottrina; e
questa ragione mosse Agustino ne le sue Confessioni a parlare di sé, ché per lo processo
de la sua vita, lo quale fu di [non] buono in buono, e di buono in migliore, e di migliore
in ottimo, ne diede essemplo e dottrina, la quale per sì vero testimonio ricevere non si
potea." Dante Alighieri, *Il convivio*, bk. 1, chap. 2, line 13ff., pp. 16–17. (Truly, turning
back to the originally intended topic, I say, as was touched on above, that on occasions
of necessity, speaking of oneself is permissible: and among the various occasions of
necessity two are quite obvious. The first is when, without speaking of oneself, great
infamy or danger cannot be avoided; and therefore it is allowed, because to take the
less bad of two routes is almost equivalent to taking one good one. And this necessity
moved Boethius to talk about himself, so that under the pretext of consolation he could
exonerate himself of the unending infamy of exile, showing it to be unjust, since no
other exonerator stood up on his behalf. The other justification for speaking of oneself
is when, by talking about oneself, an extremely great usefulness flows out to others

Convivio to that very goal. In so doing, Dante aligns himself and this, his second prosimetric project, with Boethius explicitly and directly. Dante thus establishes Boethius as an authority for the apologetic mode of literary self-narration.[28]

We do not need to rely exclusively on Dante to establish a broad-based medieval awareness of Boethius as an apologist. Medieval commentators and translators also note the apologetic force in Boethius's work. William of Conches takes the frame narrative of Boethius's imprisonment as literal and historical and suggests that Boethius tells his tale, in part, to clear his own name and to explain the context and circumstance by which he, formerly a man of high station, now finds himself in prison and condemned to die.[29] Perhaps following William's commentary, Chaucer, in his *Boece*, amplifies the apologetic aspect of Boethius's narrative, adding to Boece's self-justification several glosses that give historical context and specificity to his claims. When, for instance, Boece attempts to justify his policy decisions during Theodoric's rule, Chaucer includes extenuating historical information to explain why Boece made the choices he made:

> Glosa. Whan that Theodoric, the kyng of Gothes, in a dere yeer, hadde his gerneeris ful of corn, and comaundede that no man ne schulde byen no coorn til his corn were soold, and that at a grevous dere prys, Boece withstood that ordenaunce and overcome it, knowynge al this the kyng hymselve. Coempcioun is to seyn comune achat or beyinge

through that teaching; and this is what moved Augustine in his *Confessions* to talk about himself, because by the process of his life, which went from bad to good, and from good to better, and from better to best, he gave example and doctrine, which could not be conferred by any truer testimony.)

28. Although it is inconclusive, there is considerable evidence that Chaucer knew the *Convivio* (Lowes, "Chaucer and Dante's *Convivio*"). There is no evidence that Usk had direct contact with the text, but it is quite possible that the *Convivio* was already a presence in the English literary imagination by the time Usk wrote his *Testament*.

29. William of Conches calls Boethius a "most noble Roman and faithful Catholic" (Boetius iste nobilissimus ciuis Romanus et fide catholicus extitit), who fought heresies and injustices during the reign of Theodoric (Deinde tempore Theodorici regis Gothorum). Despite his unfailing good intentions, Boethius is convicted of crimes against the king unfairly—"defenseless and absent" from his own trial (indefensus et absens)—and is sentenced to imprisonment. To comfort himself and give comfort to others in his position, according to William, Boethius decided to compose his consolation against the mutability of fortune (Vt ergo unusquisque quo se solaretur haberet, si aliqua aduersitas sibi contingeret, contra mutabilitatem fortunae philosophicam consolationem composuit) (*Glosae super Boetium*, pp. 3–4, lines 8–32).

togidre, that were establissed upon the peple by swich a manere impo-
sicioun, as whoso boughte a busschel corn, he moste yyve the kyng the
fyfte part.[30]

Chaucer amplifies the apologetic impact of the *Consolation* and situates
Boethius firmly within English literary consciousness as an apologetic
writer.

Given Dante's, Chaucer's, and commentators' tendencies to think, first,
that Boethius's protreptic narrative is written while he is in prison for political reasons and, second, that it is deliberately composed as a defense of
its author against the accusations his detractors brought to bear against
him, it seems natural that Usk would find in the *Consolation* a particularly apt literary inspiration for his own politically motivated narrative of
ethical transformation.[31] When Lady Love first appears on the scene, she
immediately identifies her narrative goal as, in part, to make an apologia
for Usk. She offers to set the record straight regarding Usk's public reputation and his imprisonment for supposedly evil deeds.

> And bycause that men ben of dyvers condycions, some adradde to saye a
> sothe, and some for a sothe anone redy to fyght; and also that I maye not
> myselfe ben in place to withsay thilke men that of thee speken othe-
> rwyse than the sothe, I wol and I charge thee in vertue of obedyence
> that thou to me owest, to writen my wordes and sette hem in writynges
> that they mowe as my witnessynge ben noted amonge the people.[32]

Like the *Consolation* and the *Boece*, the *Testament* uses its salvific interlocutor to account for and justify the intentions of its narrator-hero. As
in the *Consolation* and the *Boece*, so in the *Testament*, that interlocutor
will "withsay" the malevolent gossip of the hero's detractors by urging the
hero to write down and record the coming dialogue, which will, in turn,
bear "witness" to the hero's good character "amonge the people." Thus,
in the tradition of Boethius's self-exonerating *Consolation* and Chaucer's
Englishing of it, the *Testament* offers itself as a public record of its hero
and narrator's good conscience and irreproachable intentions.

Because of its apologetic ambitions, the *Testament* seeks to promote

---

30. Bk. 1, pr. 4.
31. See also Galloway, "Private Selves and the Intellectual Marketplace," 294–95.
32. Bk. 1, chap. 2, lines 161–66.

an image of its author-narrator as a good person, deserving of sympathy. It does so not only narratively, by insisting on Usk's good service, but also through its formal choices, especially its inclusion of extremely artificed, songful prose passages. The *Testament* deploys its most intricate rhythms and ornamentations in scenes of heightened emotional intensity, especially in moments of despair:

> Howe shulde the grounde without kyndly noriture bringen forthe any frutes? Howe shulde a shippe withouten a sterne in the great see be governed? Howe shulde I, withouten my blysse, my herte, my desyre, my joye, my goodnesse, endure in this contrarious prison, that thynke every hour in the day an hundred wynter?[33]

Here, the anaphoric repetition "howe shulde," combined with the repetition of "withouten," creates an incantatory rhythm for the passage. Usk may claim "rude" lack of ornament for his writing, but what he actually produces is often a rather conspicuously songful mode of prose. Shortly after this anaphoric sequence, another anaphoric series of incantatory lamentations ensues, this time beginning with the lyrical exclamation "O":

> O, love, whan shal I ben pleased? O, charyte, whan shal I ben eased? O, good goodly, what shal the dyce turne? O, ful of vertue, do the chaunce of comforte upward to fal. O, love, whan wolt thou thynke on thy servaunt?[34]

Usk augments the rhythmical ornamentation of this anaphoric "O" passage by fitting the first two phrases with nearly the same stress pattern and the same syllabic count. Further, the first two questions end-rhyme with each other. The subsequent three questions, though less tightly fettered to the exact sonic patterning of the first two, are comparable in length, have common apostrophic beginnings and similar stress patterns. Through their highly structured and repetitive form, these two passages render an aesthetic experience of likeness. Much as in Boethius's own meters and in Chaucer's reinvention of them in the *Boece*'s and the *Troilus*'s aesthetic sentence, the architectures of likeness in these songful prose passages promote a reader's ability to identify with the narrating hero. Ap-

---

33. Bk. 1, chap. 1, lines 31–35.
34. Bk. 1, chap. 1, lines 73–76.

ologia necessitates not only narrative explication of the apologist's deeds
and intentions but also songfulness, just as it did in the *Consolation*, and
the intermittent ornateness of Usk's prose serves his apologetic agenda.

Paradoxically, even as the apologetic thrust of the *Testament* explains
its swerves into peri-song, it simultaneously helps more fully to account
for Usk's rigidly expressed commitment to "rude" prose. Through his
prose form and his explicit justification of its "rude" style, Usk casts himself, by judicious embodiment of contemporary literary theory, as a simple, straightforward, truthful person, not as a liar or practitioner of poetic
fiction. By extension, the *Testament* casts itself not as a "poetic fiction"
but as a true and simple display of its author's good intention, as a true
literary apology. The prose of the *Testament* thus works to promote the
image of Usk as an honest man, while it simultaneously works, on the local level of practice, to curry affective identification between narrator and
reader by creating architectures of sonic and rhythmical likeness in its
songful prose.

As a Boethian apologist and a self-conscious prose stylist of the late
fourteenth century, Usk both registers the formal power of poetry (it promotes identification between reader and narrator) and simultaneously registers its dangers (it reads as fiction, false, and artificial). Thus, his prose
work is designed both to draw on poetry's aesthetic efficacy and to locate
actual song elsewhere—in the imaginary Latin beyond of his Middle English work. It is designed to evoke the Boethian theory and practice of
verse and to ignite its apologetic potential, but also to sap poetry's power
to fictionalize and complicate his putatively "rude" and truthful prose
narrative. The *Testament* manifests a canny recognition that because of
its particular cultural weight in the late Middle Ages, prose—no matter
how ornate—can insist on its own clarity and, by extension, truthfulness
in a way that metrical writing cannot. Thus, the *Testament* is very much
in the experimental tradition of Chaucer's *Boece*, exploring and exploiting
the logic and limits of prose style to produce a transformative work.

But the *Testament*'s commitment to the single form of prose goes beyond the *Boece*, beyond contemporary prose theory, and beyond apologetics. In the *Testament*, the single form of English prose *must* be enough to
do the work of literary transformation and political apology in order for
the work to be aesthetically consistent with its own deep-seated ethical
commitments. To show how, I will return to and reconsider Usk's love
object, the Margarite or "pearl," to whom all of Usk's love is directed from
the very beginning of his work.

Early on, "Margarite" denotes a real, human woman; in the tradition of Dante's *Vita nuova* and Guillaume's *Remède,* Usk's early, agonized love is decidedly earthly and decidedly amatory.[35] As Love's healing of Usk progresses, however, his affections are reconfigured, so that he is able to understand Margarite, his beloved pearl, not only as a real human woman but also as a figure for a love of larger scope. In the *Testament,* the Margarite is a love object in transition from being a single, atomistic human being to representing something much more social and much more sacred: "Ryght so a jewel betokeneth a gemme, and that is a stone vertuous, or els a perle. Margarite a woman betokeneth grace, lernyng, or wisdom of God, or els holy church."[36] Although united by the single signifier "Margarite," Margarite's modes of being are multiplicitous.

This ontological unity-in-multiplicity of the Margarite-pearl—her encompassing of many kinds of love—is crucial not just to the *Testament*'s representation of how Usk's psyche transforms over the course of the narrative but also to its vision both of how the *Testament* itself works and of how society should function. The Margarite-pearl becomes, in the *Testament,* a manifestation of the "knot," to which the book refers time and again, and which signifies the unity of all people in the love of God and obedience to natural, human, and divine laws. The *Testament* registers that this concept of the knot of unity derives directly from Boethius: "Boece sheweth this thynge at the ful, that this name good is, in general, name in kynde, as it is comparysoned generally to his principal ende, which is God, knotte of al goodnesse."[37] That God is the knot that ties all good together has important consequences for the *Testament,* both metapoetically and

35. The reality of "Margarite" as an actual woman Usk loved during his life, outside of his literary self-representation, is further attested by the acrostic that he programs into his book, which reads "Margarete of Vertw Have Merci on thin Vsk" (Middleton, "Usk's Perdurable Letters," 69).

36. Bk. 3, chap. 9, lines 90–92.

37. Bk. 2, chap. 13, lines 46–48. According to Allen Shoaf, "After the Margarite, the most important as it is also the most unusual image in *TL* is that of the knot. The knot figures centrally and extensively in Book 2 and serves there, as Jellech observes, as an equivalent to Boethius's *summum bonum* and *beatitudo:* at one point, God himself is said to be the 'knotte of al goodnesse'" (bk. 2, line 1286). And yet this is hardly all that can be said, especially if one simply lists all the definitions of the knot in *Testament of Love* book 2, chaps. 4 and following. J. A. W. Bennett makes the very important observation that as a scrivener, Usk would have been intimately familiar with the practice of flourishing signatures with knots so as to make them unique and immune to forgery." Introduction, *Testament of Love,* ed. Shoaf, 10. See also Jellech, "*Testament of Love* by Thomas Usk," 99–100; Bennett and Gray, *Middle English Literature,* 350.

philosophically. Because God is the knot of all goodness, and because God is the source of biblical law, the guarantor of human laws, and the originator of natural laws, Love reminds Usk both early and late in the *Testament* that all laws are one law, knit together by God's loving goodness. Eventually, Usk explicitly associates this knotlike unification of the laws of love with the round, unbroken, perfect, and pure surface of the pearl.

> But in conclusyon of my boke and of this Margarite peerle in knyttynge togider, lawe by thre sondrie maners shal be lykened, that is to saye, lawe, right, and custome, whiche I wol declare. Al that is lawe cometh of Goddes ordynance by kyndly worchyng . . . Trewly, lawe of kynde, for Goddes own lusty wyl, is verily to maintayne, under which lawe—and unworthy—bothe professe and reguler arne obedyencer and bounden to this Margarite perle, as by knotte of loves statutes and stablysshment in kynde, whiche that goodly maye not ben withsetten.[38]

Salvific connection with the smooth surface of the pearl happens when people obey the "knotte of loves statutes," the union of many different types of love and law. Attaining oneness with the beloved "Margarite perle" means finding a way to participate in the "knot" of love, in the according of discord, in the unity from multiplicity that the law embodies in the social world. In order to be healed of his disorderly and imbalanced love of Margarite, Usk must learn and remember the unity of all loves and must promise to obey "lawe, right, and custome" as they are joined together under the statutes of love, and he must let go of any singular love, which is, by definition, a lesser love.

The *Testament*'s conceptual commitment to the possibility of deriving unity from multiplicity inflects not only how it understands the social world but also how it understands and integrates a mixed style into an all-prose work of transformation. If Usk were to break out of prose form, not only would that break overtly signal the abrogation of the putative ease, honesty, and clarity of the *Testament*'s style by constraining that style to fit an artificial meter, but it would also—and perhaps more insidiously—create a formal reflex of the kind of division and disunity about which the *Testament* is so critical. It would create a twinned kind of sensation, a split literary experience, when the rhetorical arc of the work is ever toward unity and synthesis. Such a break would, in form, unravel the "knot of love" to produce duality, alterity, and aesthetic rupture in Usk's work.

38. Bk. 3, chap. 1, lines 90–94, 116–20.

In realizing its thematic commitment to unity in its prose form, Usk's work makes oblique and revisionist contact with Alain de Lille's *De planctu naturae*. As I discussed in chapter 1, Alain's work deploys the mixed form as a figure for unification of two different things, for a harmony drawn from disharmony, for an accord from discord, for, in effect, a heterosexual marriage of form. Like Alain's, Usk's work functions as an aesthetic reflex of the highest ethical idea that it propounds. Unlike *De planctu*, however, the *Testament* does not create a heterosexual marriage of forms, based on fundamental and sustained differences between prose and meter. Quite the contrary, Usk couches his own protrepsis as a process of getting over the desire for heterosexual union, a process of learning the higher order of love that prosocial and Christian affective behavior strives toward. Alain's narrative produces an awareness of the possibility of uniting two different modes of being, be it male/female or prose/poetry, while Usk's produces an awareness that all referents of the Margarite—be it a pearl, a woman, the church, God's wisdom, grace, or common laws—should coincide in an ideal world. The *Testament*'s vision of ideal love is thus not dyadic but social.[39] In effect, then, the *Testament*'s formal embodiment of protrepsis is diametrically opposed to *De planctu*'s. Though the *Testament* recognizes *in theory* the importance of song—the Latin songs that Love sings but that Usk does not represent— to a process of philosophical transformation, it reveals *in practice* that variably artful prose can contain a fiction of social transformation better than prosimetrum can, since "rude" and "knotty" prose embodies the ideally "knit" social world in a way that Boethius's prosimetrum does not even imagine and Alain's prosimetrum would reject as morally perfidious.

In the *Testament*, the mode of transformative literary apologia has become a scaffold from which to launch a vision of sociopolitical idealism, in which all different modes of "love" and all different levels of style are collected under the single unifying image of the prosaic pearl. The stylistic realization of the Margarite-pearl, then, is where Usk's transformation edges over into readerly protreptic. The *Testament*'s prose, unified in

---

39. Anne Middleton has associated Usk's *Testament* with a Ricardian poetic genre she calls "public poetry." Public poetry, in her assessment, is "defined by a constant relation of speaker to audience within an ideally conceived worldly community, a relation which has become the poetic subject . . . The voice of public poetry is neither courtly, nor spiritual, nor popular. It is pious, but its central pieties are worldly felicity, and peaceful, harmonious, communal existence" ("Idea of Public Poetry," 95).

form and multiple in style, formally renders the knot that binds a reader
to the smooth unification of the pearl itself. Usk's narratorial transformation couches, then, a readerly protrepsis of a far more *social* ethical scope
than we have seen in any other protreptic work so far: readers are not simply meant to come to a closer understanding of the relationship between
their soul and God. They are also meant to build on that understanding to
realize a greater integration between their individual selves and the larger
social world to which they belong.

The social protrepsis that Usk's work offers is not limited to the av-
erage reader. Quite the contrary, as becomes clear in the third book, the
Testament's protreptic agenda is aimed rather high on the sociopolitical
hierarchy. Ultimately, the *Testament*'s ethical ambitions transform into
full-scale political ambitions. Usk himself signals that this encrypting of
politics into fictive form and genre is part of his plan when he explains
why he has composed his book:

> And, for this booke is al of Love, and therafter beareth his name,
> and phylosophie and lawe must here-to acorden by their clergyal
> discriptions—as phylosophie for love of wisdome is declared, lawe for
> mainteynaunce of peace is holden—and these with love must nedes
> acorden, therfore of hem in this place have I touched. Ordre of homly
> thinges and honest maner of lyvynge in vertue, with rightful jugement
> in causes and profitable administration in commynalties of realmes
> and cytes by evenhed profitably to raigne, nat by singuler avauntage, ne
> by prive envy, ne by soleyn purpose in covetise of worship or of goodes,
> ben disposed in open rule shewed, by love, philosophy, and lawe; and
> yet love toforn al other.[40]

Toward the end, Usk's *Testament* casts itself not simply as a prose, vernacular, amatory revision of the *Consolation of Philosophy* and its apologetic
agenda, or even a protreptic on the right way for members of the common-
wealth to love in society. Instead, it is a manual aimed at the uppermost
echelons of society, promoting "rightful jugement," "profitable adminis-
tration," and good "raigne," to be achieved by a union of love, philosophy,
and law.

When Usk urges a new and loving law in his third book, he stands
on Boethius's authoritative literary example as a soapbox from which to

---

40. Bk. 3, chap. 1, lines 74–84.

launch a critique of a governmental system gone astray.[41] Retrospectively, Usk's experiments with mixed styles and apologetic genres earlier in his *Testament* have served as a framework for introducing this decidedly political agenda—the cultivation of a new, society-saving and synergistic kind of "love" of governor for governed—as a work of literary fiction. The apologetic frame of the work and its pointedly artful mixing of styles allow the *Testament* to hover somewhere between literary experimentation and political critique. In Usk's hands, textured by the literary topoi of his own historical moment, the mixed form paradigm for apologetic consolation becomes not just a protreptic for an everyman reader but also a slyly encrypted manual for right rule, a vernacular mirror for princes.

O PHILOSOPHICAL GENIUS: GOWER'S MIXED PROTREPSIS

Like Usk, John Gower uses his sustained engagement with protreptic literary logic as a platform for sociopolitical critique, though he does so in a manner all his own. Gower's *Confessio amantis* has long been recognized for its Boethian thematic echoes: throughout the poem, Gower analyzes problems of free will versus fate, the nature of fortune, the dangers of focusing excessively on the material pleasures of life, and, eventually, the necessity of turning toward divine contemplation as the only legitimate mode of living. But Gower's poem also, and perhaps more loudly, announces itself as Boethian in its basic narrative framework: the narrating main character, Amans, initially trapped in a state of psychological woe, is gradually brought back to consciousness of himself and to correct thinking and feeling via an extended dialogue with the personification of all he holds dear.[42] But Gower's poem avails itself of Boethian literary theory in order to parody some of the basic, underlying principles of literary transformation that have, by the 1390s, begun to become commonplace. It signals that Boethian literary modes will be under pressure in

41. Galloway notes that the Margarite is an increasingly elusive allegory that justifies Usk's literary pursuits ("Private Selves and the Intellectual Marketplace," 295), and he also suggests that Usk's "knot," toward which all rightly directed love tends, is both erotic and a figure for the social contract (296). Ultimately, Galloway sees Usk's writing as protohumanistic and his protohumanism as geared partially toward an apologetic self-exoneration, but more broadly toward a call for larger social values and civic virtues (305).

42. Michael Cherniss suggests that "Venus and Genius share the role of Boethian authority figure" (*Boethian Apocalypse*, 100).

two overt, large-scale ways. First, it positions its *consolatio* somewhere in the generic hinterlands between Martianus Capellus and penitential manuals. The *Confessio* is modeled on the seven-part defense and explication of the seven liberal arts that arises in Martianus's *De nuptiis*, but rather than the seven arts, Gower presents the seven sins, following in rough outline the structure of penitential manuals. Second, the poem undercuts any strict identification as "Boethian" by drawing pervasively on Alain de Lille's *De planctu naturae*, with its concern to revisit and revise Boethius's joining of the mixed form with protreptic function. Highlighting its affiliation with the *De planctu*, the *Confessio*'s salvific interlocutor is named not Philosophy but Genius.

As I have suggested, one way in which Alain revises Boethian literary theory and practice is through his sexualization of the mixed form itself, but that overt formal revision is by no means his only disruption of the Boethian paradigm of literary transformation. As James Simpson has shown, Alain's *De planctu naturae* deploys Genius, the narrator's putatively salvific interlocutor, precisely so as to highlight Genius's own ethical and psychological instabilities.[43] In deploying a philosophical healer whose own plasticity of self contributes to the narrator's ethical uncertainty, Alain destabilizes the unified protreptic project of the *Consolation*, in which Philosophy's ethical righteousness is never called into question. Gower's *Confessio* is infused with a similar spirit of revision and reimagination—very likely originating in Gower's exposure to Alain's writings—though Gower's narrative of transformation will be considerably more ironic than Alain's, considerably more optimistic about the possibility of ethical redemption for a narrating hero, considerably lighter-hearted about the possibility that a narratorial transformation could work a salvific protrepsis for a reader, and considerably more willing to reinvent prosimetrum radically in the process.

Although, like the *Troilus*, the *Confessio* is more often recognized as Boethian in its thematic echoes, Winthrop Wetherbee has also recognized it as Boethian in its form.[44] In Wetherbee's reading, Gower emulates Boethian prosimetrum by dividing his work first into two distinct parts: a

---

43. "Genius accounts himself an imperfect figure, whose own judgment has been narrowed by the deformed vices of men . . . So Genius, in Alan's *De Planctu*, is not simply the solution to the problem of human deformity, but he is also a part of the problem itself" (*Sciences and the Self in Medieval Poetry*, 183).

44. "Latin Structure and Vernacular Space." See also Olsen, *Betwene Ernest and Game*.

set of short, lyrical Latin poems, and the long, continuous English narrative that they interrupt. From there, Gower adds in a set of prose, Latin
marginal glosses, putatively as an interpretive apparatus for the rest of the
poem. These divisions of the *Confessio* into Latin and English and into
meter and prose, Wetherbee suggests, recreate and reinvent the formal dialectics of the *Consolatio*.[45] Ultimately, however, Wetherbee argues that the
net effect of this dual recreation and reinvention is to point to the difficulty of reconciling the classical tradition with a vernacular poem.[46] Prosimetrum becomes, for Wetherbee, a formal arena for staging a meditation
about the incommensurability of Latin and vernacular. In my view, the
Confessio's linguistic and formal revision of prosimetrum shows quite the
opposite—the power of vernacular poetry to remake meaning and reinvent
inherited classical traditions. In the *Confessio*'s reinvention of mixed-form
protrepsis, Boethius becomes not simply a source of philosophical consolation but also a source of learned, high-concept, literary comedy.

To show how, I will first look deeper into the aesthetic interactions
between English and Latin verse in Gower's poem. Siân Echard and Claire
Fanger have suggested that the relation of the vernacular narrative poem
to the Latin lyrical poems is exegetical; the vernacular poem attempts to
spell out the meaning of the Latin headings, which often contain ideas
and images too abstruse for ready comprehension.[47] In its exegetical function, the switching between English and Latin in the poem replicates an
aspect of how the mixed form works in the *Consolation*: Philosophy often
presents complexly related images of comfort to Boethius in her meters

---

45. He notes that Gower's "Boethianism" is discernible even "in the very format
of his pages," in which the "English text . . . is framed by Latin marginal glosses,
which summarize and often moralize the individual tales, and its principal divisions
are marked by Latin head-verses," so that "the interplay between vernacular text and
Latin apparatus becomes in many respects a substitute for the traditional Boethian
dialogue" ("Latin Structure," 9–10). He further argues that Gower may have derived his
Boethian formal impulse not directly from Boethius himself but via the mediation of
the Boethian mixed form through French writers like Alain de Lille: "It is precisely the
dialogic aspect of the *Consolation* and the challenge to philosophical resolution posed
by the interplay of its poetry and prose that most strongly influenced the first major
imitation of Boethius, the *De planctu naturae* of Alain de Lille" (13).

46. "Classical and Boethian Tradition in *Confessio Amantis*," 183.

47. Echard and Fanger, *Latin Verses in the Confessio amantis*, li. "The English
may also expand upon the Latin by offering images that are clearly related to, but not
directly presented in, the Latin." Echard and Fanger also note that the Latin verses tend
to "compress" the meaning of what lies around them (xxiii). Wetherbee notes that the
vernacular "discursively" spells out the meaning of the Latin ("Latin Structure," 18–19).

and then glosses them for him in the subsequent proses. This reading of the *Confessio*'s formal gesture toward Boethius, however true, tells only part of the story: the *aesthetic* manner in which the Latin verses function as revisions of Boethian meters and the English narrative poem functions as Boethian proses has yet fully to be accounted for.

In what follows, I suggest that the English/Latin verse dialectic, much like the revisionist prosimetric dialectic in the eighth fragment of the *Canterbury Tales*, is designed, first, to prompt two conflicting sense experiences of reading poetry and thereby to explore the kinds of cognitive and aesthetic demands those experiences of reading can make on an audience. From there, the *Confessio* moves deeper and deeper into the logic of prose and verse and into whether and how those two forms might combine to produce protrepsis.

As a specific example, the second Latin verse of the prologue mourns the passage of former times when justice governed the earth in perfect harmony, but it does so in language that makes full comprehension deliberately difficult:

> Tempus preteritum presens fortuna beatum
> Linquit, et antiquas vertit in orbe vias.
> Progenuit veterem concors dileccio pacem,
> Dum facies hominis nuncia mentis erat:
> Legibus vnicolor tunc temporis aura refulsit,
> Iusticie plane tuncque fuere vie.
> Nuncque latens odium vultum depingit amoris,
> Paceque sub ficta tempus ad arma tegit;
> Instar et ex variis mutabile Camelionitis
> Lex gerit, et regnis sunt noua iura novis:
> Climata que fuerant solidissima sicque per orbem
> Soluuntur, nec eo centra quietis habent.[48]

---

48. Gower, *Confessio amantis*, 6. "Now Fortune leaves the blessed time of yore, / And turns the antique customs on her wheel. / Harmonious love begat the ancient peace, / When yet man's face was herald of his mind: / The air of that age shone, one-hued, with laws; / The paths of justice then were plain and smooth. / Now hidden hatred paints a loving face, / And hides a time of war beneath feigned peace. / The law, chameleon-like, transforms and shifts: / In novel realms, new laws; and regions which / Were strong, through Fortune's wheel are rendered weak, / Now there a hub of quiet do they find" (Echard and Fanger, *Latin Verses in the Confessio amantis*, 5 and 7).

This poem, typical of the Latin verse in the *Confessio*, is characterized by highly wrought syntax: verbs are often decoupled from nouns, verbs often begin lines of verse, and modifiers are often separated from the nouns they modify. Indeed, in their introduction to the Latin verses and in their translations of them, Echard and Fanger call attention to their unusual syntactic wroughtness, noting how difficult it is to render these Latin verses into English.[49] These intricate syntactic effects make demands on a reader's Latin fluency precisely by refusing to superimpose rules of English word order onto Latin. Put otherwise, the poem exploits Latin syntax in order to frustrate vernacular reading competencies, since English is a language driven by word order, while Latin, with its inflections, does not need word order to make meaning. In the Latin verse, then, a space is created in which the temporal linearity of the reading experience is constantly destabilized; one must read, as it were, backward and forward, pulling together object and subject, noun and verb, modifier and modified from syntactically noncontiguous positions.

This nonlinear experience of reading the Latin head verses is brought into sharper relief—and is brought into relief specifically as a Boethian aesthetic experiment—by the English narrative poem that surrounds them. The English passage that immediately follows the Latin passage above is built around a Boethian thematic and reads as follows:

If I schal drawe in to my mynde
The tyme passed, thanne I fynde
The world stod thanne in al his welthe:
Tho was the lif of man in helthe,
Tho was plente, tho was richesse,
Tho was the fortune of prouesse,
Tho was knyhthode in pris be name,
Wherof the wyde worldes fame
Write in Cronique is yit withholde;
Justice of lawe tho was holde,
The privilege of regalie
Was sauf, and al the baronie

49. "The very things that make the verses of interest to us are often those that are least amenable to representation in English—his play upon Latin etymologies for example, or his idiosyncratic use of Latin's flexible word order" (*Latin Verses in the Confessio amantis*, xxx).

Worshiped was in his astat;
The citees knewen no debat,
The people stod in obeissance
Under the reule of governance

. . .

Now stant the crop under the rote,
The world is changed overal,
And therof most in special
That love is falle into discord.[50]

From this point, the vernacular narrative goes on for another seventy lines, continuing to develop the distinctly Boethian theme that this world, the "now" of lived experience, is a fallen world in comparison with the just and noble world of the past.[51] It is true, then, that the English poem that follows the Latin expands upon the meaning of the Latin, and does so by amplifying the latter's thematic Boethianness. But this amplification of Boethian thematics is not an end unto itself; instead it serves to ground the aesthetic experiment that subtends both the Latin lyric and the English narrative poems: the English here functions according to a radically different syntactic logic than that which governs the Latin. Whereas the word order of the Latin is complex and hard to unpack, the syntax in the Middle English is extremely straightforward—to such an extent that it seems to be a deliberate element of the *Confessio*'s style. Even though the poem does separate a few verbs from their subjects across line breaks ("was sauf" and "worshiped"), it nevertheless replicates the natural syntax of Middle English as closely as possible, rarely breaking with standard practices of word order simply to suit the exigencies of meter.

In apposition with each other, Gower's Latin poems show how Latin strategies of reading differ from those of English, highlighting how English is a language that aestheticizes linear order in language, while Latin, by dint of its relative freedom from word order, promotes recursion and

---

50. Gower, *Confessio amantis*, 93–108, 118–21.

51. In particular the fifth meter of book 2, which begins, "Felix nimium prior aetas / contenta fidelibus aruis / nec inerti perdita luxu, / facili quae sera solebat / ieiunia soluere glande. / Non Bacchica munera norant / liquido confundere melle / nec lucida uellera Serum / Tyrio miscere ueneno. / Somnos dabat herba salubres, / potum quoque lubricus amnis, / umbras altissima pinus. / Nondum maris alta secabat / nec mercibus undique lectis / noua litora uiderat hospes." (Bk. 2, m. 5, lines 1–15). As Gower may well have been aware, Chaucer reconceives this meter in his short lyric "The Former Age." See *Riverside Chaucer*, 650–51, and the note on p. 1083.

nonlinearity. Thus, Gower's English section replicates the cardinal aesthetic effect of Boethian prose—it renders sense-perceptible the causal order that comes with linear narrative—and the Latin replicates the time-bending aesthetics of Boethian meter, requiring readers to find words with like endings and map them onto each other, to construe the grammar and sense of the Latin poems. The *Confessio*'s particular reinvention of prosimetrum is in some ways very much in line with the eighth fragment of the *Canterbury Tales*: on the one hand, the *Confessio* presents a narrative form that makes temporal order palpable; on the other, it presents a lyrical form that makes temporal disorder palpable.

This reading of how the Latin and English work together resolves a central interpretive problem that has long perplexed Gower scholars. Many scholars of the Gowerian Latin lyrics, including those who are inclined to read them as "Boethian," note that while the relation of vernacular to Latin often seems to be a relation of discursive explanation to proverbial utterance, there are numerous instances in the *Confessio* where it is far from clear what interpretive work, exactly, the vernacular poem is designed to do on the Latin verses. Despite their supposed vernacular glosses in the English narrative, the Latin proems at the head of each book of the *Confessio* remain particularly difficult interpretive cruces: the Latin itself is challenging, the meaning of each proem is often unclear, as is the relation of each to both the book it precedes and the whole poem. In their introduction to these problems, Echard and Fanger suggest that Gower often uses the forbidding Latin to draw the reader in: by being "more demanding of the reader's involvement and attention," the Latin proems are "in keeping with Gower's overall endeavor in the *Confessio Amantis* to put the reader in the picture, to demand that he see and judge the action described in the poem for himself."[52] This may well be true, but the fact remains that while seeming to invite the greater engagement of the reader, Gower actually frustrates that involvement by blurring the meaning of the Latin poems through highly wrought syntax and by occulting their exact relation to the English vernacular narratives that follow them. Understanding the Latin and English as being marshaled and deployed for their syntactic renderings of nonlinearity and linear order, respectively, resolves this difficulty by suggesting that the English is there neither to expand upon nor to diminish the Latin, but instead to make the central realization of Boethius's consolation—the supervening presence of order—*felt*, in the vernacular's apposition with the Latin. The Latin/English verse dialectic is

52. Echard and Fanger, *Latin Verses in the Confessio amantis*, xxxvii.

not interpretative but aesthetic. The *Confessio* understands Boethius's formal investment in creating a feeling of order via linear narration and realizes that the vernacular has a particular syntactic capacity to create that feeling. Thus, the *Confessio* recreates Boethius's mixed form as a mixing of languages, in which the Latin functions as "meter" and the vernacular as "prose," each because of the particular strategies of reading that it necessitates through its level of syntactic complexity.

On one level, this set of observations suggests that the *Confessio* and Usk's *Testament* have strategic investments in common: both reconceive Boethius's formal twinning of prose and meter in part as a linguistic challenge. Both works, moreover, seem quick to associate English with prose and to use English in a way that replicates the function of prose in Boethius's *Consolation*. Seemingly, that is, both the *Confessio* and the *Testament* find in Boethius's twin form a way of representing the tense relationship between Latinity and vernacularity as a relationship between recursive, songful artistry and linear, prosaic elucidation, between complexity and simplicity, between lyrical monologism and "rude" dialogism.

But that mapping of English onto prosaicness, of vernacularity onto clarity, is as readily problematized by both authors as it is raised. As we have seen, the *Testament* explores the association between English prose and its supposed "rudeness," ultimately to demonstrate the possibility of holding simplicity and artfulness together in the single language and single form of English prose. The *Confessio*, too, deploys an easy dialectic between Latinate complexity and vernacular simplicity precisely to destabilize it and to suggest a new way of understanding the relationship between Latinity and vernacularity and between poetry and prose.

It does so first by introducing a secondary mode of Latinity—one that is straightforward, prosaic, and linear—in the form of the aforementioned prose Latin commentary in the margins of the poem. The Latin prose comments do not offer glosses on the Latin lyrics but instead appear toward the beginning of new Middle English sections of versified narrative. They call attention to what is about to transpire in the Middle English, forecasting narrated events yet to come in vernacular verse. Indeed, the vast majority of the glosses begin in one of three ways: with "hic" and a verb of narration ("narrat," "scribat," "describat," "loquitur," "queritur," "dicit," "declarat," "incipit," "ponit," and "tractat" all appear), with "de" plus an ablative noun phrase, or with "nota." All of these grammatical structures signal the primary purpose of the prose Latin glosses to be deictic, calling attention to the writtenness of the Middle English, its status as a textual object needing summary and unpacking.

Because of its fairly straightforward glossing function, the Latin prose of Gower's book is often passed over in the scholarship. But the Latin prose serves two important purposes. First, by implicitly asserting that the Middle English verse passages need glossing, the Latin proses construct the English as a language of complexity and alterity rather than a language of simplicity and familiarity. In so doing, they call into question the linguistic dyad that the *Confessio* creates between Latin lyric poetry and Middle English narrative. In that dyad, the English narratives read as easy, clear, syntactically linear elucidations of and expansions upon the compact and overwrought Latin lyrics. When the *Confessio* implicitly asserts, by this second linguistic dyad—between Latin prose glosses and Middle English verse—that Middle English verse itself needs prefacing and glossing, English verse becomes the new "Latin," the new learned discourse in need of unpacking and contextualization. Thus, by interspersing the Latin proses in the margins, the *Confessio* formally undermines any distinction between English as an open, clear, and linear language and Latin as a difficult, wrought, and recursive one.

Second, by introducing the Latin prose commentary, the *Confessio* creates a third formal term in its linguistic revision of prosimetrum, so that Gower's work begins to read as a triune compilation of lyric, narrative, and commentary—much like Dante's *Vita nuova*, though here the narrative part is Middle English, and both lyric and commentary are Latin.[53] In its relation to the lyrics, the Middle English functions as prose—discursive, clear, and linear. In its relation to the Latin prose commentaries, however, the Middle English seems more complex, more intricate, and decidedly more poetic. What this inclusion of the Latin proses does, then, is to disavow an easy binary between either Latin and English or poetry and prose. The Latin prose undercuts binaristic assumptions about the nature and purpose of each form and each language, showing the boundaries among lyric, narrative, and commentary, as well as between Latin and English, to be far more porous and shifting than the Boethian paradigm would allow. There is, in the *Confessio*, no absolute "Latin," no absolute vernacular, no absolute meter, no absolute prose. Latin and English, just like verse and prose, are relative categories, which have meaning only in comparison with another language or form.[54]

53. Olsen argues indeed that the *Confessio* is an English analogue for Dante's *Vita nuova*. (*Betwene Ernest and Game*, 6).

54. David Townsend suggests indeed that Latin(s) and vernacular(s) should be seen not as existing in dialectical opposition to each other but rather as on a continuum

The relativity of prose and poetry arises not only between Latin and English, and not only between the highly wrought and lyrical Latin head verses and the relatively straightforward Latin prose glosses, but also within the English poetry of the *Confessio*'s main narrative. Toward the end, in book 8, the narrator-poet Amans includes his epistle to Venus, in which he laments "the wofull peine of loves maladie."[55] As is clear from this first line, in this letter the vernacular poetic form shifts—suddenly and for the only time in the poem—from rhymed, octosyllabic, four-stress couplets to meticulous five-beat decasyllabic lines. Simultaneously, a stanzaic form appears, not surprisingly in the rime royal rhyme scheme of *ababbcc*. Suddenly, for the duration of the epistle, the *Confessio* follows the form of the *Troilus*.[56]

This is true not just in overt form but also in how syntax folds into stanzas and lines. Whereas in the four-stress rhymed couplets of the rest of the poem, there are no solid rhythmical markers for the ends of full sense units, in the rime royal epistle, the *Confessio*, like the *Troilus*, uses stanzas to bumper syntactic units at the level of the sentence. All of the twelve rime royal stanzas end at a full stop, at the end of a sentence. This increased metrical and syntactic organization extends down from the level of the stanza to the level of the line: whereas the rest of the *Confessio* manifests a good deal of enjambment, the rime royal letter is careful to tailor clauses to full line lengths make sense units sense-perceptible through the rhythmical regularity of the rime royal stanzaic verse. In effect, rime royal in the *Confessio*, as in the *Troilus*, becomes a mode of rendering syntax, and thereby ideation, sense-perceptible.

When the epistle does create strong enjambments between lines, they are motivated by immediate context, usually to highlight the division in Amans's own psyche. Describing the woful pain of love's malady, the poem reads, "I finde it evere redy to assaile / Mi resoun, which that can him noght defende," using the line break to render sonically and rhythmi-

---

with each other, interpenetrating and fluid, multiple and ever-shifting in their precise relation to each other. Townsend, "Latinities in England: 894–1135," workshop at New York University, January 22, 2010. Townsend has subsequently and recently published an essay on the methodological and theoretical problems and opportunites of medieval Latin studies that elaborates on these notions. See Townsend, "Current Questions and Future Prospects of Medieval Latin Studies," 15–19.

55. Bk. 8, line 2217.

56. Gower may well also be drawing on the interpolated verse epistles that appear in contemporary French romances. For discussion of such letters, see Boulton, *Song in the Story*, 152–70.

cally perceptible Amans's own amatory self-alienation.[57] The pinnacle of this practice arrives in the letter's third stanza, when Amans wonders, "Hou I schal spede, and thus betwen the tweie / I stonde, and not if I schal live or deie."[58] Here, through the formal break, the poetic speaker literally stands at the fulcrum between the two lines—"thus between the two / he stands"—thereby aestheticizing the liminality of his own state, standing between life and death, as a state that straddles two lines of verse. This usage of rime royal's metrical and stanzaic structure not only promotes order and the sensory perception of syntactic boundaries but also, and perhaps more powerfully, allows divergences from that pattern to be perceived all the more readily—much as we saw in the *Troilus*. Amans's letter to Venus, like Chaucer's letter from Troilus to Criseyde, seems keen to show how poetic form could make answer to the syntactic and aesthetic demands of epistolary theories of prose, to show how rhythm, rhyme, and stanzaic form could create sensible order for syntax and meaning. It is, in the *Confessio* as in the *Troilus*, the task of poetry—not prose—to create epistolary structure, and to do so by relying on meter, rhythm, rhyme, and stanzaic construction as the edifices of syntax, cadencing, and sentence. With its inclusion of the five-beat lines and stanzaic form in the letter, the *Confessio* again shows "prose" and "meter" to be relative states; just as there are two levels of Latin in the poem, there are two levels of Middle English verse, one that operates in a fashion fairly close to natural speech, while the other uses the full arsenal of artificial form to structure its syntactic order and to aestheticize epistolary "sentence," meaning both content and syntactic structure.

The *Confessio*'s revision of the prosimetric formal embodiment of ethical transformation does not end with the inclusion of a prose commentary to unmoor the Latin-English and prose-verse dialectics, nor does it end with the inclusion of a rime royal letter to complicate how vernacular verse can work to aestheticize meaning. Instead, the revision reaches its fullest articulation when the narrator-hero Amans finally meets Venus. Being the goddess of love, she seems a reasonable person for Amans to ask for counsel, but Venus and Amans seem characterologically unable to understand each other—despite Amans's well-crafted rime royal letter. Wetherbee sees Amans and Venus's interlocutory standstill as a troubling, ongoing manifestation of the interpretive stymieing that the work creates in the incommensurability between the Latin prose, the Latin songs, and

57. Bk. 8, lines 2221–22.
58. Bk. 8, lines 2234–35.

the English narrative.[59] To be sure, the formal tension between Latin and English serves to set up the poem's eventual standstill, but it does so by gesturing toward transformative prosimetrum as a set of literary topoi of form and function, not by radically questioning the very possibility of making meaning. The final scene of the poem constitutes its most savvy and fluent engagement with the paradigm of mixed-form protrepsis. In that scene, all expectations are reversed; in that reversal comes the *Confessio*'s final and fullest appropriation of Boethian form and function as a joint resource for a cross-linguistic comedy of ethical transformation in a narrator-author-hero.

The end of the poem reveals two things: first, Amans is old, far past his sexual prime and thus a bizarre candidate for being a "lover" in the first place. Second, Amans is none other than John Gower himself. Ardis Butterfield sees this moment as the high-water mark of the complexity of Gower's representation of his own authorship:

> Through this disorienting revelation, the distinction between author and persona that had seemed so clear earlier in the work appears to fail. *Confessio amantis* causes the collapse of its distinction between *auctor* and *amans* to upset that between *auctor* and narrator. This is a powerfully unsettling manoeuvre, especially since it is performed both within and without the narrative frame of the work. It heavily qualifies our ability to regard author, narrator, and lover as either stable or distinct categories.[60]

True, the collapse of distinctions among levels of narration is unsettling within the *Confessio*, but it also serves precisely to settle the work more deeply into a larger literary-historical frame. Similar to how the *Retractions* works for Chaucer, this collapse of author, narrator, and character into one revealed identity in the person of John Gower also collapses the generic distance between the *Confessio* and the *Consolation* yet further than all the Boethian thematic and formal echoes in the poem have already done. For Boethius, the identity between character, narrator, and author is central to the poem's logic of teaching: the recursive mapping of character onto narrator, narrator onto author, and, eventually, author onto audience is designed to make the audience feel implicated in the learning

---

59. "The impasse between Venus and Amans is in large part a failure of communication between the Latin and vernacular traditions" ("Latin Structure," 24).

60. Butterfield, "Articulating the Author," 80.

process—it is designed to create protrepsis. By reading the *Consolation*, a reader learns that like the writing, narrating, and acting Boethius, he or she is a lover of worldly delights. By reading the *Consolation*, a reader, along with Boethius, gradually learns the limitations of his or her own physical powers, the inevitability of his or her mortality, and the wisdom of a turn toward God.

All of these narrative elements ostensibly exist in Gower's narrative as well: he writes his poem to invite his readers into a higher state of understanding, and he makes this protreptic intent quite clear at the very end, when he shifts from self-narration to gnomic proclamation.

> Bot thilke love which that is
> Withinne a mannes herte affermed,
> And stant of charite confermed,
> Such love is goodly forto have,
> Such love mai the body save,
> Such love mai the soule amende,
> The hyhe God such love ous sende
> Forthwith the remenant of grace;
> So that above in thilke place
> Wher resteth love and alle pes,
> Oure joie mai ben endeles.[61]

This set of insistences replicates what Boethius presents at the end of the *Consolation* and what Chaucer presents at the end of the *Troilus*, suggesting that the audience's capacity for love and understanding should have been reformed over the course of reading the foregoing poem, "standing confirmed in charity" from the reading process so that "oure joie mai ben endeles." The poem, then, should have been ethically transformative for us, as it has been for Amans.[62] At this late moment, it unveils itself as a protreptic work.

The passage grounds its own modeling function grammatically, in its

---

61. Bk. 8, lines 3162–72; cf. lines 3098–3114.

62. Focusing on the prologues of each work rather than their ends, and on choice of vernacular language rather than local instances of grammar, Olsen notes that Gower and Dante share a common will to endorse the vernacular language as a means of connecting with the "lust" of the common audiences (*Betwene Ernest and Game*, 9) and that both of their mixed-form poems are designed to reach outward to implicate readers in the transformations undergone by narrators and authors.

switch from "I" or "the lover" to "we" and "us." But there is something deeply ironic in this turn toward "us," because it is unclear exactly what ethical lessons Amans is supposed to take away from his interactions with Genius at this point. Instead of clarifying that problem, what happens is the demystification of the putatively amorous narrator, Amans, via the revelation that he is the old, hoar, and moral author, John Gower.

> Wherinne anon myn hertes yhe
> I caste, and sih my colour fade,
> Myn yhen dymme and al unglade,
> Mi chiekes thinne, and al my face
> With Elde I myhte se deface,
> So riveled and so wo besein,
> That ther was nothing full ne plein,
> I syh also myn heres hore.
> Mi will was tho to se nomore
> Outwith, for ther was no plesance.[63]

This is why Amans *cum* Gower is so quick—even eager—to accept the verdict that he should turn his attention away from the amatory and toward the contemplative: he is made to see himself, his true nature, and to register that nature as aged and unfit for lovemaking. Whereas, for Boethius the gradual recuperation of the narrator's sense of self entails a recovery of ideas of harmonic likeness and divine order, and for Chaucer in the *Troilus* the narrator's turn to God is born of a tragic recognition of the futility of earthly delights, for Gower the turn toward divine love is based on the entirely bathetic recognition that one cannot gracefully continue to be a lover in any other sense than the spiritual once one has reached a certain age. Gower's disclosure not only of his identity but, more importantly, of his age thus demystifies the ethically transformative logic of the *Consolatio* genre and its formal mode of creating protrepsis, showing that ethical transformation is a function of aging and that it need not necessarily come of learning to feel and believe in the comforting order of the universe through the aesthetic action of literature. Whereas Boethius begins his narrative by lamenting how old age has deformed and reduced his body—in Chaucer's rendering, "For eelde is comyn unwarly upon me, hasted by the harmes that Y have, and sorwe hath comandid his age to ben in me. Heeris hore arn schad overtymeliche upon myn heved, and the

63. Bk. 8, lines 2824–33.

slakke skyn trembleth of myn emptid body"[64]—and Philosophy's project thenceforward is, in effect, to rejuvenate his soul, Gower suggests a far more practical and more comically inevitable trajectory for self-knowledge. The object of his narrative is to show how the body, not the mind or soul, is preprogrammed to shunt a person's energies, at the end of life, away from the world and toward divine contemplation. One's aging sex drive, by its naturally planned obsolescence, urges one inevitably toward the kind of salvation that Boethius understands and represents only as hard-won by an unflagging devotion to philosophy and a carefully scripted exposure to songful meter and argumentative prose.[65]

With this final revelation, suddenly, the reader, like Amans-Gower, is made to realize that he or she is implicated in this final turn from love toward mortality. With dour old Gower, "we" the readers now turn toward the necessity of taking comfort not in desire for worldly, sexual love but in the divine "pes" of the "hyhe love" of God's "charite." "We," who might not have been able to attain philosophical learning about the futility of worldly desire from the poem that has gone before, can relax, since "we" can rely on another source of ethical salvation: these mortal coils will mandate a turn away from lust and toward the divine, whether "we" like it or not. The end of the *Confessio* offers a pragmatic reprise of the final literary dynamics of the *Consolation*. In this pragmatic turn, Gower's adaptation of transformative literature does a particular kind of work that neither Boethius in the *Consolation* nor Alain in *De planctu* nor even Chaucer in the *Troilus* or the *Canterbury Tales* does: it calls into question the tone of all of the foregoing, suddenly fitting a comical lens into a reader's eye as she recognizes her own mortal frailty in the aged and withered body of John Gower.[66]

In conjunction with its bathetic but nevertheless transformative out-

---

64. *Boece*, bk.1, m. 1, lines 13–17.

65. Rather than focusing on the aging process as a demystification of Boethius, Michael Cherniss reads the end as acutely and unironically Boethian: "By the end of the vision Amans has in fact been purged of his love for his uncooperative lady: his circumstances are unchanged, but his concerns have shifted from earthly to moral wisdom" (*Boethian Apocalypse*, 102). He reads Gower, that is, as a straight Boethian. Michael Means, similarly, sees the *Confessio* as a "pure" consolatio (Consolatio *Genre in Medieval English Literature*, 59–65).

66. As Watt has shown, Gower's long-standing reputation as "moral" and hence stolid, rigid, and unfunny grossly mischaracterizes his poetics: Gower is a poet who deliberately and consistently "undermines . . . by an alternative, ludic self-portrayal" the authoritative and moralizing voices that he so often sets up (*Amoral Gower*, 153).

come, the *Confessio*'s deliberately difficult formal oscillation among Latin lyric, English narrative, and Latin prose commentary pushes a reader to encounter the poem, overall, as a gentle but focused parody of the *Conso-latio*, a coy destabilization of the very literary-theoretical parameters that animate Boethius's work and that Chaucer familiarizes and domesticates into vernacular, fictive, poetic discourse in both the *Troilus* and the *Canterbury Tales*. Once "we" realize that Amans, the lover, is an impotent, old John Gower, the Latin head verses retroactively appear as a collection of miniature jokes. At the end of the poem, we readers are made to realize that our drive to make a coherent and revelatory sense of the dialogue between English narrative and Latin lyrics, or between Latin prose glosses and English poem, is symptomatic of our larger tendency to look outside ourselves and our own lived, bodily experiences for some fetishized, supervening truth—a truth Gower demonstrates in his final bathetic turn.

In revising the *Consolation* toward an ironic conclusion, particularly a conclusion whose irony inheres in biological realism about sexual potency, Gower's *Confessio* again lays bare its perforation by other protreptics, written after and in response to the *Consolation* itself.[67] At its end, as at its beginning, the *Confessio* is informed by Alain de Lille's *De planctu naturae*. Throughout *De planctu*, Alain represents ethical error as sexually deviant behavior. For him, damaged or destabilized masculinity is a sign of ethical weakness and vice, and Gower responds to this mapping of sexual deviance onto ethical error throughout his *Confessio*.[68] The final scenes of the *Confessio*, however, engage with Alain's sexual ethics in order to rethink Boethian protrepsis: here, a problematized and traduced masculine self appears as a surefire way out of ethical uncertainty, rather than, as it had been for Alain, the quickest way into that uncertainty. *De planctu*'s nightmare scenario, in other words, becomes the *Confessio*'s protreptic transcendence, through Gower's nimble weaving together of two different protreptic models in his intertextual and culturally fluent conclusion.[69]

---

67. For analyses of other medieval and late antique works that inform Gower's synthetic *Confessio*, see Minnis, "John Gower, Sapiens in Ethics and Politics." According to Minnis, "Gower's *Confessio Amantis* seems to work by assimilation of materials which, although they may appear to be heterogeneous to the modern reader, would have been regarded as quite compatible by the learned mediaeval reader" (225).

68. See Watt, *Amoral Gower*, 28.

69. For a reading of Gower's intertextual writing strategy, see Economou, "Character Genius." For the larger literary history of the figure of "Genius," see also Baker, "Priesthood of Genius."

The *Confessio* registers the complexity of the historical linkage of the mixed form with literary protrepsis and asserts that a comic realization can contain as many revelations as hard-going philosophical work. In the end of his work, Gower makes his most playful and most authoritative Boethian gesture: he demonstrates that he, the author and creator of the *Confessio*, can play the protreptic game according to his own formal rules. He can deploy Latin and English as though they are linguistic analogues for meter and prose but can then undercut that ready dialectical identification by introducing the prose Latin commentaries on the one hand and the rime royal English epistle on the other. Having reinvented the mixed form, he reveals at the very end of his poem that these intricate forms are not essential to finding transcendence or to escaping worldly affections— our human, mortal bodies will do the "philosophizing" for us. Gower's work deploys Boethian literary practice and theory as topoi of spiritually transformative, didactic literature, and it uses them as a springboard for a comical revision and reinterrogation of philosophical protrepsis. Thus, in the *Confessio*, Boethius, Alain, and Chaucer have become available as provocations not just for serious literary and philosophical work but also and perhaps more fully for a comical revelation of readerly naïveté and for a concomitant display of authorial mastery of Gower's Latin and vernacular literary precedents.

This setting up of readers to become aware of their own naïve engagement with protreptic narrative is not malicious but generous: the poem provides an opportunity to recognize the artificiality of ethical literature, to recognize that ethical writing is tropaic, ornamented, culturally inflected, and fictive and that it relies on readers' expectations for its efficacy. This final turn toward a demystification of ethics urges a greater awareness of how literature works, in part, by its reliance on familiar tropes of form and function. The comic revelation at the end of Gower's poem is not a snub directed at the reader but an impetus to think more deeply about how and whether literature can—or even needs to—embody ethical learning. The *Confessio* invites readers to laugh at their own understandings of ethically salvific literature, of what that literature should look like, and of how it should work. The *Confessio* is bent on debunking the idea that any one-to-one relationship could stably exist between aesthetic form and ethical transformation. The poem moves away from a mixed-form protreptic precisely by inviting readers to expect a transformation and then suggesting that that expectation does not even need to be fulfilled in order for the poem to have stable ethical meaning for the reader and the narrator.

This revelation of the inevitability of personal transformation—from

youth to age—is not, in itself, the only payoff in the poem. Quite the contrary, it serves a leveling function, drawing the author-narrator-hero and all
possible readers onto the same ontological playing field: human mortality.
That leveling function proves crucial to the larger political ambitions of
the poem. Much like Usk, Gower builds into his protreptic poem a section
that is decidedly political in tenor and subject: the seventh book of the
Confessio amantis in particular meditates on the nature of governmental ethics and makes prescriptive recommendations for right rule.[70] Often noted as a *Fürstenspiegel*, this book sets forth the rules and principles
by which good rule can be assured and sustained.[71] In this book, Gower
repurposes his own protreptic narrative—ostensibly inward-focused, self-
critical, and amatory—as an outward-focused narrative of counsel to the
rulers of England. In the best of times, offering advice to monarchs can be
a dicey business; during the sociopolitical upheaval of the end of the fourteenth and beginning of the fifteenth century, Gower chooses to couch his
counsel with extra care.[72] First, of course, being positioned toward the end
of the *Confessio*, the seventh book does not read as central to the book's
overall project, which dampens some of its potentially incendiary impact.
Second, the penitential framework of the entire *Confessio*, arcing through
the seven deadly sins, implicates the narrator himself first and foremost
in all the vices against which he later cautions rulers in the seventh book.
Thus, the ethical accountability that could fall too squarely on the shoul-

70. Alastair Minnis has shown that Gower set up his work to explore vernacular
responses to the problems of ethics that he laid out in his extrinsic, Latin prologue. In
Minnis's view, although Gower "cannot solve all the problems which he canvassed in
the extrinsic prologue," he can devise a vast series of vernacular meditations on ethics,
in which ethical questions are addressed initially within an amatory framework. For
Minnis, Gower is a poet who filters Latinate ethical questions through the conven-
tionally recognizable and parsable frameworks of vernacular amatory poetics. Minnis
also notes that "Gower's principalis materia falls within the subject-area of ethics; his
other material falls within the subject-area of politics which, according to Aristotle,
embraces the subject-area of ethics" (*Medieval Theory of Authorship*, 183); see also
Nicholson, *Love and Ethics in Gower's* Confessio amantis, 8–27, 103.

71. Indeed, in the last few decades of Gower criticism, the function of his massive
Middle English poem has been determined to be largely political and public; what reads,
on the surface, as a poem about romantic love is, on a deeper level, about the love that a
ruler should show toward his people. See Peck, *Kingship and Common Profit*; Middleton, "Idea of Public Poetry"; and Simpson, *Sciences and the Self*, 217–29.

72. His two dedications to the *Confessio*, one of which addresses Richard II and the
other Henry IV, make plain that Gower was keenly aware of his need to tailor his work
to his monarch with some degree of sensitivity from the very outset of his project.

ders of a royal reader is distributed instead between him and his hero-narrator-author. Third, and perhaps most important, positioned hard upon the heels of the seventh book's explicit advice, the eighth book's revelation of John Gower's own physical frailty and apparent mortality serves an important purpose: by foregrounding his own mortality and frailty—by, indeed, performing his own sexual impotence—at the end of his poem, Gower takes the sting out of his royal advice-giving.[73] Gower casts himself as a depleted old man—as Boethius cast himself at the beginning of the *Consolation*—and as anything but a political upstart or insurgent. Fourth and finally, Gower situates his political writings within a mode, both formal and functional, that has become recognizable in Middle English literary culture as ethical fiction: the mixed-form protreptic. Like Usk, through his carefully crafted literary fiction Gower makes his political recommendations without seeming fully to leave the realm of recognizable and culturally acceptable literary topoi of fictive self-representation.

73. Lynn Staley suggests how the public and political culture of late medieval England was created in part by literary experimentation; she uses the dual dedication of Gower's poem as a starting point and touchstone for this reading ("Gower, Richard II, Henry of Derby, and the Making of Public Culture").

CHAPTER SIX

Hoccleve and the Convention
of Mixed-Form Protrepsis

The playfully iconoclastic and profoundly intertextual spirit of revision to the twin paradigm of prosimetrum and protrepsis that we find in Gower's poem reaches its apogee in the late works of Thomas Hoccleve. In the 1380s and early 1390s, when Chaucer, Gower, and Usk compose their reengagements with and reinventions of prosimetrum, Hoccleve begins a career in the court of the Privy Seal, and his years as a public bureaucrat bring him into close contact with the literary oeuvres of both Chaucer and Gower.[1] During his public service, however, he is stricken with a severe mental illness, resulting in an extended leave of absence from public office.[2] After his return to sanity and to office, he composes two poems, "The Complaint" and "The Dialogue."[3] Both of these works, which Hoccleve places next to each other at the beginning of his self-compiled collection *The Series*, are couched as autobiographical, seeking to account for his period of madness and to assure any reader that the madness will not return.[4] Because of their feeling of genuineness and immediacy, the "Com-

1. See Bowers "Thomas Hoccleve and the Politics of Tradition," for a detailing of Hoccleve's twin indebtedness to both Chaucer and Gower. Hoccleve's extensive scribal exposure to Gower as well as to Chaucer is also laid out in Doyle and Parkes, "Productions of Copies," esp. 182–85 and 199–203, and in J. J. Smith, "Trinity Gower D-Scribe."

2. For a full description of what is known of Hoccleve's life, see Burrow, *Thomas Hoccleve*, 1–29.

3. Burrow notes that the *Dialogue* may have been written as early as the beginning of 1420, despite a majority of scholars who think 1421–22, during Gloucester's second regency ("Thomas Hoccleve: Some Redatings," 366–70).

4. Durham University Library MS Cosin V.iii.9. See Hoccleve, *Thomas Hoccleve: A Facsimile of the Autograph Verse Manuscripts*, xvii, xxviii–xxxiii, xxxvii.

plaint" and the "Dialogue" are usually read "straight" by critics.[5] More specifically, they are read as manifestations of Hoccleve's serious desire to justify himself and vindicate his mental health before his peers and imagined detractors.[6] In what follows, I will suggest that these two poems together enact a literary meditation that, although pronouncedly autobiographical in outline, is anything but "straight" in its formal execution. The "Complaint" and "Dialogue" together constitute a supple and comical engagement with literary theory and practice of mixed-form protreptic writing in the late English Middle Ages—though in a manner quite different from what appears in Gower's *Confessio*. This engagement originates in Hoccleve's combined awareness and suspicion of the mixed form as the sine qua non of protreptic writing, and that dual awareness and suspicion proves a springboard for his eventual disassembling of prosimetrum and protrepsis in the rest of his *Series*.[7]

"THE COMPLAINT" AND "THE DIALOGUE": EVOKING BOETHIAN PROSIMETRUM IN A NARRATIVE OF TRANSFORMATION

Like Chaucer, Usk, and Gower, Hoccleve encourages readers to discern Boethian valences in his poems by peppering them with Boethian echoes: he interpolates Boethian thematics and deals explicitly with the problem of consolation in both the "Complaint" and the "Dialogue." But because

5. In this vein, Jennifer Bryan calls Hoccleve "the most inward of poets," who "cannot possibly be accused of doubleness, because he has already displayed his inner life to such an intimate degree that we can hardly suspect him of harboring anything deeper" ("Hoccleve, the Virgin, and the Politics of Complaint," 1172, 1175, 1184). Though this trend predominates in scholarship, Hoccleve's authorial persona has not always been read as entirely sincere or unartificed; David Greetham argues that Hoccleve deliberately crafts a literary persona that would allow him to achieve his aesthetic and sociopolitical goals ("Self-Referential Artifacts," 242–43). This reading of Hoccleve's depiction of himself strikes me as absolutely right, and I will return to it later in this chapter, and in my conclusion.

6. Many champions of reading Hoccleve as a bureaucratic and Lancastrian subject still tend to read him "seriously." For a review of earlier works that take Hoccleve seriously and "at his word," see Greetham, "Self-Referential Artifacts," 243 n. 10.

7. Greetham acknowledges Hoccleve's debt to Boethius, saying that "much of Hoccleve's work in the *Regiment*, the *Series* and elsewhere is derived from, and an imitation of, Boethius, the generic archetype for the medieval Menippean anatomy" ("Self-Referential Artifacts," 248).

of his overdetermined pose of personal authenticity and his seeming inability to take the very consolations toward which his writing repeatedly gestures, "the Boethian label has never really stuck" as a way of understanding Hoccleve's poetic project in composing the *Series*.[8] Instead,
critics have lately focused on the relation of Hoccleve's constantly fore-
grounded interiority to his professional life as a bureaucrat and scribe.[9]
Fair enough, but the looming question remains: Why does he make those
gestures toward Boethius and his ideas, given that Hoccleve himself seems
so invested in the authority of his own personal experience? Why does he
align his writings with a seminal philosophical work of the Middle Ages
if his own sensibilities are so comfortably aligned with the office of the
Privy Seal? In what follows, I will suggest that the "Complaint" and "Dialogue" constitute a miniature and polemical reinvention of mixed-form
protrepsis. From their demonstration of Hoccleve's fluency in the literary
mode of mixed-form protreptic, these two poems then inaugurate a highly
experimental set of literary pairings in the rest of his *Series*. Together, the
various short pieces that Hoccleve collects and serializes in the *Series* constitute a sustained critique of how literary writing and reading use form to
convey a narrator's ethical transformation and initiate readerly protrepsis.

The *Series* first signals its investment in how literature works on the
human psyche about two-thirds of the way through the "Complaint."

> This othir day / a lamentacioun
> Of a woful man / in a book I sy,
> To whom wordes / of consolacioun
> Resoun yaf / spekynge effectuelly;
> And well esid / myn herte was therby,
> For whan I had a whyle / in the book red
> With the speeche of Resoun / was I wel fed.[10]

This stanza, and those that follow it, are among the most densely intertextual in the "Complaint." As A. G. Rigg has shown, this section of Hoccleve's

8. See Bryan, "Hoccleve, the Virgin, and the Politics of Complaint," 1172.

9. See E. Knapp, "Bureaucratic Identity and the Construction of the Self " and
"Eulogies and Usurpations"; Simpson, "Nobody's Man"; Scanlon, "King's Two Voices";
Pearsall, "Hoccleve's *Regement of Princes*."

10. Thomas Hoccleve, "The Complaint," in *Thomas Hoccleve's Complaint and
Dialogue*, lines 309–15. All further citations from "The Complaint" are taken from this
text, from Burrow's "edited text."

poem is patterned closely after Isidore of Seville's *Synonyma*, another late antique protreptic work, in which a personified Reason offers consolation to her pupil.[11] But writing a century after Boethius, Isidore's own sense of what might constitute a rational, consoling dialogue is informed by the *Consolation of Philosophy*. Hoccleve amplifies this intertextual echo by situating his calque on Isidore in the larger framework of his own illness-and-recovery narrative. After indicating that he was "well fed" by the speech of "Reason"—equally a reenvisioning of Boethius's Lady Philosophy and an Englishing of Isidore's *Ratio*—Hoccleve presents at once a vernacular synopsis of the *Consolation* and a borrowing from Isidore's *Synonyma*. This synoptic and intertextual aria reveals Hoccleve's own sense of how consolation is meant to take its effect via literature. In Hoccleve's understanding of literary consolation, by reading through the "wordes of consolacioun" of Reason, a reader is meant to take "effectuel" nourishment and to have his heart "esid." The reading experience that the "Complaint" describes seems quite able to initiate a psychological transformation for the narrating Hoccleve, a transformation of cognition and affect in him that parallels that which takes place in the "woeful man" to whom Reason effectually speaks.

But Hoccleve's literary analysis of how literary consolation works quickly becomes deeply challenging to protreptic literary philosophy. His admiring synopsis of the *Synonyma* and his framing of it with his own illness narrative, reminiscent of the *Consolation*, last only for a few stanzas before he interrupts himself to ironize how the reading of these consoling works affected him. Hoccleve reveals that he has read only part of the book his friend loaned him, and for the most mundane of reasons: the friend who loaned it to him has asked for it back. Even so, Hoccleve affirms that he has learned his ethically-transformative lesson from his reading:

> Yit haue I caght
> Sum of the doctrine / by Resoun taght
> To the man / as aboue haue I said,
> Whereof I holde me / ful wel apaid.

11. "[W]hatever the personal, autobiographical, content of the Complaint, it is functionally a lesson for other men: Hoccleve presents an exemplum of a man (narrated in the first person) suffering, just as Isidore did (dramatizing the lament of the man as part of a dialogue.) The function, and I would assume the intention, of both works was to act as a consolation to other men—just as Boethius did in the *Consolatio philosophiae* or Petrarch in the *De remediis utriusque fortunae*, to name only two outstanding works of the genre—and especially to justify the works of God to men." Rigg, "Hoccleve's Complaint and Isidore of Seville," 574.

> For euere sythen / set haue I the lesse
> By the peples / ymaginacioun,
> Talkynge this and that / of my seeknesse
>
> . . .
>
> Farwel my sorwe / I caste it to the cok!
>
> . . .
>
> Make al myn olde / affeccioun resorte,
> And in hope of that / wole I me conforte.[12]

Evidently, even reading only a part of Reason's comforting words has had a profound effect on Hoccleve: he asserts to his own audience that he has "caght" Reason's lessons, despite not having read the whole book. In this seeming homage to the efficacy of transformative writing and its ability to "conforte" a reader, then, Hoccleve deftly ironizes the very idea that literary work, by virtue of its form overall or its contents taken as a whole, could produce a transformation for its narrator, much less model one for its reader. The suggestion that a reader could be fully healed or ethically renewed by a partial, selective, or interrupted reading of a narrative of transformation, be it the *Synonyma* or the *Consolation*, undercuts the cardinal principles on which authors of protreptic fictions base their theories of literary efficacy and learning. Namely, it undercuts the notion that protrepsis consists in a sustained experience of witnessing the full and successful transformation of a narrator/hero from a state of despair to a state of joy. Interrupted reading should forestall the gradual, cumulative learning process that protreptics represent and embody. Indeed, to read only part of a protreptic, to be stopped before one has reached the end, is to fail to witness the would-be transformed narrating character's final turn from worldly concerns to divine faith and philosophical well-being—the turn that perfects and concludes the foregoing process of ethical reeducation. Hoccleve's insistence that, despite his not having finished reading through his borrowed book, he has nevertheless taken some kind of consolation calls into question the basic premises of how protreptic narrative works to represent and model the reattainment of mental health.[13]

---

12. "Complaint," lines 375–81, 386, 391–92.

13. Karen Smyth suggests that Hoccleve's various "misreadings" enable him to render multiple temporalities available in his *Series* ("Reading Misreadings in Thomas Hoccleve's *Series*"). My reading of Hoccleve's deliberate Boethianness builds on this observation; his willful and comical misreading of the *Consolation* makes Boethius

The "Complaint" carries this reinterrogation of how transformation might take place via literary reading through to its end. In the final three stanzas, Hoccleve represents himself as the successful convert to healthier thinking and feeling: he gives thanks to God, recognizing that his madness and recovery were both produced by divine will. Then, like Chaucer in his *Retractions*, he turns from his worldly writings to holy prayer. The poem ends as follows:

> And hens forward / to sette myn entente
> Vnto his deitee / to do plesance
> And tamende / my synful gouernance.
>
> Laude and honour / and thanke vnto thee be,
> Lord God / that salue art / to al heuynesse:
> Thank of my welthe / and myn aduersitee,
> Thank of myn elde / and of my seeknesse,
> And thank be / to thyn infynyt goodnesse
> For thy yiftes / and benefices alle;
> And vnto thy mercy / and grace I calle.[14]

Like the *Troilus* narrator at the end of the *Troilus*, Hoccleve sees that God alone is the solution to heaviness and sorrow, and he can now promise "hence forward" to set his intention on God; like the Chaucer pilgrim at the end of the *Canterbury Tales*, Hoccleve seems now able "to amend his sinful governance" and thank God for all his "gifts and benefices." Like Boethius, Hoccleve seems to register God's "infinite goodness" as the final and only true source of comfort for an ailing soul. Ending his poem in the way he does, Hoccleve deliberately and recognizably aligns himself and his project with protreptic writing, a tradition embodied at once by Chaucer, Boethius, and Isidore.

But Hoccleve's final protreptic turn, rooted in a willful misapprehension of the nature of protreptic reading, remains ironic, becoming only more so as Hoccleve moves from the "Complaint" not, in fact, to holy prayer but instead to the decidedly worldly "Dialogue with a Friend." This move reveals that Hoccleve's work of healing is half achieved at best: now

---

at once present, a living part of the contemporary readerly landscape of late medieval England, and profoundly past, a literary forebear so always already overfamiliar that his work's power is more talismanic than actual.

14. "Complaint," lines 404–13.

that he has internalized ethically transformative lessons from his abortive reading of Reason's book, it seems, he must enter into and represent in writing a salvific and rational dialogue with his unnamed "Friend" who comes to visit him after his recovery from madness. Once the Friend arrives, Hoccleve begins by reading him "The Complaint"; in so doing, he mimics the beginning of the *Consolation*, in which Boethius pens his own lamentations and then recounts the reasons he has written them to Philosophy, and thus he steers his *Series* more decisively toward the Boethian tradition.[15] In mentioning that he "redde hym my conpleynte," Hoccleve casts himself again as a new Boethius and casts his Friend as a presumptive Philosophy.[16]

But it becomes immediately clear that the reworking of the *Consolation* that we find in the "Dialogue" is anything but naïve or obeisant mimicry. Whereas Philosophy urged Boethius (and Pandarus urged Troilus) to lay forth all his sorrows, arguing that divulgence of pain would ease it,[17] Hoccleve's Friend urges him at first to keep his sorrows to himself, when confronted with Hoccleve's desire to publish his complaint:

> "Nay, Thomas, waar / do nat so.
> If thow be wys / of that mateere ho!
> Reherce thow it nat / ne it awake;
> Keepe al that cloos / for thyn honoures sake."[18]

Thus, the "Dialogue" reveals a comical slippage between Hoccleve's potentially salvific dialogue with a friend and Boethius's discussions with Philosophy: unlike Boethius, sealed up in a prison cell with only his fair

15. In Chaucer's translation, Boece begins, "Allas! I wepynge am constreyned to bygynnen vers of sorwful matere . . . For lo, rendynge muses of poetes enditen to me thynges to ben writen." *Boece*, bk. 1, pr. 1, sentences 1–2, 3–5. At the end of this lamentation penned under constraint, Philosophy appears, and Boece quickly turns to explain to her why he is writing his lamentations. See bk. 1, pr. 4.

16. Hoccleve, "The Dialogue," in *Thomas Hoccleve's Complaint and Dialogue*, line 17. All further quotations from this poem will be drawn from this edition, from Burrow's "edited text" when the lines are before line 302, and from the "Durham MS" text thereafter.

17. In the *Boece*, Philosophy urges her pupil, "Yif thou abides after helpe of thi leche, the byhoveth discovere thy wownde." Bk. 1, pr. 4, sentences 4–6. In the *Troilus*, Pandarus urges, "For whoso list have helyng of his leche, / To hym byhoveth first unwre his wownde." Bk. 1, lines 857–58.

18. "Dialogue," lines 25–28.

Lady Philosophy, Hoccleve is a public servant and thus lives in the public eye. For this reason, he should consider the impact his writings might have on the opinions of those around him. Hoccleve's Friend, that is, reveals the gap that exists between the somewhat idealistic *Consolation* and the pragmatic realities of Hoccleve's own life, suggesting that Hoccleve cannot expect to receive approbation and absolution just because of his writings. Literature, the Friend suggests, does not solve all problems; it also creates them, especially when one is an author of one's own experiences, since any act of self-narration is a public performance of one's internal state that might simply create new problems. As Hoccleve's Friend begins to sound more like a mock Philosophy than like Philosophy's latest sincere incarnation, Hoccleve's work becomes increasingly critical of and eager to destabilize its "straight" relation to any Boethian analogue.

The slippage between Hoccleve's *Series* and protreptic literature gains momentum as the "Dialogue" proceeds. Rather than being gradually led to reason by the measured and authoritative counsels of the Friend who acts as both mentor and healer, Hoccleve himself takes on a role much closer to Philosophy's than to Boethius's, explaining to his passive Friend the truth of his recovery from madness and counseling the Friend not to worry so desperately about him. Hoccleve summons Boethian literary theory and practice as a guiding presence within his putatively autobiographical writing only to satirize them, showing the roles of tutor and pupil to be less self-evident and rigidly fixed than one might expect. By thus undermining a basic principle of protrepsis, Hoccleve carves out his own unique space in the literary landscape, using Boethian literary-theoretical paradigms as straight men to his decidedly revisionist literary act.

Hoccleve's iconoclastic evocation of and engagement with Boethian "consolation" extends even to the announced forms of his twinned poems. Although both the "Complaint" and the "Dialogue" are composed in stanzaic rime royal verse, Hoccleve uses them together to parody the prosimetric literary practice that animates Boethius's work and formally embodies its autobiographical narrative of transformation. By dividing his autobiographical narrative into a "Complaint" and a "Dialogue," Hoccleve offers his twin memoir as a prosimetrum, since "complaint" is a traditionally metrical form, one lyrical and monologic, while a "dialogue," in Boethius's paradigm, is exactly what takes place in prose. But Hoccleve's labeling of his work as a prosimetrum is purely gestural: while the Chaucer pilgrim repeatedly reinvents prosimetrum formally, the *Troilus* narrator divides his poem into lyrical proems and dialogic narrative, Usk includes passages of conspicuous rhythmical regularity in his prose, and Gower composes his monological "lyrics" in Latin and his dialogical "narratives" in English, Hoccleve does not differentiate the form and style in his "Complaint" from what exists in his "Dialogue." As embodied in the "Complaint" and "Dialogue," his protreptic prosimetrum is prosimetric in labels only.

As one reads through the two poems, however, it becomes clear that Hoccleve's poetic dyad works not simply as an underformed prosimetrum but actively as an antiprosimetrum. In addition to a lack of formal differentiation between the two poems on a large scale, each poem audaciously violates on a local scale the function of the half of Boethian form that it purports by its title to fulfill. Specifically, the complaint fails to be truly monologic, in the sense of being articulated by a single, lyrical subject, and the dialogue fails to be dialogic, in the sense of being articulated by two rational subjects in conversation with each other.

The "Complaint," though putatively in Hoccleve's voice throughout, repeatedly parrots the voices of other people, Hoccleve's many unnamed critics and detractors:

> Thus spak many oon / and seide by me:
> "Althogh from him / his seeknesse sauage
> Withdrawe and past / as for a tyme be,
> Resorte it wole / namly in swich age
> As he is of . . ."[19]

> "Whan passynge hete is," quod they / "trustith this,
> Assaile him wole ageyn / that maladie."[20]

Though included as reported speech, rather than direct discourse, these passages do something utterly foreign to Boethian metrical practice and foreign to Gower's Latin revision of that practice, by creating heteroglossia within a notionally lyrical, monologic mode of expression. This drive to make dialogue out of monologue suffuses Hoccleve's complaint: he even uses his own perspective dialogically when, in a distinctively Hocclevian scene, he peers into a mirror and wonders at himself and his appearance.

> Many a saut made I / to this mirour
> Thynkynge / "If that I looke / in this maneere

19. "Complaint," lines 85–89.
20. "Complaint," lines 92–93.

Among folk / as I now do / noon errour
Of suspect look / may in my face appeere.
This contenance / I am seur / and this cheere
If I foorth vse / is no thyng repreeuable
To hem that han / conceites resonable."[21]

Here, Hoccleve reports thoughts he had in his own mind. Although monologic in that these are Hoccleve's thoughts, reported by Hoccleve himself, the scene is dialogic in two ways. First, these internal thoughts are reported back retrospectively; thus, Hoccleve's own persona is implicitly separated between two timescales, the one that thinks and the one that remembers thinking. Second, Hoccleve is thinking these things while regarding himself in the mirror; thus, there is an implicit witnessing going on, in that Hoccleve has an audience for his thoughts and facial expressions even in the moment he makes them: he is his own audience, watching his face change in the mirror and engaging in a conversation with himself. Thus, this mirror scene devises and deploys a subtle and comical critique of the possibility of true lyrical isolation.

The "Complaint" amplifies this critique of the fantasy of isolation that lyric promises when Hoccleve begins literally to debate with himself. First, he thinks about how well he has done in managing his emotions since his mental breakdown:

Syn I recouered was / haue I ful ofte
Cause had of anger / and inpacience,
Where I borne haue it / esily and softe,
Suffryng wrong be doon / to me and offense
And nat answerd ageyn / but kept silence,
Lest that men of me / deeme wolde and seyn
"See how this man / is fallen in ageyn."[22]

Even in this rumination, he imagines the thoughts of other people, thus forging dialogism in his complaint, his putatively monologic moment of lamentation. But more than simply parroting the imagined thoughts of other people, as this passage goes on, the poem projectively imagines another self within Hoccleve's speaking self.

21. "Complaint," lines 162–68.
22. "Complaint," lines 176–82.

And thanne thoghte I / on that othir syde:
"If that I nat be seen / among the prees
Men deeme wole / that I myn heed hyde
And am wers than I am / it is no lees."[23]

This passage divides Hoccleve's consciousness in two, calling attention to how his monological "lamentation" is always a negotiation with another voice, whether that voice is one's own alternate perspective or the imagined voice of another audience or interlocutor. This poem reveals itself as, in effect, a dialogic monologue. It suggests that there is no truly monological discourse: all lamentation is both private and public, both internal and projective. This literary-theoretical awareness unravels part of the literary theory and practice implicit in the *Consolation*, showing the fallaciousness of the notion that any kind of written speech can be truly monologic, can be, indeed, anything other than public, dialogic, and witnessed.

The revision to the traditional dialogue/monologue division in how prosimetrum works bleeds over into the "Dialogue." The designation "dialogue" for Hoccleve's "conversation" with his Friend is as much a misnomer as is "complaint": rather than reproducing the Socratic exchange that governs Boethius's dialogues, the "Dialogue" is actually far closer to a monologue. Whereas Boethius modeled a process of dialectical reasoning in his conversation with Philosophy, Hoccleve merely uses the conceit of the dialogue as a framework for projecting his own perspective onto a passive audience—his "Friend." In fact, the Friend scarcely speaks a word until the forty-third stanza, so that Hoccleve's "dialogue" is not much of a dialogue at all.

Pointedly, when the Friend finally does speak, he mouths a critique of precisely the kind of psychological transformation and healing that the protreptic tradition offers: confronted with Hoccleve's determination to continue writing and working, the Friend reminds him that "bisy studie" is what first addled his brain.[24] The Friend urges, thus, that Hoccleve not take up any activity of study or learning. This reasonable piece of advice is an indirect corrective to the *Consolation*'s claim that study, logic, and learning—Philosophy's ministers of healing—are key to a recovery from despair. By urging Hoccleve not to resume his obsessively studious labors, the Friend injects yet another ironic dose of reality into the story, suggesting that not all study is salutary and reminding Hoccleve that, despite

23. "Complaint," lines 190–93.
24. "Dialogue," line 302.

Boethius's successful healing by Philosophy, and despite the pupil's successful healing in the *Synonyma*, Hoccleve's own life experiences should lead him to be suspicious of too much time spent in study.

Composed in the first quarter of the fifteenth century, after Chaucer's experiments with and Gower's demystifications of protreptic theory and the mixed form, the "Complaint" and "Dialogue" register that the topos of prosimetrum as the form of protrepsis has become a *convention*. In designating this topos a "convention," I do not mean to undersell its significance in Hoccleve's works. Quite the contrary, "convention" is a term that maps specific formal choices onto particular historical periods of literary invention, a term that signals not a transhistorical topos but rather one that, within a thin slice of time, has accumulated enough cultural force to draw experimental literary writers inexorably into its orbit. Conventions are not inert, static literary choices. They are sites at which literary experimentation is maximally possible, precisely through their having attained a cultural heft substantial enough to facilitate and even to invite creative reinvestigation.

For Hoccleve, this convention of poetic self-representation is subject to ironic revision and is useful in a project of creating an artful and recognizable authorial identity. Hoccleve registers the mixed-form protreptic as a well-established mode of vernacular literary writing: Chaucer did it thrice over, and Gower did it in his *Confessio*. Hoccleve's particular mode of mixed-form protrepsis relies on his audience's having a fully shaped habit of reading and understanding, not just the association between the mixed form and transformative fiction, but also and perhaps more importantly a vernacular revision of that association. He writes under the assumption that his readers' sensitivities to a theory and practice of literature as potentially ethically salvific are already awake and in play. In Hoccleve's narrative, the convention of mixed-form, protreptic writing has shifted from being a framework within which serious literary-theoretical thought takes place and has become, instead, a foundation on which to build an authoritative vernacular poetic voice, whose power derives from its own canny cultural iconoclasm.

UNMAKING THE MIXED FORM: THE *SERIES*

Having been introduced by the antiprosimetric antiprotreptic of the "Complaint" and "Dialogue," Hoccleve's iconoclastic relation to literary history is only fully on view when we examine the *Series* as a whole. After the "Complaint" and "Dialogue" have concluded, the frame narrative, in which Hoccleve and his Friend talk through what Hoccleve needs to do in order to secure his reemergence into public life as an author, continues for the duration of the *Series*. It is in that dialogic frame narrative that Hoccleve fully dissects the mixed-form paradigm for vernacular protrepsis.

As Hoccleve and his Friend continue to talk, they light upon new works of poetry that they feel that Hoccleve should undertake to translate from Latin sources. Since the *Series* is a fairly unfamiliar work, even to medievalists, its contents merit a quick review. After much consideration, Hoccleve and the Friend decide that Hoccleve's next literary move should be the translation of the story "Jereslaus's Wife," which tells the tale of a highly ethical and sexually faithful, though sorely tested, empress.[25] After this narrative, Hoccleve decides he will translate another Latin protreptic, which he titles "Lerne to Dye," that will explain the art of dying well via a dialogue between Wisdom and her Disciple and their shared conversation with an "Ymage" of a man who is dying in sin.[26] Next, having already presented a virtuous woman in the tale of Jereslaus's wife, Hoccleve and his Friend decide that he should also translate a Latin work that narrates the evils of wicked, sexually profligate, and greedy women, so he translates the story "Jonathas," which describes how an innocent and highly gullible man is defrauded of three magical objects he has inherited from his father by a seductive and avaricious woman named Fellicula. Between each of his poems, Hoccleve also—often at the behest of his Friend—interpolates a moralization, in which he explains the allegorical meaning of each of his tales within a Christian referential framework.

Responding to the *Series* as a whole, putatively concerted authorial effort, most scholars note its seemingly piecemeal construction, its randomness, and its refusal to cluster around a single narrative through-line or thematic focus.[27] But the *Series* is deliberately constructed as a whole

25. This work is translated from the *Gesta romanorum*. Karen Winstead has read Hoccleve's decision to include this particular tale, putatively about female virtue, as an index of the misogyny that runs through the entire *Series* ("'I am al other to yow than yee weene'").

26. As Benjamin Kurtz demonstrated, this work translates Henry of Suso's *Horologium sapientiae* ("Source of Occleve's *Lerne to Dye*").

27. As Burrow puts it, "The *Series* is in fact a loosely knit sequence of narrative and didactic units: Complaint, Dialogue with a Friend, The Tale of Jereslaus, Learn to Die, and the Tale of Jonathas. Admittedly, these units are enclosed within a narrative that purports to identify their order of composition." "Thomas Hoccleve: Some Redatings," 371.

production, animated by a single literary experiment. Indeed, it is really only after the "Dialogue" that Hoccleve's *Series* emerges as a fully unified artistic production. It emerges moreover as a unified metapoetic work, designed to make a commentary on and critique of the tradition of mixed-form protreptics, as well as of the commentary tradition itself. The "Complaint" and "Dialogue" have thus served an end analogous to the thematizing of Boethian theory in the *Troilus*: the two initial poems quicken an awareness of Boethian literary theory and practice, so that the rest of the *Series* and its metapoetic experiments can appear in sharper relief.[28]

The mixed form of the rest of the *Series* is overt and programmatic. "Jereslaus's Wife," "Lerne to Dye," and "Jonathas" are all taken from prose sources: the first and third from the *Gesta romanorum*; the second from Henry Suso's *Horologium sapientiae*. When Hoccleve translates them into English, however, he converts them all into rime royal verse. The sources for the moralizations of these three tales—the first and third again taken from the *Gesta* and the second taken from the *Sarum Breviary*—are all also composed originally in prose, and Hoccleve leaves them in prose. Hoccleve thus takes six pieces of prose and creates from them three prosimetric dyads.

Not only does the *Series* morph into an overt prosimetrum when it transitions from the notionally autobiographical first two poems and into the notionally fictive final three and their moralizations, but it also calls attention to its status as a mixed-form work, raising formal variation to the level of an enunciated theme in the frame narrative in which Hoccleve self-consciously assembles his work. After "Jereslaus's Wife," the Friend appears, to ask Hoccleve in rime royal about his progress and to ask him why he has not included a moralization along with his poem. Hoccleve complains that his own Latin source did not contain one, so the Friend obliges by supplying his own copy of "Jereslaus's Wife," which does include a moralization. Hoccleve promises the Friend to take up this mor-

28. In his edition of *The Complaint and Dialogue*, Burrow notes that the *Series* acts as though it was intended for duke of Gloucester (lv–lvii). As to the *Series* overall, Burrow says, "The resulting structure resembles that of the *dits* of Middle French poets such as Machaut or Froissart (though with very different content). Like them, the English poet represents himself, in the foreground, as the author of those various texts that the work incorporates. The technique is described as 'montage' by one writer on the French *dit*, Jacqueline Cerquiglini" (lx). Burrow also suggests that with the possible exception of "Learn to Die," the whole series seems to have been composed together, intended to be strung together into a coherent work.

alization, "[i]n prose wrytynge it / hoomly and pleyn."[29] With this promise, Hoccleve makes a metapoetic move. He aligns his theory of prose and
its usefulness alongside contemporary vernacular theorists, including
Chaucer, Usk, Trevisa, and the Wycliffites: for Hoccleve, apparently, prose
is the form appropriate to "hoomly and pleyn" discourse.

The ascription of "homeliness and plainness" to his coming prose
translation retroactively sheds light on the formal intricacy of "Jereslaus's
Wife" itself. Hoccleve is unusually rigid in his theory and practice of ver-
sification: throughout the poems of the *Series*, Hoccleve's ironclad rule
for composition is that each line must contain exactly ten syllables. The
number of lines that part from this rule is tiny.[30] Scholars of Hoccleve's
metrics have tended to regard this formal rigidity as a sign of his less sophisticated poetic skills, as compared with Chaucer.[31] But I would suggest
that something rather different is going on. Where Chaucer, in his use of
rime royal, experiments with its capacity to aestheticize sense and syntax,
where he experiments, in effect, with how verse can be used to shore up
sense, Hoccleve is far more invested in meter for meter's sake. He carefully enfolds Latin prose into English ten-syllable lines, allowing the metrical form itself to take primacy over all other concerns.

The poetic wroughtness of his "Jereslaus's Wife" is not limited to
the intricacy of the verse form and the meticulousness of syllabic count.
Hoccleve also adds to his source texts a recurring type of lyrical interruption. He breaks in to comment upon the emotional import of the events
he narrates—much as the *Troilus* narrator does in the *Troilus*. Hoccleve
often marks his insertions as departures from the narrative by introducing
them, at the beginning of a new stanza, with a lyrical "O," a call to songfulness akin to what we saw in Usk's prose *Testament*. About Jereslaus's
wife, Hoccleve adds the following passage:

O noble lady / symple and Innocent,
Trustynge vp-on his ooth and his promesse,
fful wo is me / for thy wo consequent!
Often happith / wommannes tendrenesse

---

29. Thomas Hoccleve, *Hoccleve's Works 1 and 2*, p. 174, line 25. All quotations of
the "Lerne to Dye," "Jereslaus's Wife," and "Jonathas," as well as from their "moralizations," are drawn from this source.

30. Burrow, introduction, *Thomas Hoccleve's Complaint and Dialogue*, xxviii–
xxvix, xlviii.

31. Ibid., xxvii–xxvix.

Torneth hir vn-to harm / and to duresse:
This Emperice fond it so by preef,
Whom that forsworn man / greet harm dide, & greef.[32]

In this passage, Hoccleve introduces the apostrophic phrase "O noble lady, symple and Innocent," as well as the proleptic and affective expletive "fful wo is me, for thy wo consequent!" Both the apostrophe and the added affective signposting here augment the lyrical aura of his work. By contrast, the original *Gesta*, in both Latin and English versions, lack these affective excursuses and lack apostrophic calls to the heroine of the tale.[33] Hoccleve makes his tale not only far more metrically ornate but also far more invested in exporting affective cues to his readership—much as Chaucer does in his translation of Boccaccio's *Filostrato* into the *Troilus*.

In addition to his affective cues, Hoccleve adds gnomic assessments of the ethical meaning of this moment in his narrative: "Often happith / wommannes tendrenesse // Tornith hir vn-to harm." This autoexegetical drive does not appear in the *Gesta* version but appears in Hoccleve's poem at intervals and is often associated with the superadded lyrical and affective passages. Frequently, these autoexegetical excursuses are couched in apostrophic arias. About Jereslaus's treacherous brother, Hoccleve adds another narratorial commentary:

O false lyer / o thow cofre and cheste,
Of vnclennesse / o stynkynge Aduotour
In wil, seye I / and willy to inceste;
O false man to god / and thow traitour
To thy lord and brothir, the Emperour;
O enemy to wyfly chastitee,
And in thy wirkes ful of crueltee.[34]

Apostrophe, in this passage, constitutes a powerful stylistic drive: over the course of eight lines, Hoccleve weaves in five "O" apostrophes, indicating the severity of his censure of the Emperor's brother on the level of story but also indicating the salience of the lyrical mode in this passage on the level of literary self-positioning. Hoccleve's versified translation of

32. P. 146, lines 169–75.
33. For reference, see *Early English Versions of the Gesta romanorum*, 312, which includes no such lyrical interpolation.
34. P. 148, lines 246–52.

the *Gesta* tale, that is, is pervasively concerned to signal its own status as a lamentation, as a lyrical composition capable of providing ethical guidance to its readers. In these apostrophic exclamations, Hoccleve chooses to add a set of pejorative terms to characterize the brother and his behavior— false, stinking, unclean, treacherous, and cruel—whereas his source material contains none of these ethical judgments. This indictment of the Emperor's brother continues for another fourteen lines, culminating in the recognition that Hoccleve has now significantly departed from his sources when he dives into ethical commentary—"Nathelees / of this tretith nat the book."[35] Hoccleve's poem, unlike its source, has swerved into the realm of commentary, ethical analysis, and lyrical perseveration—much as Chaucer's *Troilus* diverges from its own source when his narrator conducts his affect-shepherding excursuses. Flagging his departures from the *Gesta*, the narrating Hoccleve seems to want to pull his poem back from the brink of lyric and into the realm of what his source "tretith." The poem thus creates a tension between the story of the source and the formal artifice and ethical editorializing of the translation.

Try as it might to remain close to what its source "tretith," the Hocclevian "Tale of Jereslaus's Wife" veers again and again into superadded ethical commentary. As the poem goes on, these commentaries are often directed specifically toward its readers, so that the poem makes its own relationship with an imagined readership a subtheme of its narrative—once again, in a manner reminiscent of the *Troilus*.

> O yee that seyn / wommen be variant,
> And can nat sad been / if they been assailed;
> Yee been ful vnkonnynge and ignorant,
> And of the soothe / foule yee han faillid;
> Constance is vn-to wommanhode entaillid;
> Out of that fee / they nat be dryue may;
> Swich hir nature is, thogh sum men seyn nay.[36]

Here, the poem turns outward, addressing its readership as "yee" and critiquing that "yee" for its ignorant adherence to tired literary stereotypes, such as the idea that women are "variant." The poem chastens the "yee" of the audience, most tellingly, for running afoul of "the soothe," indicating that this poem expects its readers to read for ethical truth-value and

---

35. P. 149, line 264.
36. P. 157, lines 484–490.

not simply for entertainment. In this insistence, the narrating Hoccleve reminds us of a cardinal principle of protreptic literature: it is supposed to transform its readership to a greater understanding of ethical "soothe."

Hoccleve's repeated interruptions of his narrative to provide affective, lyrical, and normative commentaries on the action take on a greater significance when seen in the context of the moralization that Hoccleve ends up appending, at the urging of his Friend, to the end of his tale. For the narrating Hoccleve, the ethical message of "Jereslaus's Wife" has been mostly concerned with female virtue, male vice, and the wrongheadedness of ascribing ethical pusillanimity to women. He has made that ethical message available endogenously in the poem itself, not exogenous to it, through his lyrical excursuses and ethical editorializing.

When Hoccleve adds the *Gesta*'s moralization, then, it contradicts and undermines the relation of the tale to the commentary that Hoccleve himself has already supplied. The *Gesta*'s moralization is bluntly Christian, interpreting everything from within an exceedingly conservative exegetical framework: those who seek to harm Jereslaus's wife are construed as the vices and temptations that beset the soul; her drive to get back to her husband is construed as the true soul's desire to be close to God. Given the added attention that Hoccleve as narrator has given to the endogenous ethical messages of the story, the exogenous prose Christian moralization feels forced, overdetermined, and superfluous. Why should we think that all the characters, whom the narrating Hoccleve has taken so very seriously for nearly a thousand lines, need to be or even can be subordinated to a supervening mandate of Christian exegesis? That interpretive modality may work in the *Gesta romanorum* itself, in which Christianizing moralizations are appended to every tale, but it surely cannot work in Hoccleve's *Series*, which has already evoked and undermined its own relation to literary genres and has emphasized, in the ongoing dialogue between Hoccleve and the Friend, the constructedness and artificiality of literary writing.

Given the generic and registral slipperiness of the *Series* as a whole, how are the intratale lyrical moralizations meant to work with or against the superimposed moralizations that Hoccleve receives in a deus ex machina fashion from his Friend? The narrating Hoccleve suggests, in the last rime royal line before he switches into his homely and plain prose, that the moralization "to that tale is good be knyt, in feith,"[37] but there remains unsatisfied tension between what readers are urged, again and

37. P. 174, line 28.

again, to take as the ethical meaning of the tale and what the narrating Hoccleve is coerced by his Friend into endorsing as its true, deeply "knyt" ethical meaning. The dyad of tale and moralization thus becomes a platform for interrogating the idea that any necessary or stable relation could exist between the versified story and its prosaic and moralistic exogenous commentary. Like Gower's *Confessio*, Hoccleve's *Series* is eager to expose the seductive but fallacious normative relation of commentary to poem.

The unsatisfied tension between poem and commentary spills over into the next mixed-form dyad in Hoccleve's work. From his translation of the prose moralization to "Jereslaus's Wife," Hoccleve transitions to another rime royal rendering of another originally all-prose Latin work: the second part of the second book of Henry Suso's *Horologium sapientiae*. Just as do the "Complaint," "Dialogue," and "Jereslaus," "Lerne to Dye" valorizes the decasyllabic count and the *ababbcc* rhyme scheme over all other formal considerations: where it suits his syllabic meter, Hoccleve breaks syntax across line breaks and sometimes across stanza breaks.[38]

Though construed by Hoccleve scholars as a sign of poetic inferiority,[39] the rigid maintenance of a ten-syllable line takes on greater literary-theoretical significance when put into conversation with the other driving force in the poem, which is the accurate translation of Suso's Latin into Middle English. As Benjamin Kurtz demonstrated decades ago, "Lerne to Dye" is quite faithful to the Latin original, omitting little of the original work, although adding many new words and short passages.[40] Kurtz

38. There is marked syntactic overflow between stanzas 1 and 2, 13 and 14, 15 and 16, 33 and 34, 115 and 116, and 121 and 122. There are weaker instances as well (as when a new stanza begins with "but" or "and," suggesting a possible syntactic connection with the previous stanza but also inaugurating a new independent clause), and numerous examples of lines that contain whole syntactic units only when read in pairs or triplets of lines.

39. As Kurtz puts it, "A sententious and melancholy reflection on the brevity of this life [in Suso] may be sacrificed to an insipid rhyme [in Hoccleve's translation]" ("Relation of Occleve's *Lerne to Dye* to Its Source," 258). Kurtz pervasively construes the changes Hoccleve makes to Suso's original as clumsy degradations of the elegance of the Latin.

40. Ibid., 256. Kurtz's article focuses closely on the differences between the Latin source and Hoccleve's English poem, however, so that his argument ends up, on the surface, reading as a suggestion that Hoccleve did change the original a great deal—just not to any concerted aesthetic or thematic effect. But Kurtz's argument works against itself: by pointing up the instances in which Hoccleve changes individual words and rhythms to maintain his rhyme scheme, Kurtz also invariably points up how very close Hoccleve's translation is to Suso's at any level larger than word by word.

understands this translational precision as one among many signs of the relatively small poetic ambitions of "Lerne to Dye," but I would construe it differently. To make a precise translation of a Latin work into English, the easiest form to translate into is, without a doubt, prose. As the dictaminists, Wycliffite translators, Usk, Chaucer, and Hoccleve himself all understand, it is much harder to render sense, theme, and argument when one is constrained by the strictures of an artificial meter. Harder, but not impossible, the *Series* seems to say. The fact, then, that "Lerne to Dye" maintains a highly restrictive decasyllabic line and the rime royal rhyme scheme and still manages to be an accurate translation of Suso's prose *Horologium* is remarkable, and it is an index of Hoccleve's own metapoetic interests. The poem is wedded at once to the accurate rendering of sense and to the construction of intricate aesthetic form, thus exposing the Wycliffite, Trevisan, Chaucerian, and Uskian commitment to prose as the necessary and obvious choice for "true" and "accurate" writing as a fallacy. The *Series* does not, as *Troilus and Criseyde* does, use the stanzaic form to aestheticize sense, but instead it allows poetic meter to hold sway.

Hoccleve's privileging of decasyllabic lines does not mean that he steers clear of other ornament in his verse. Quite the contrary, he relies heavily on various poetic devices throughout his poem, especially anaphora, apostrophe, chiasmus, simile, and exclamation. But in most instances, when Hoccleve introduces these poetic devices he is following the example of his Latin prose source, which is, in its own right, notable for its density of poetic devices. Where Suso writes,

> "*Finis venit, venit finis.* Decretum est, impleri optet." O mi Deus, oportet me iam mori? Non potest haec sententia mutari? Debeo iam tam cito de hoc mundo recedere? O mortis immensa crudelitas. O impietas et indignatio miseranda. Parce quaeso, parce iuventuti, parce nondum maturae aetati,[41]

Hoccleve translates as follows:

> "Thyn eende is comen / comen is thyn eende,
> It is decreed / ther is no resistence."
> lord god / shal y now die / and hennes weende?
> Whethir not changed may be this sentence;

41. Henry Suso, *Heinrich Seuses Horologium sapientiae*, p. 528, lines 25–29.

O lord, may it nat put been in suspense?
Shal y out of this world so soone go?
Allas / wole it noon other be than so?

O deeth, o deeth, greet is thy crueltee!
Thyn office al to sodeynly doost thow.
Is ther no grace? lakkist thow pitee?
Spare my youth / of age rype ynow
To dye am y nat yit / spare me now![42]

Where Suso deploys a chiasmus—"Finis venit, venit finis"—Hoccleve follows suit, though he augments the bleakness and intimacy of Suso's utterance by adding the second person singular possessive pronoun: "Thyn
eende is comen / comen is thyn eende." Suso's single "O Deus" becomes
doubled for Hoccleve as "lord God" and then "O lord," indicating that Hoccleve perceived the stylistic salience of apostrophe in Suso's original and
amplified it in his translation by repetition; this amplification of apostrophe occurs again when Suso's lyrical "O mortis" becomes Hoccleve's re-
duplicative "O deeth, o deeth." Though Hoccleve does not preserve Suso's
tripled "Parce" anaphora, he does render the emphasis that the anaphora
produces, first by creating a double anaphora in the final lines of the stanza
and, second, by augmenting the formal ornamentation of that anaphora by
converting it also into a chiastic structure, in which the clause "of age
rype ynow // to dye am y nat yit" functions as a fulcrum around which the
two anaphoric clauses "spare my youth" and "spare me now" balance.

    Though Kurtz's observation is absolutely correct that Hoccleve's main
compositional concern is the preservation of syllabic count, and though
his observation is equally correct that Hoccleve's translation is not particularly innovative in terms of content, those two criticisms elide the
primary achievement of Hoccleve's verse: he manages to conserve Suso's
content and the formal choices Suso makes, while also adhering to the
restrictive metrical requirements that he imports from Chaucerian poetic
practice. Rather than a slavish translation of Suso and a cheap knockoff of
Chaucerian poetic form, Hoccleve presents an intricately crafted and carefully executed verse form, in which syllabic count structures but does not
constrain sense, and in which intra- as well as interlinear aesthetic effects,
including anaphora, apostrophe, and chiasmus, are maintained in the transition from Latin to English. Hoccleve's "Lerne to Dye" is, in many ways,

42. P. 183, lines 134–45.

the high point of the *Series*'s metapoetic investment in showing that meter, however highly wrought, can still accurately carry sense.

Upon arriving at the end of Suso's second part of his second book, Hoccleve seems ready to acknowledge the difficulty and intensity of his poetic labors: he breaks off his own translation in sheer exhaustion, saying that he "forsooke" the "greet thyng" of working to translate the rest of the *Horologium*.[43] After thus calling attention to the sheer difficulty of translating the Latin work into his own meticulously accurate and rigidly ornamented rime royal stanzas, Hoccleve switches sources, to tip into his translation of the *Horologium* a section of the *Sarum Breviary* as another prose moralization.[44]

> But as the ix lesson which is rad
> in holy chirche / vp-on all halwen day
> witnessith / syn it ioieful is and glad
> ffor hem that hens shuln wel departe away,
> And to the blisse go that lastith ay,
> Translate wole y / nat in rym, but prose,
> ffor so it best is / as that y suppose.[45]

Hoccleve again makes a metapoetic move, calling attention to the tension between "rym" and "prose," first suggesting that prose is somehow "best" for conveying information that might help the soul find "the blisse . . . that lastith ay" and, second, reminding his audience that he could have translated the "ix lesson" into rhyme, as he did with "Lerne to Dye." Hoccleve's calling attention to form here and his ellipticism about why he would switch form work in two ways. First, they remind his readers that they are reading a self-consciously prosimetric work. But, second, they undercut the notion that the formal switching originates from any consistent or recoverable motivation. The formal switching sometimes seems to originate in Hoccleve's wish to curtail his "labour"; for him, it seems, prose is "hoomly and playn," and hence an easier form to compose, while "rym" is harder to maintain. Prose seems actively to be associated with an exportable ethical value: when Hoccleve turns to the *Breviary*, he switches to prose, saying that he supposes that form is "best" to capture and convey lessons for the soul's immortality. This claim that salvific messages

---

43. P. 212, lines 920–21.
44. Kurtz, "Prose of Occleve's *Lerne to Dye*," 56–57.
45. P. 212, lines 925–31.

are better encoded in prose than in "rym" implicitly undercuts the verse translation of the *Horologium*, a treatise of soul-saving didacticism par excellence. It is as though, having worked Suso's artful Latin prose into artful English verse, without sacrificing the former's ideational content or his own rigid metrics, Hoccleve now disavows that very impulse and bows to the contemporary notion that didactic writing is best done in prose. Hoccleve's metapoetic statements and his practices of poetics seem at loggerheads with each other.

Complicating matters, the prose style in this prose section from the *Breviary*, as throughout the proses of the *Series*, is far from "hoomly and playn." It is riddled with anaphora, frequently in the form of negations.

> [W]hat is more blissful / than that lyf is / where no dreede is of pouerte / of maladie / no feeblenesse / there is no wight hurt / no wight wrooth / no wight hath enuye / there is no brennynge or hete of couetyse / no desir of mete / noon ambicioun of honour or of power / no dreede of the feend / noon awaytes of deueles.[46]

To describe the eternal and unchanging state of heavenly peace that exists after death for good Christians, this passage recurs, again and again, to short clauses that begin with negating particles, thereby apophatically rendering both the unthinkability of eternal life and its unchangingness, its identity through time. This stylistic amplification of ideation continues, when the passage switches focus to describe not the unthinkable eternity of salvation but instead the nature of its oneness, its capacity to unify all things: "no diuision, but onhede / for ther shal been o concord of all seintes / o pees & gladnesse continuel / all thynges peisible / all in quiete and reste."[47] Rather than relying on a negating anaphora, this passage deploys two concatenated "o" clauses, rendering both the idea of unity and the feeling of lyric apostrophe, and then two concatenated "all" clauses, contributing a feeling of plenitude and universality to the passage. Thus, despite the contention in the preface to this prose section that prose is somehow lighter, easier, and more appropriate, it is, like Usk's prose in the *Testament* or Chaucer's in the *Boece*, nevertheless pervasively wrought, highly ornate, and stylistically geared to bring to aesthetic crisis the ideas it contains.

Hoccleve does not, however, derive his prose stylistics out of the ether.

46. P. 213.
47. P. 213.

Quite the contrary, once again his stylistic choices are motivated by his serious engagement with his Latin source. The negative anaphoras of Hoc-cleve's translation read in the Latin *Sarum Breviary,*

> Quid hac vita beatius, ubi non est paupertatis metus, non aegritudinis imbecillitas? Nemo laeditur, nemo irascitur, nemo invidet: cupiditas nulla exardescit. Nullum cibi desiderium: nulla honoris pulsat aut po-testatis ambitio. Nullus ibi diaboli metus, insidiae daemonum nullae: terror gehennae procul.[48]

Hoccleve derives his anaphoric impulse directly from the Latin, which, like his Middle English rendering, relies on concatenated negative clauses to render at once the eternal stability and the unthinkability of divine salvation. The passage that Hoccleve translates with the doubled "o" and "all" anaphoras, however, appears as follows in the Latin: "Nulla erit tunc usquam discordia: sed cuncta consona, cuncta convenientia: quia om-nium sanctorum una concordia, pax certa et laetitia continua. Tranquilla sunt omnia et quieta."[49] Though the "cuncta/cuncta" conjunction does ap-pear, translating into the "o/o" conjunction in Hoccleve's prose, the Latin anaphora does not do the doubled aesthetic work of Hoccleve's English; it does not simultaneously render the idea of oneness and the style of song-ful apostrophe. Hoccleve, then, in his translational choice, amplifies the poetic artistry and lyricism of the passage. Moreover, the Latin original does not contain the "all/all" anaphora found in the Middle English; in-stead, the Latin *Sarum* buries the "omnium" and "omnia" in the middle of clauses, rather than promoting them to a more rhythmically or syntac-tically salient position. Hoccleve finds an aesthetic pattern for rendering ethical sense in his Latin original and amplifies it in his putatively simple, unadorned Middle English prose—much as Chaucer finds alliteration in the Latin *Consolation* and amplifies it in his *Boece.*

After his artful prose rendering of the Latin *Sarum,* the narrating Hoc-cleve turns back to verse and indicates that he intended at this point to end his book but that his Friend arrived once again, this time to ask him to translate the tale of "Jonathas," also from the *Gesta.*

> "Thomas," he saide / "at Estren that was last,
> I redde a tale / which y am agast

48. *Breviarium ad usum insignis ecclesiae Sarum,* vol. 3, col. 976.
49. Ibid.

To preye thee, for the laboures sake
That thow haast had / for to translate & make."[50]

Not only does the Friend want Hoccleve to "translate" this tale, but he also specifically wants Hoccleve to make it into versified poetry—to "make" the translation. Thus, this interstitial moment between the end of the *Sarum* moralization and the coming "making" of "Jonathas" becomes another metaliterary moment, at which the Friend draws attention to the fact that there is an asymmetry between translation and *poiesis*.

He quickly expands on this asymmetry to suggest that "making" somehow conduces to the didactic work of exemplarity: he wants Hoccleve's poetic translation to serve as "ensaumple" to other men, including and especially to his own son, who cannot read Latin but needs to read it in English, because he is susceptible to the temptations of the flesh: "wylde is he / and likly to foleye."[51] The tale of Jonathas follows, which narrates how a young man, through incautious behavior, loses his patrimony but ultimately regains everything. Hoccleve's Friend thus sets up the story as an exemplum to wild and unruly young men, a cautionary tale against the poor decisions one may make about one's material resources when under the bewitching effects of sexual desire. The introduction to the tale, then, raises two interrelated metapoetic problems. The first, which has been on the horizon throughout the *Series*, is the problem of how to "translate & make" a Latin work not simply into English but specifically into English verse. The second is the problem of protrepsis: how to create salvific discourse, how to marshal a narrative in the service of a specific didactic agenda to change a reader from "wildness" to being "bettre of gouernaill" by modeling that very transformation in its main character.[52]

How Hoccleve "makes" this poem seems straightforward enough at first, but that straightforwardness quickly evaporates when one reads the tale in the context of the *Series* overall. When Hoccleve translates the prose tale of Jonathas from the *Gesta romanorum* into his own English verse, he again, as he has done throughout the *Series*, works it into rime royal stanzas. In this rime royal translation, he once again follows his source's content meticulously: Jonathas is a phenomenally naïve young man, who inherits three magical boons from his father—a ring, a brooch, and a carpet.

50. P. 216, lines 4–7.
51. P. 216, lines 9 and 27.
52. P. 216, line 11.

When he travels to the city for his education, he falls in love with the das-
tardly and promiscuous Fellicula, who cheats him of his belongings and
leaves him alone in a vast wilderness, until he wises up and comes home
to recover his belongings and take gruesome vengeance on her.[53] Though
Hoccleve follows the source tale closely in all these plot points, there is
nevertheless a significant slippage between his source material and his
"translation" of it into English prose—a slippage that emerges when he
turns to translate the *Gesta*'s prose moralization of this tale into his own
Middle English one.

The *Gesta*'s moralization is, once again, rigidly Christian. It explains
that Jonathas represents the human soul searching for Jesus, while Fellicula represents diabolical temptation, and the three magical boons are the
resources of the soul on its quest for union with the divine. In the *Gesta*,
the moralization reads straight: there is neither commentary nor contextualization to destabilize a reader's sense that the tale of Jonathas does indeed allegorically signify the quest of the human soul for a purer relationship with Jesus via its exercise of faith.[54] In Hoccleve's work, on the other
hand, the Friend's injunction that Hoccleve should translate the story of
Jonathas specifically to help safeguard the Friend's son from his tendency
to wildness shifts a reader's sense of how the moralization can be read in
apposition with the tale itself. The tale, after all, is supposed to be tailored
to the particular problems the Friend is having with his son. Its literal
meaning, its narrative surface, is what the Friend seeks to have "translated and made" into English for the benefit of his son. When Hoccleve
then turns to the moralization, it seems excessive, and seems even to vitiate the Friend's express purpose in asking Hoccleve to render "Jonathas"
into English, since it suggests that the allegorical level of interpretation,
not the literal, is what matters. But because the reader has encountered,
throughout the *Series*, the Friend as a serious character and shaping influence not only on Hoccleve's psyche but also on the works that are included
in the *Series* itself, the allegorizing moralization, which cuts against the

53. Though it is not known exactly which manuscript he was following, or whether
it was Latin or an early English translation, I have compared Hoccleve's writings with
two late medieval English-language translations of the *Gesta*, an his translation is
extremely close to them both. The two mauscripts are HL 7333 and AD 9066, as edited
in *Early English Versions of the Gesta romanorum*, 180–96. Hoccleve's moralization is
slightly closer to Additional 9066 than to HL 7333, in both word choice and syntax.

54. See *Early English Versions of the Gesta romanorum*, 193–96; *Hoccleve's Works
1 and 2*, pp. 240–42.

Friend's immediate didactic goals, seems parodic. The "Jonathas"/moralization dyad, then, reads as a critique—more pronounced than the one that emerged in the "Jereslaus's Wife" dyad—of the very possibility of exemplary discourse.[55] It begins to appear more as a commentary on the oblique relation of readerly desire—as embodied in the Friend—to the moralization tradition that would deny and override all but its own authoritative, explicit, and monolithic interpretation. The "Jonathas" dyad, then, begins to read as a final critique of the putatively natural relationship of story to moralization, of exemplum to extractable meaning, or of poetry to prose. It begins to read as a defamiliarization of how literature can or should contribute to ethically transformative learning, and of how commentaries relate to imaginative works.

In suggesting that the "moralization" tradition somehow misses the point of fulfilling readerly desire, Hoccleve arrives at a mode of prosimetrum analogous to Dante's project in the *Vita nuova* or Gower's in the *Confessio amantis*. Dante, as I discussed in my first chapter, responds to the prosimetric provocation by changing the terms of the formal opposition so that the versified sections of his composition are where the lion's share of his aesthetic and philosophical attention is situated, while his prose sections become, quite simply, narrative frames for and commentaries upon his poems. In Gower's *Confessio*, the relation of putative "commentary" to "poem" is constantly and multifariously under pressure, showing the very enterprise of glossing and marginal interpretation to be deeply problematic. For Hoccleve, the prose moralizations, especially the one that follows his "making" of "Jonathas" into verse, seem likewise otiose, obliquely related to the contents of the poem at best. The moralizations seem, then, to ironize the idea of using an explanatory prose to make sense of a poetic, fictive narrative. The poetry is where the real action happens; the proses are superfluous and are included in a way that highlights their own superfluity.

Adding to this sense that Hoccleve's prosimetrum serves to deemphasize the necessity of prose explication and to amplify the possibility that

---

55. In this, Hoccleve's *Series* seems to understand exemplarity much in the same way as Mitchell, who calls it "a function rather than a form of rhetoric. The exemplary text is, simply, one in which *we recognize what we should be doing*" (*Ethics and Exemplary Narrative*, 14). But it seems that in his ironic juxtaposition of poem with prose, Hoccleve suggests that at the end of the day there is always a slippage between what we read, how we interpret it, and its functional ability to shape what we do.

vernacular poetry itself can be a protreptic *telos*, Hoccleve's final move in his *Series* is to add an adaptation of Chaucer's famous palinode to *Troilus and Criseyde*. The beginning of the end of the *Troilus* reads,

> Go, litel bok, go, litel myn tragedye,
> Ther God thi makere yet, er that he dye,
> So sende myght to make in some comedye!
> But litel book, no making thow n'envie,
> But subgit be to alle poesye;
> And kis the steppes where as thow seest pace
> Vergile, Ovide, Omer, Lucan, and Stace.[56]

Leveraging the sociopoetical weight of the Chaucerian exemplar in bidding farewell to his work and his reader, Hoccleve says,

> Go, small book / to the noble excellence
> Of my lady / of Westmerland / and seye,
> Hir humble seruant / with al reuerence
> Him recommandith vn-to hir nobleye;
> And byseeche hire / on my behalue, & preye,
> Thee to receyue / for hire owne right;
> And looke thow / in al manere weye
> To plese hir wommanhede / do thy might.[57]

But even as Hoccleve mimics Chaucer's famous palinode, he radically reinvents what it expresses and how it works in his overall composition. What is, for Chaucer, a dual gesture of literary self-abasement and self-aggrandizement—he directs his poem to kiss the steps where great classical poets walk, a move of humility, but humility within a supremely lofty clique—becomes for Hoccleve a far more savvy gesture of social obeisance. Where Chaucer asks leave of God that he, Chaucer the "makere" of poetry, might compose a comical work, Hoccleve simply dedicates this work to the discretion of his would-be patroness, the "lady of Westmerland." Chaucer's moment of literary transformation turns into Hoccleve's moment of submission to his own economic and social bottom line.

The disparity between the two authors is borne out in the fact that Hoccleve, after this stanza, simply moves on to a conclusory salutation:

56. Bk. 5, lines 1786–92.
57. P. 242.

Humble seruant
to your gracious
noblesse
    T. Hoccleue[58]

Chaucer, by contrast, adds an additional eleven stanzas after his "Go, litel bok" stanza, in which he at least performatively laments the fates of ancient pagans and turns his attention, much as Boethius does, to the consolation of divine eternity:

Thow oon, and two, and thre, eterne on lyve,
That regnest ay in thre, and two, and oon,
Uncirsumscript, and al maist circumscrive,
Us from visible and invisible foon
Defende, and to thy mercy, everichon,
So make us, Jesus, for thi mercy, digne,
For love of mayde and moder thyn benigne. Amen.[59]

Chaucer's palinode to his "litel bok" culminates in what reads as an ethical transformation: through the act of reading and then retelling the story of *Troilus and Criseyde*, the narrator arrives at a renewed understanding of the supervening truth of divine goodness and eternity. By contrast, Hoccleve's verbal curtsy to his lady reads as an ethical anticlimax, in the tradition of the *Confessio amantis*'s bathetic denouement: it is not so much that Hoccleve has arrived at a transcendent understanding of divine goodness as that he has arrived at an awareness of how beside the point transcendence may be when one has at last newly restabilized a position in one's own socioeconomic and sociopolitical world. He has, in effect, used the device Chaucer uses to claim his spiritual growth in order to claim his own social growth, his recovery from isolated madness and his reemergence into the world of political and financial relationality. For Hoccleve, the mixed-form transformative fiction has become a mode of courtly address, grounded in his ability to demonstrate cultural mastery by manifesting literary iconoclasm.

Hoccleve's literary iconoclasm is not born of despair or a desire to deny the power of literary work and literary experience. His performative denial of the mystical power of the mixed form to couch a narrator's

58. P. 242.
59. Bk. 5, lines 1863–70.

transformation—much less work a parallel transformation in an audience, as embodied by the ever-skeptical and unchanging Friend—does not bring with it a profound sense of literature's inertness or inutility. Instead, what Hoccleve's iconoclasm brings about is an awareness of the literary field as a domain of play, renewal, and experimentation with the limits of form and form's relation to contents. At the same time, it reads as the dawning of a new kind of authorship, in which the author toys with his readers, not maliciously, but generously—a dynamic that exists in Chaucer's and Gower's works as well, though not so pervasively. For Hoccleve, the idea that an author could write himself or his audience out of a state of distracted despair and into a state of illuminated hope, combined with the idea that he could do so by alternating prose with verse, has become an authorizing trope, a mode of situating his own work somewhere on a legible map of literary convention and simultaneously of showing his mastery over a convention that had become, in the generation before him, a tremendously exciting literary provocation around which some of the great late Middle English experiments with prose and meter gathered, and in response to which some of the great works of enacted literary theory were written.

A Mixed-Form Tradition of
Literary Theory and Practice

The *Consolation of Philosophy* is a protreptic, designed not simply to tell of its hero-narrator-author's ethical transformation but to export that renewal to a readership through a literary encounter with the aesthetics of the mixed form. For Boethius, prosimetrum and protrepsis are two necessary, interlocking modes—one aesthetic, one ethical—that join to model a transformation of the human soul. In the works of Alain, Dante, and Guillaume, cracks already appear in the literary-theoretical foundation of mixed-form protrepsis: each of these medieval authors use and construe the mixed form in a different way, none quite reproducing the consoling outcome of the Boethian exemplar or quite reproducing his form. Alain creates in his *De planctu* a large-scale, structural reflex of his dogmatic approbation for heterosexual marriage. Dante reinvents prosimetrum as a mode of autocommentary for his poetry. Guillaume amplifies the salience of musicality to the mixed-form project and executes his work in such a way as to take prose out of the equation entirely, thus valorizing poetry as the sine qua non of ethical transformation. By the middle of the fourteenth century, the precise cultural meaning of the twin form and function of mixed-form ethical writing has come under great pressure.

The claims that a narrator's putative transformation does, should, or even could ground readers' parallel transformations of ethics and that those transformations could inhere in form are yet more complex for the Middle English authors I have studied. In the works of Chaucer, Gower, Usk, and Hoccleve, the idea that a narrator's transformation could be salvific for a reader, the topos of protrepsis itself, is just that: a topos. It works by offering itself up as a recognizable literary mode, as a palimpsestic allusion to a particular theory and practice of literature that has accumulated enough cultural critical mass in this period of literary history to become available for complex meditations on the nature of literary experience itself. The Middle English poems in this book all capitalize on the received cultural value of the mixed-form protreptic as an ethically justifiable mode of fictive writing, a way of couching new, fictive literary work as ethically grounded because it both represents transformation in its own author-narrator-hero and offers a parallel avenue to ethical renewal for a reader.

But each of these works reinvents the mixed-form method by which literary learning within the narrative—the narrator's own transformation—might be exportable to the imagined reading audience as protrepsis. In reinventing the mixed form, these works call into question the notion that aesthetic experience has or could have any absolute, stable, or natural relation to ethical learning. For Chaucer, receiving literary impulses not only from Boethius but also from Guillaume, Dante, and contemporary theorists of prose and tragedy, the practiced and theorized assertion of the utility of the mixed form in the composition of ethically salvific literature provides a provocation for the formal and structural organization and framing of three great literary projects. Chaucer's engagement with mixed-form protrepsis is largely as a theory of literature, a formal scaffold on which to experiment with how and whether aesthetic experience might bring about some new kind of understanding for a narrator and/or reader. Chaucer's experiments with the mixed-form rendering of protrepsis shape the aesthetic construction of the *Boece* toward the aesthetic *sentence*, they undergird the toggling between causality and likeness that characterizes the *Troilus*, and they provide the seed crystals for the literary philosophy of the *Canterbury Tales*.

For Usk and Gower, the reengagement with the mixed-form protreptic is more social, geared to help narrators and readers envision and participate in a new, more affectively balanced society. That is, the eventual protrepsis that their works gesture toward is not simply a contemplative transformation, by which a reader is taken to a higher level of self-knowledge, but one by which a reader is taken to a higher level of social consciousness. In this turn toward the social as the eventual *telos* of Boethian writing, Gower and Usk push the Boethian paradigm a step further than Chaucer does, a step away from the realm of literary theory and into the realm of social practice. However social, multiple, and political Chaucer's writings are in thematics, his literary-theoretical engagement with Boethius is more acutely formalist: he takes Boethius as a provocation for considering the power of form, style, and aesthetic experience to represent transformation for a narrator or to model one for a reader.

When Hoccleve composes his *Series*, the dynamic integration of mixed-form logic into a narrative of transformation shifts again: now, rather than prescribing any set ethically transformative goal for his readers by model-ing transformation in himself, Hoccleve performs a concerted and fluent send-up of the very idea that literary work—simply by virtue of its toggling between meter and prose or between fiction and commentary—could pos-sibly be innately transformative for anyone. For Hoccleve, the payoff in lit-erary experimentation lies elsewhere. Hoccleve's concern, in appropriating and undercutting the logic of mixed-form writing and the logic of transfor-mation by writing or reading, is to toy with the interpretive horizons of readers of Boethius, Alain, Dante, Guillaume, Chaucer, and Usk. He is keen to engage with and frustrate his readers' expectations, in an instanti-ation of what Victor Shklovsky calls defamiliarization. For Shklovsky, the fundamental function of art, both aesthetically and ethically, is to work against the bugbear of human existence, which is "habitualization."

> Habitualization devours works, clothes, furniture, one's wife, and the fear of war . . . And art exists that one may recover the sensation of life; it exists to make one feel things, to make the stone *stony*. The purpose of art is to import the sensation of things as they are perceived and not as they are known. The technique of art is to make objects 'unfamil-iar,' to make forms difficult, to increase the difficulty and length of perception because the process of perception is an aesthetic end in it-self and must be prolonged. *Art is a way of experiencing the artfulness of an object; the object itself is not important.*[1]

For Hoccleve, the literary experiment with the mixed form and its puta-tively transformative function is an occasion for a display of culturally vir-tuosic defamiliarization: he weaves himself into the burgeoning history of mixed-form transformative works only to dishabituate readers from their comfort with that literary mode, showing at all junctures between meters and proses the constructedness and artificiality of form. Hoccleve's *Se-ries* makes the category of the literary felt as unnatural, constructed, art-ful, and, in a word, *literary*. Indeed, it is Hoccleve's *Series* that recognizes mixed-form protreptic works precisely as literary fictions and seems to see that process of recognition as an end unto itself.

To what might we attribute this sudden surge of interest in the ethics of form and the forms of ethical literature in the late fourteenth and early

---

1. Shklovsky, "Art as Technique," 12.

fifteenth centuries in England? The timing of this intensive experimentation with the mixed form and its putatively ethically transformative function undoubtedly is to be explained in part by changes in the political and social landscape of late medieval England. English poetry from the late fourteenth century, as Anne Middleton has demonstrated, is pervasively concerned to produce a "common voice" for the "common good," with a sense of duty to an emergent notion of the "public."[2] The experimentation with how ethics might be able to inhere in form, I would suggest, constitutes a particular formation of that cultural investment in the common good. This is especially true in the works of Usk and Gower, who, as I have discussed, shepherd their ethical meditations quite boldly into the world of politics.

But there is a second factor in the surge of experimental poetics in the period, one that might seem, prima facie, less "historical" than the sociopolitical changes England undergoes in the period. The second factor of late medieval English culture that contributes to this intensive attention to form and ethics is, simply put, literary. What sets off the cascade of reinvestigations and reinventings of the mixed-form protreptic in the late fourteenth century is a criticality that is achieved by earlier medieval experiments with the mixed form. In nature, a "criticality" occurs when a structure or system has achieved its maximum state of some property—mass, density, volume, color, and so on.[3] If even one additional unit of that property is added to the system in its criticality, the entire system begins to come undone. A cone of sand, for instance, will reach a point of criticality after which the addition of a single grain of sand will cause the structure to collapse. The topos of the mixed-form protreptic reached, by the late fourteenth century, a literary criticality through the continental writings not just of Boethius but also of Alain, Guillaume, and Dante. At that point, Chaucer drops his grain of sand onto the pile, in the form of the *Boece*, and the whole tropaic structure begins to collapse. But that collapse, far from being destructive, ignites the curiosity of a set of interrelated, courtly writers—Chaucer himself, Usk, Gower, and Hoccleve—as to how and why the mixed form might (or might not) promote protreptic transformation. The ruins of the collapsing structure of Boethian metapoetics then provide the basic building materials for some of the greatest late Middle English long-form fictive writings. The rebuilt structures of the

2. Middleton, "Idea of Public Poetry," 95.

3. For the concept of criticality as a metapoetic construct, see Joron, *Cry at Zero*, 8.

works I have examined in this book are deliberately rickety and programmatically artful, designed both to make their own literary constructedness felt and to encourage readers to meditate on the aesthetic experience of the literary encounter and on how, whether, and why that encounter might prove in some way transformative. The criticality of the mixed-form paradigm for protreptic writing facilitates a synergistic construction of a vernacular literary theory that explores the relation of aesthetics to ethical learning and does so not by discursive explication but by embodying that relation in experimental literary forms.

BIBLIOGRAPHY

PRIMARY SOURCES

Alanus de Insulis. *De planctu naturae.* Ed. J. P. Migne. Patrologia Latina, 210. Paris: Grenier, 1865.

———. *Plaint of Nature.* Trans. James Sheridan. Toronto: Pontifical Institute of Mediaeval Studies, 1980.

Aristotle. *Poetics.* Trans. Penelope Murray and T. S. Dorsch. London: Penguin Classics, 2000.

The Berlin Commentary on Martianus Capella's De nuptiis Philologiae et Mercurii. Ed. Haijo Jan Westra. 2 vols. Leiden: Brill, 1994.

Bernard of Silvester. "Il 'Dictamen' di Bernardo Silvestre." Ed. Mirella Brini Savorelli. *Rivista critica della storia filosofia, testi e documenti* 20 (1965): 182–230.

Boethius. *Boethii: Philosophiae consolatio.* Ed. Ludwig Bieler. Corpus Christianorum, series Latina, 94. Turnhout: Brepols, 1957.

———. *De institutione musica.* Ed. J. P. Migne. Patrologia Latina, 63. Paris: Grenier, 1865.

———. *Fundamentals of Music.* Trans. Calvin Bower. Ed. Claude Polisca. New Haven: Yale University Press, 1989.

———. *Quomodo trinitas unus Deus ac non tres dii and Utrum Pater et Filius et Spiritus sanctus de divinitate substantialiter praedicantur.* In *Theological Tractates and the Consolation of Philosophy,* by Boethius, ed. and trans. H. F. Stewart, E. K. Rand, and S. J. Tester. Cambridge: Harvard University Press, 1973.

Breviarium ad usum insignis ecclesiae Sarum. Ed. Francis Procter and Christopher Wordsworth. London: C. J. Clay and Sons, 1886.

Buridan, John. "Questions on the Ten Books of the Nicomachean Ethics of Aristotle." In *Philosophy of the Middle Ages,* ed. Arthur Hyman and James J. Walsh. Indianapolis: Hackett, 1973.

Chaucer, Geoffrey. *Boece.* In *The Riverside Chaucer,* ed. Larry D. Benson. Boston: Houghton Mifflin, 1987.

———. *Canterbury Tales.* In *The Riverside Chaucer,* ed. Larry D. Benson. Boston: Houghton Mifflin, 1987.

————. *The House of Fame.* In *The Riverside Chaucer*, ed. Larry D. Benson. Boston: Houghton Mifflin, 1987.

————. *Troilus and Criseyde.* In *The Riverside Chaucer*, ed. Larry D. Benson. Boston: Houghton Mifflin, 1987.

————. *Troilus and Criseyde.* Ed. Stephen A. Barney. New York: Norton, 2005.

The Cloud of Unknowing. Ed. Phyllis Hodgson. Oxford: Early English Text Society, 1958.

The Commentary on Martianus Capella's De nuptiis Philologiae et Mercurii *Attributed to Bernardus Silvestris.* Ed. Haijo Jan Westra. Toronto: Pontifical Institute of Medieval Studies Publications, 1986.

Cursor mundi (the Cursur of the World): A Northumbrian Poem of the XIVth Century in Four Versions. Ed. Richard Morris. Original Series 57, 59, 62, 66, 68, 99, 101. London: Early English Text Society, 1874–93.

Dante Alighieri. *Il convivio.* Ed. G. Busnelli and G. Vandelli. Florence: Felice le Monnier, 1968.

————. *Paradiso.* Ed. and trans. Alan Mandelbaum. New York: Bantam, 1984.

————. *Vita nuova.* Ed. Domenico de Robertis. Milan: Roberto Ricciardi, 1980.

Early English Versions of the Gesta romanorum. Ed. Sidney Herrtage. London: Oxford University Press, 1879.

Gower, John. *Confessio amantis.* In *The Complete Works of John Gower*, ed. G. C. Macaulay. Oxford: Clarendon Press, 1899–1902.

Guillaume de Machaut. *Le jugement du roy de Behaigne et Remède de Fortune.* Ed. James I. Wimsatt and William Kibler. Atlanta: University of Georgia Press, 1988.

Hoccleve, Thomas. *Hoccleve's Works 1 and 2: The Minor Poems.* Ed. F. J. Furnivall. London: Early English Text Society, 1892.

————. *Thomas Hoccleve: A Facsimile of the Autograph Verse Manuscripts.* Ed. J. A. Burrow and A. I. Doyle. Oxford: Oxford University Press, Early English Text Society, 2002.

————. *Thomas Hoccleve's Complaint and Dialogue.* Ed. J. A. Burrow. Oxford: Oxford University Press, Early English Text Society, 1999.

Horace. *Satires, Epistles, and Ars poetica.* Ed. H. Rushton Fairclough. Loeb Classical Library. Cambridge: Harvard University Press, 1966.

Isidore of Seville. *Etymologiae.* Ed. W. M. Lindsay. Oxford: Oxford University Press, 1911.

John of Briggis. *Compilacio de arte dictandi.* In *Medieval Rhetorics of Prose Composition*, ed. Martin Camargo. Binghamton: Medieval and Renaissance Texts and Studies, 1995.

John of Garland. *Parisiana poetria of John of Garland.* Ed. Traugott Lawler New Haven: Yale University Press, 1974.

Merke, Thomas. *Formula dictandi et usitati dictaminis.* In *Medieval Rhetorics of Prose Composition*, ed. Martin Camargo. Binghamton: Medieval and Renaissance Texts and Studies, 1995.

Michel, Dan. *Dan Michel's Ayenbite of Inwyt: or, Remorse of Conscience.* Ed. Richard Morris and Reverend P. Gradon. London: Early English Text Society, 1965.

Neckam, Alexander. *Commentum super Martianum*. Ed. Christopher J. McDonough. Florence: Edizioni del Galuzzo, 2006.

Peter of Blois. *Libellus de arte dictandi rhetorice*. In *Medieval Rhetorics of Prose Composition*, ed. Martin Camargo. Binghamton: Medieval and Renaissance Texts and Studies, 1995.

"A Prolog to Jeremiah." In *The Holy Bible, containing the Old and New Testaments, with the Apocryphal Books*. Ed. Josiah Forshall and Frederic Madden. Oxford: Clarendon, 1879.

Saeculi noni auctoris in Boetii Consolationem philosophiae Commentarius. Ed. E. T. Silk. Papers and Monographs of the American Academy in Rome, 9. Rome: American Academy, 1935.

Sampson, Thomas. *Modus dictandi*. In *Medieval Rhetorics of Prose Composition*, ed. Martin Camargo. Binghamton: Medieval and Renaissance Texts and Studies, 1995.

Suso, Henry. *Heinrich Seuses Horologium sapientiae*. Ed. and trans. Pius Künzle. Freiburg: Universitätsverlag Freiburg Schweiz, 1977.

Thomas von Capua. *Die ars dictandi des Thomas von Capua*. Ed. Emmy Heller. Heidelberg: Carl Winters Universitätsbuchhandlung, 1929.

Transmundus. *Transmundus' Introductiones dictandi*. Ed. Ann Dalzell. Toronto: Pontifical Institute of Medieval Studies, 1995.

Trevet, Nicholas. *Exposicio Fratris Nicolai Trevethi Anglici Ordinis Predicatorum super Boecio "De consolatione."* Ed. E. T. Silk. Yale University, Sterling Memorial Library, MS 1614.

Trevisa, John. *Polychronicon Ranulphi Higden monachi Cestrensis; together with the English translations of John Trevisa and of an unknown writer of the fifteenth century*. Ed. Churchill Babington and Joseph Lumby. Rolls Series. London: Longman, 1886.

Usk, Thomas. *Testament of Love*. Ed. Gary W. Shawver. Toronto: University of Toronto Press, 2002.

William of Conches. *Glosae super Boetium*. Ed. Lodi Nauta. Corpus Christianorum Continuatio Mediaevalis, 158. Turnhout: Brepols, 1999.

SECONDARY SOURCES

Aers, David. *Faith, Ethics and Church: English Writings, 1360–1409*. Woodbridge, Suffolk, UK: Brewer, 2000.

Allen, Judson Boyce. *The Ethical Poetic of the Later Middle Ages*. Toronto: University of Toronto Press, 1982.

Andersen, Elisabeth A. *The Voices of Mechthild of Magdeburg*. Bern: Peter Lang, 2000.

Baker, Denise N. "The Priesthood of Genius: A Study of the Medieval Tradition." *Speculum* 51 (1976): 277–91.

Bakhtin, Mikhail. *The Dialogic Imagination*. Austin: University of Texas Press, 1991.

Barolini, Teodolinda. *The Undivine Comedy: Detheologizing Dante*. Princeton: Princeton University Press, 1992.

Barolini, Teodolinda, and Manuele Gragnolari, eds. *Rime giovanile e della Vita nuova*. Milan: BUR Rizzoli, 2009.

Baum, Paull Franklin. "The Canon's Yeoman's Tale." *Modern Language Notes* 40 (1925): 152–54.

———. "Chaucer's Metrical Prose." *Journal of English and Germanic Philology* 45 (1946): 38–42.

Bennett, J. A. W., and Douglas Gray, eds. *Middle English Literature*. Oxford: Clarendon Press, 1986.

Benson, C. David. *Chaucer's Drama of Style: Poetic Variety and Contrast in the Canterbury Tales*. Chapel Hill: University of North Carolina Press, 1986.

Benson, Larry D. Introduction to *Canterbury Tales*. In *The Riverside Chaucer*, ed. Benson. Boston: Houghton Mifflin, 1987.

Blamires, Alcuin. *Chaucer, Ethics, and Gender*. Oxford: Oxford University Press, 2006.

Bloomfield, Morton. "Distance and Predestination in *Troilus and Criseyde*." *PMLA* 72 (1957): 14–26.

Boffey, Julia. "Lydgate, Henryson, and the Literary Testament." *Modern Language Quarterly* 53 (1992): 41–56.

Boitani, Piero, ed. *Chaucer and the Italian Trecento*. Cambridge: Cambridge University Press, 1983.

———. *The Genius to Improve an Invention: Literary Transitions*. Notre Dame: University of Notre Dame Press, 2002.

Bonner, Francis W. "The Genesis of the Chaucer Apocrypha." *Studies in Philology* 48 (1951): 461–81.

Bornstein, Diane. "Chaucer's *Tale of Melibee* as an Example of the 'Style Clergial.'" *Chaucer Review* 12 (1978): 236–54.

Borthwick, Mary Charlotte. "Antigone's Song as Mirrour." *Modern Language Quarterly* 22 (1961): 227–35.

Boulton, Maureen Barry McCann. *The Song in the Story: Lyric Insertions in French Narrative Fictions, 1200–1400*. Philadelphia: University of Pennsylvania Press, 1993.

Bourdieu, Pierre. *Distinction: A Social Critique of the Judgment of Taste*. Trans. Richard Nice. Cambridge: Harvard University Press, 1984.

———. *Outline of a Theory of Practice*. New York: Cambridge University Press, 1997.

Bowers, John M. "Thomas Hoccleve and the Politics of Tradition." *Chaucer Review* 36 (2002): 352–69.

Brantley, Jessica. *Reading in the Wilderness: Private Devotion and Public Performance in Late Medieval England*. Chicago: University of Chicago Press, 2007.

Breen, Katharine. *Imagining an English Reading Public, 1150–1400*. Cambridge: Cambridge University Press, 2010.

Brewer, Derek. "Comedy and Tragedy in *Troilus and Criseyde*." In *The European Tragedy of Troilus*, ed. Piero Boitani, 95–109. Oxford: Clarendon Press, 1989.

Bryan, Jennifer E. "Hoccleve, the Virgin, and the Politics of Complaint." *PMLA* (2002): 1172–87.

Burnley, J. D. "Curial Prose in England." *Speculum* 61 (1986): 593–614.

Burrow, J. A. *Thomas Hoccleve*. Brookfield, VT: Ashgate, Variorum, 1994.

———. "Thomas Hoccleve: Some Redatings." *Review of English Studies* 46 (1995): 366–72.

————. "Wasting Time, Wasting Words in *Piers Plowman* B and C." *Yearbook of Langland Studies* (2003): 191–202.

Burrow, J. A., and Thorlac Turville-Petre, eds. *A Book of Middle English*. London: Blackwell, 2001.

Butterfield, Ardis. "Articulating the Author: Gower and the French Vernacular Codex." *Yearbook of English Studies* 33 (2003): 80–96.

————. *Poetry and Music in Medieval France: From Jean Renart to Guillaume de Machaut*. Cambridge: Cambridge University Press, 2002.

Camargo, Martin. "The Consolation of Pandarus." *Chaucer Review* 25 (1991): 214–28.

Campbell, Jackson J. "The Canon's Yeoman as Imperfect Paradigm." *Chaucer Review* 17 (1982):171–81.

Cannon, Christopher. *The Grounds of English Literature*. Oxford: Oxford University Press, 2008.

Carlson, David. "Chaucer's Boethius and Usk's *Testament*: Politics and Love in the Chaucerian Tradition." In *The Centre and Its Compass: Studies in Medieval Literature in Honor of Professor John Leyerle*, ed. Robert A. Taylor et al., 29–70. Kalamazoo: Western Michigan University Press, 1993.

Cervigni, Dino, and Edward Vasta, eds. *Vita nuova*, by Dante Alighieri. Notre Dame: University of Notre Dame Press, 1995.

Chadwick, Henry. *The Consolations of Music, Logic, Theology, and Philosophy*. Oxford: Clarendon, 1984.

Chaganti, Seeta. *The Medieval Poetics of the Reliquary: Enshrinement, Inscription, Performance*. New York: Palgrave, 2008.

Chamberlain, David S. "The Philosophy of Music in the *Consolatio* of Boethius." *Speculum* 45 (1970): 80–97.

Chambers, R. W. *On the Continuity of English Prose from Alfred to More and His School*. Oxford: Oxford University Press, 1957.

Cherniss, Michael. *Boethian Apocalypse: Studies in Medieval English Vision Poetry*. Norman, OK: Pilgrim Books, 1987.

Chickering, Howell. "The Poetry of Suffering in Book V of the *Troilus*." *Chaucer Review* 34 (2000): 243–68.

Cole, Andrew. "Chaucer's English Lesson." *Speculum* 77 (2002): 1128–67.

Cook, John. "The Protreptic Power of Early Christian Language: From John to Augustine." *Vigiliae Christianiae* 48 (1994): 105–34.

Cooper, Helen. "Chaucer's Poetics." In *New Readings of Chaucer's Poetry*, ed. Robert Benson, 31–50. London: Boydell, 2003.

Copeland, Rita. *Rhetoric, Hermeneutics, and Translation in the Middle Ages*. Cambridge: Cambridge University Press, 1991.

Courcelle, Pierre. *La Consolation dans la tradition littéraire*. Paris: Etudes Augustiniennes, 1967.

Crocker, Richard L. "Musica Rhythmica and Musica Metrica in Antique and Medieval Theory." *Journal of Music Theory* 2 (1958): 2–23.

Dalzell, Ann. Introduction to *Transmundus' Introductiones dictandi*, 19–20. Toronto: Pontifical Institute of Medieval Studies, 1995.

Davenport, W. A. *Chaucer: Complaint and Narrative*. Cambridge: Brewer, 1988.

David, Alfred. "The Man of Law vs. Chaucer: A Case in Poetics." *PMLA* 82 (1967): 217–25.

Dean, James. "Chaucer, Gower, and Rime royal." *Studies in Philology* 88 (1991): 251–75.

———. "Dismantling the Canterbury Book." *PMLA* (1985): 746–62.

Dedeck-Héry, V. L. "Le *Boèce* de Chaucer et les manuscrits français de la *Consolatio* de J. de Meun." *PMLA* 59 (1944): 18–25.

———. "Jean de Meun et Chaucer, Traducteurs de la *Consolation* de Boèce." *PMLA* 52 (1937): 967–91.

Deleuze, Gilles, and Felix Guattari. *A Thousand Plateaus: Capitalism and Schizophrenia.* Trans. Brian Massumi. Minneapolis: University of Minnesota Press, 1987.

Dickson, Donald. "The 'Sliding' Yeoman: The Real Drama in the Canon's Yeoman's Tale." *South Central Review* 2 (1985): 10–22.

Dinshaw, Carolyn. *Chaucer's Sexual Poetics.* Madison: University of Wisconsin Press, 1989.

Doyle, A. I., and M. B. Parkes. "The Productions of Copies of the *Canterbury Tales* and the *Confessio Amantis* in the Early Fifteenth Century." In *Medieval Scribes, Manuscripts and Libraries: Essays Presented to N. R. Ker,* ed. M. B. Parkes and A. G. Watson, 163–210. London: Scolar Press, 1978.

Dronke, Peter. *Verse with Prose from Petronius to Dante.* Cambridge: Harvard University Press, 1994.

Duffell, Martin J. "Craft so longe to lerne: Chaucer's Invention of Iambic Pentameter." *Chaucer Review* 34 (2000): 269–88.

Echard, Siân, and Claire Fanger, eds. *The Latin Verses in the Confessio amantis.* East Lansing: Colleagues Press, 1991.

Eckhardt, Carolyn. "The Medieval Prosimetrum Genre (From Boethius to Boece)." *Genre* 16 (1983): 21–38.

Economou, George D. "The Character Genius in Alan de Lille, Jean de Meun, and John Gower." In *Gower's Confessio amantis: A Critical Anthology,* ed. Peter Nicholson, 109–16. London: Brewer, 1991.

Edwards, A. S. G. "'I speke in prose': Man of Law's Tale 96." *Neuphilologische Mitteilungen* 92 (1991): 469–70.

Edwards, Robert. *Chaucer and Boccaccio: Antiquity and Modernity.* New York: Palgrave, 2002.

Elbow, Peter. "Two Boethian Speeches in *Troilus and Criseyde* and Chaucerian Irony." In *Literary Criticism and Historical Understanding,* ed. Phillip Damon, 85–107. New York: Columbia University Press, 1967.

Fleming, John. *Classical Imitation and Interpretation in Chaucer's Troilus.* Lincoln: University of Nebraska Press, 1990.

Foster, Edward. "Has Anyone Here Read *Melibee*?" *Chaucer Review* 34 (2000): 398–409.

Fradenburg, L. O. Aranye. *Sacrifice Your Love: Psychoanalysis, Historicism, Chaucer.* Minneapolis: University of Minnesota Press, 2002.

Frisardi, Andrew. Introduction. In *Vita nova: Dante.* Evanston: Northwestern University Press, 2012.

Gallagher, Catherine. "Formalism and Time." *Modern Language Quarterly* 61 (2000): 229–51.

Galloway, Andrew. "Private Selves and the Intellectual Marketplace in Late Fourteenth-Century England: The Case of the Two Usks." *New Literary History* 28 (1997): 291–318.

Gaylord, Alan. "Gentilesse in Chaucer's *Troilus*." *Studies in Philology* 61 (1964): 19–34.

———. "Uncle Pandarus as Lady Philosophy." *Papers of the Michigan Academy of Science, Arts, and Letters* 46 (1961): 571–95.

Ginsberg, Warren. *Chaucer's Italian Tradition*. Ann Arbor: University of Michigan Press, 2002.

Gordon, Ida. *The Double Sorrow of Troilus: A Study of Ambiguities in* Troilus and Criseyde. Oxford: Oxford University Press, 1970.

Green, Richard Hamilton. "Alan of Lille's *De planctu naturae*." *Speculum* 31 (1956): 649–74.

Greenblatt, Stephen. *Learning to Curse: Essays in Early Modern Culture*. New York: Routledge, 1990.

Greetham, David. "Self-Referential Artifacts: Hoccleve's Persona as a Literary Device." *Modern Philology* 86 (1989): 242–51.

Grenberg, Bruce. "The Canon's Yeoman's Tale: Boethian Wisdom and the Alchemists." *Chaucer Review* 1 (1966): 37–54.

Grennen, Joseph E. "The Canon's Yeoman and the Cosmic Furnace: Language and Meaning in the Canon's Yeoman's Tale." *Criticism* 4 (1962): 227–29.

———. "Chaucer's Characterization of the Canon and His Yeoman." *Journal of the History of Ideas* 25 (1964): 279–84.

———. "Saint Cecilia's 'Chemical Wedding': The Unity of Canterbury Tales, Fragment VIII." *Journal of English and Germanic Philology* 65 (1966): 466–81

Gualtieri, Angelo. "Lady Philosophy in Boethius and Dante." *Comparative Literature* 23 (1971): 141–50.

Halle, Morris, and Samuel Jay Keyser. "Chaucer and the Study of Prosody." *College English* 28 (1966): 187–219.

Halpern, Richard. *Shakespeare among the Moderns*. Ithaca: Cornell University Press, 1997.

Hanna, Ralph, and Traugott Lawler. "*Boece*." In *The Riverside Chaucer*, ed. Larry D. Benson, 395–97. Boston: Houghton Mifflin, 1987.

Hayton, Heather Richardson. "Many Privy Thinges Wimpled and Folde." *Studies in Philology* 96 (1999): 22–41.

Heinrichs, Katherine. *The Myths of Love: Classical Lovers in Medieval Literature*. University Park: Pennsylvania State University Press, 1990.

Herz, Judith Scherer. "The Canon's Yeoman's Prologue and Tale." *Modern Philology* 58 (1961): 231–37.

Holsinger, Bruce. "Lyrics and Short Poems." In *Yale Companion to Chaucer*, ed. Seth Lerer, 187–90. New Haven: Yale University Press, 2006.

Howard, Donald R. *The Idea of the Canterbury Tales*. Berkeley: University of California Press, 1987.

Huber, John. "Troilus' Predestination Soliloquy." *Neuphilologische Mitteilungen* 66 (1965): 120–25.

Hunt, Tony. "Precursors and Progenitors of *Aucussin et Nicolette*." *Studies in Philology* 74 (1977): 1–19.

Huot, Sylvia. "Guillaume de Machaut and the Consolation of Poetry." *Modern Philology* 100 (2002): 169–95.

Huppe, Bernard F. "The Unlikely Narrator: The Narrative Strategy of the *Troilus.*" In *Signs and Symbols in Chaucer's Poetry,* ed. John P. Hermann and John J. Burke Jr., 174–91. Tuscaloosa: University of Alabama Press, 1981.

Jakobson, Roman. "Two Aspects of Language and Two Types of Aphasic Disturbances." In *Fundamentals of Language,* 67–96. The Hague: Mouton, 1980.

Jankowski, Eileen. "Chaucer's Second Nun's Tale and the Apocalyptic Imagination." *Chaucer Review* 36 (2001): 128–48.

Jefferson, Bernard L. *Chaucer and the Consolation of Philosophy of Boethius.* Princeton: Princeton University Press, 1917.

Jellech, Virginia Boarding. "*The Testament of Love* by Thomas Usk: A New Edition." Ph.D. diss., Washington University, 1970.

Johnson, Eleanor. "Chaucer and the Consolation of Prosimetrum." *Chaucer Review* 43 (2009): 455–72.

———. "Feeling Time, Words, and Will: Vernacular Devotion in the *Cloud of Unknowing.*" *Journal of Medieval and Early Modern Studies* (2011): 345–68.

Jordan, Mark D. "Ancient Philosophic Protreptic and the Problem of Persuasive Genres." *Rhetorica* 4 (1986): 309–33.

Jordan, Robert M. "The Narrator in Chaucer's *Troilus.*" *English Literary History* (1958): 237–57.

Joron, Andrew. *The Cry at Zero: Selected Prose.* Denver: Counterpath Press, 2007.

Kaminsky, Alice. *Chaucer's* Troilus and Criseyde *and the Critics.* Columbus: Ohio State University Press, 1980.

Kay, Sarah. *The "Chansons de geste" in the Age of Romance: Political Fictions.* Oxford: Oxford University Press, 1995.

Kean, P. M. "Chaucer, an Englishman Elusively Italianate." *Review of English Studies* 34 (1983): 388–94.

Kelly, Henry Ansgar. *Chaucerian Tragedy.* Cambridge, UK: Brewer, 1997.

———. *Ideas and Forms of Tragedy from Aristotle to the Middle Ages.* Cambridge: Cambridge University Press, 1993.

Kittay, Jeffrey, and Wlad Godzich. *The Emergence of Prose: An Essay in Prosaics.* Minneapolis: University of Minnesota Press, 1987.

Knapp, Ethan. "Bureaucratic Identity and the Construction of the Self in Hoccleve's *Formulary* and *La male regle.*" *Speculum* 74 (1999): 357–76.

———. "Eulogies and Usurpations: Hoccleve and Chaucer Revisited." *Studies in the Age of Chaucer* 21 (1999): 247–73.

Knapp, Peggy. "Aesthetic Attention and the Chaucerian Text." *Chaucer Review* 39 (2005): 241–58.

Knopp, Sherron. "The Narrator and His Audience in Chaucer's *Troilus and Criseyde.*" *Studies in Philology* 78 (1981): 323–40.

Kolve, V. A. "Chaucer's *Second Nun's Tale* and the Iconography of Saint Cecilia." In *New Perspectives in Chaucer Criticism,* ed. Donald H. Rose, 137–76. Norman, OK: Pilgrim Press, 1981.

Krapp, George Philip. *The Rise of Early English Literary Prose.* Oxford: Oxford University Press, 1915.

Kreuzer, James. "A Note on Chaucer's *Tale of Melibee.*" *Modern Language Notes* 63 (1948): 53–54.

Kuhn, Sherman M. "Cursus in Old English: Rhetorical Ornament or Linguistic Phenomenon?" *Speculum* 47 (1972): 188–206.

Kurtz, Benjamin. "The Prose of Occleve's *Lerne to Dye.*" *Modern Language Notes* 39 (1924): 56–57.

———. "The Relation of Occleve's *Lerne to Dye* to Its Source." *PMLA* 40 (1925): 252–75.

———. "The Source of Occleve's *Lerne to Dye.*" *Modern Language Notes* 38 (1923): 337–40.

Lage, G. Reynaud de. *Alain de Lille, poète du XIIe siècle.* Montreal: Institut d'Etudes Medievales, 1951.

Lambert, Mark. "Telling the Story in *Troilus and Criseyde.*" In *Cambridge Companion to Chaucer,* ed. Piero Boitani and Jill Mann, 78–92. Cambridge: Cambridge University Press, 2003.

Lawler, Traugott. *The One and the Many in the Canterbury Tales.* Hamden, CT: Archon, 1980.

Lerer, Seth. *Boethius and Dialogue: Literary Method in the Consolation of Philosophy.* Princeton: Princeton University Press, 1985.

———. "The Endurance of Formalism in Middle English Studies." *Literature Compass* 1 (2003): 1–15.

———. Introduction. In *La vita nuova,* trans. David R. Slavitt. Cambridge: Harvard University Press, 2010.

Levinson, Marjorie. "What Is New Formalism?" *PMLA* 122 (2007): 558–69.

Lewis, C. S. "What Chaucer Really Did to *Il filostrato.*" *Essays and Studies* 17 (1932): 56–75.

Liu, Alan. "The Power of Formalism." *English Literary History* 56 (1989): 721–71.

Lowes, John Livingston. "Chaucer and Dante's *Convivio.*" *Studies in Philology* 13 (1915): 19–33.

Machan, Tim William. *Techniques of Translation: Chaucer's Boece.* Norman, OK: Pilgrim Press, 1985.

McAlpine, Monica. *The Genre of Troilus and Criseyde.* Ithaca: Cornell University Press, 1978.

Means, Michael. *The Consolatio Genre in Medieval English Literature.* Gainesville: University of Florida Press, 1972.

Middleton, Anne. "Aelfric's Answerable Style: The Rhetoric of Alliterative Prose." *Mediaeval Studies* 4 (1973): 83–91.

———. "The Idea of Public Poetry in the Reign of Richard II." *Speculum* 53 (1978): 94–114.

———. "Thomas Usk's 'Perdurable Letters': The *Testament of Love* from Script to Print," *Studies in Bibliography* 51 (1998): 63–116.

Miller, Mark. *Philosophical Chaucer: Love, Sex and Agency in the Canterbury Tales.* Cambridge: Cambridge University Press, 2004.

Minnis, A. J., ed. *Chaucer's "Boece" and the Medieval Tradition of Boethius.* Wood-
    bridge, Suffolk, UK: Boydell and Brewer, 1993.
———. "John Gower, Sapiens in Ethics and Politics." *Medium Aevum* 49 (1980): 207–29.
———, ed. *The Medieval Boethius: Studies in the Vernacular Translations of "De con-
    solatione philosophiae."* Woodbridge, Suffolk, UK: Boydell and Brewer, 1987.
———. *Medieval Theory of Authorship: Scholastic Literary Attitudes in the Later
    Middle Ages.* London: Scolar Press, 1984.
Minnis, A. J., and Tim Machan. *The Sources of Chaucer's 'Boece.'* Athens: University
    of Georgia Press, 2005.
Minnis, A. J., and A. B. Scott, eds., with David Wallace. *Medieval Literary Theory and
    Criticism, 1100–1375: The Commentary Tradition.* Oxford: Clarendon, 2000.
Mitchell, J. Allan. *Ethics and Eventfulness in Middle English Literature.* New York:
    Palgrave, 2009.
———. *Ethics and Exemplary Narrative in Chaucer and Gower.* Cambridge, UK:
    Brewer, 2004.
Morgan, Margery. "A Treatise in Cadence." *Modern Language Review* 47 (1952): 156–64.
Mueller, Janel. *The Native Tongue and the Word.* Chicago: University of Chicago Press,
    1985.
Murphy, J. J. *Rhetoric in the Middle Ages.* Berkeley: University of California Press,
    1974.
Musa, Mark. "An Essay." In *Dante's Vita nuova: A Translation and Essay.* Blooming-
    ton: Indiana University Press, 1973.
Newman, Barbara. *God and the Goddesses: Vision, Poetry, and Belief in the Middle
    Ages.* Philadelphia: University of Pennsylvania Press, 2003.
Nicholson, Peter. *Love and Ethics in Gower's* Confessio amantis. Ann Arbor: Univer-
    sity of Michigan Press, 2005.
Nietzsche, Frederic. *The Birth of Tragedy.* Trans. Douglas Smith. Oxford: Oxford Uni-
    versity Press, 2000.
Nolan, Barbara. "Chaucer's Tales of Transcendence: Rhyme Royal and Christian Prayer
    in the *Canterbury Tales.*" In *Chaucer's Religious Tales,* ed. C. David Benson and
    Elizabeth Robertson, 21–37. London: Brewer, 1990.
Nolan, Maura. *John Lydgate and the Making of Public Culture.* Cambridge: Cambridge
    University Press, 2005.
Olsen, Alexandra Hennessey. *Betwene Ernest and Game: The Literary Artistry of the
    Confessio Amantis.* New York: Peter Lang, 1990.
Olson, Glending. "Chaucer, Dante, and the Structure of Fragment VIII (G) of the *Can-
    terbury Tales.*" *Chaucer Review* 16 (1982): 222–36.
———. *Literature as Recreation in the Middle Ages.* Ithaca: Cornell University Press,
    1982.
Owen, Charles A. "The Significance of Chaucer's Revisions to the *Troilus and Cri-
    seyde.*" *Modern Philology* 55 (1957): 1–5.
———. "Thy Drasty Rhymyng." *Studies in Philology* 63 (1966): 533–64.
Parkes, Malcolm. "The Literacy of the Laity." In *The Medieval World,* ed. David
    Daiches and Anthony Thorlby, 555–77. Literature and Western Civilization. Lon-
    don: Aldus, 1973.

———. *Pause and Effect: An Introduction to the History of Punctuation in the West.* Berkeley: University of California Press, 1993.

Pasnau, Robert. *Theories of Cognition in the Later Middle Ages.* Cambridge: Cambridge University Press, 1997.

Patch, Howard R. *The Tradition of Boethius: A Study of His Importance in Late Medieval Culture.* Oxford: Oxford University Press, 1935.

———. "Troilus on Determinism." *Speculum* 6 (1931): 225–43.

Patterson, Lee. *Chaucer and the Subject of History.* Madison: University of Wisconsin Press, 1991.

———. "Perpetual Motion: Alchemy and the Technology of the Self." *Studies in the Age of Chaucer* 15 (1993): 50–51.

———. "'What man artow?' Authorial Self-Definition in the *Tale of Sir Thopas* and the *Tale of Melibee.*" *Studies in the Age of Chaucer* 11 (1989): 117–75.

Payne, Anne. *Chaucer and Menippean Satire.* Madison: University of Wisconsin Press, 1981.

Pearsall, Derek. "Hoccleve's *Regement of Princes*: The Poetics of Royal Self-Representation." *Speculum* 69 (1994): 386–405.

Peck, Russell. *Kingship and Common Profit in John Gower's* Confessio Amantis. Carbondale: Southern Illinois University Press, 1978.

Price, Thomas R. "*Troilus and Criseyde*, a Study in Chaucer's Method of Construction." *PMLA* 11 (1896): 307–22.

Rand, E. K. "On the Composition of Boethius' *Consolatio philosophiae.*" *Harvard Studies* 15 (1904): 1–28.

Reinhard, John R. "The Literary Background of the Chantefable." *Speculum* 1 (1926): 157–69.

Richardson, Malcolm. "The Dictamen and Its Influence on Fifteenth-Century English Prose." *Rhetorica* 2 (1984): 207–26.

———. "The Fading Influence of the Medieval *Ars dictaminis* in England after 1400." *Rhetorica* 19 (2001): 225–47.

Rigg, A. G. "Hoccleve's Complaint and Isidore of Seville." *Speculum* 45 (1970): 564–74.

Robinson, Ian. *Chaucer's Prosody.* Cambridge: Cambridge University Press, 1971.

Rosenberg, Bruce A. "The Contrary Tales of the Second Nun and the Canon's Yeoman." *Chaucer Review* 2 (1968): 278–91.

Rosenfeld, Jessica. "The Doubled Joys of *Troilus and Criseyde.*" In *The Erotics of Consolation,* ed. Catherine Léglu and Stephen Milner, 39–59. New York: Palgrave, 2008.

———. *Ethics and Enjoyment in Late Medieval Poetry.* Cambridge: Cambridge University Press, 2011.

Saintsbury, George. *A History of English Prose Rhythm.* Bloomington: Indiana University Press, 1965.

Salter, Elizabeth. "Troilus and Criseyde: Poet and Narrator." In *Acts of Interpretation: The Text and Its Context, 700–1400: Essays on Medieval and Renaissance Literature in Honor of E. Talbot Donaldson,* ed. Mary Carruthers and Elizabeth Kirk, 281–91. Norman, OK: Pilgrim Books, 1982.

Scanlon, Larry. "The King's Two Voices: Narrative and Power in Hoccleve's *Regement*

of Princes." In *Literary Practice and Social Change in Britain, 1380–1530*, ed. Lee
    Patterson, 216–47. Berkeley: University of California Press, 1990.

Scarry, Elaine. "The Well-Rounded Sphere: The Metaphysical Structure of the *Consola-
    tion of Philosophy.*" In *Essays in the Numerical Criticism of Medieval Literature*,
    ed. Carolyn Eckhardt, 91–140. Lewisburg, PA: Bucknell University Press, 1980.

Schlauch, Margaret. "Chaucer's Prose Rhythms." PMLA 65 (1950): 568–89.

———. "Stylistic Attributes of John Lydgate's Prose." In *To Honor Roman Jakobson*:
    Essays on the Occasion of His Seventieth Birthday, October 11, 1966, 1757–68. The
    Hague: Mouton, 1967.

Shanzer, Danuta. *A Philosophical and Literary Commentary on Martianus Capella's*
    De nuptiis Philologiae et Mercurii. Berkeley: University of California Press, 1986.

Shklovsky, Victor. "Art as Technique." In *Russian Formalist Criticism*, ed. Lee T.
    Lemon and Marion Reis, 3–24. Lincoln: University of Nebraska Press, 1965.

Shoaf, Allen. Introduction. In *The Testament of Love*, by Thomas Usk. Kalamazoo:
    TEAMS, 1998.

Simpson, James. "Nobody's Man: Thomas Hoccleve's *Regement of Princes.*" In *London
    and Europe in the Later Middle Ages*, ed. Julia Boffey and Pamela King, 149–80.
    London: Queen Mary and Westfield College, 1995.

———. *Sciences and the Self in Medieval Poetry: Alan of Lille's* Anticlaudianus *and
    John Gower's* Confessio amantis. Cambridge: Cambridge University Press, 1995.

Skeat, W. W. Introduction. In *The Complete Works of Geoffrey Chaucer*. Oxford: Oxford
    University Press, 1880.

Smith, J. J. "The Trinity Gower D-Scribe and His Work on Two Early *Canterbury Tales*
    Manuscripts." In *The English of Chaucer and His Contemporaries*, ed. Smith,
    51–69. Aberdeen: Aberdeen University Press, 1989.

Smith, Thomas. "The Protreptic Character of the Nicomachean Ethics." *Polity* 27
    (1994): 307–30.

Smyth, Karen. "Reading Misreadings in Thomas Hoccleve's *Series.*" *English Studies* 87
    (2006): 3–22.

Spearing, A. C. *"A Ricardian 'I': Essays on Ricardian Literature*. Ed. Alastair Minnis.
    Oxford: Clarendon, 1997.

Spiegel, Gabrielle. "Forging the Past: The Language of Historical Truth in the Middle
    Ages." *History Teacher* 17 (1984): 267–88.

———. *Romancing the Past*. Berkeley: University of California Press, 1995.

Stahl, William. "To a Better Understanding of Martianus Capella." *Speculum* 40 (1965):
    102–15.

Staley, Lynn. "Gower, Richard II, Henry of Derby, and the Making of Public Culture."
    Speculum 75 (2000): 68–96.

Steadman, John. *Disembodied Laughter*. Berkeley: University of California Press, 1972.

Stevens, Martin. "The Royal Stanza in Early English Literature." *PMLA* 94 (1979):
    62–76.

Stewart, Garrett. "The Foreign Offices of British Fiction." *MLQ* 61 (2000): 181–206.

Stillinger, Thomas C. *The Song of Troilus: Lyrical Authority in the Medieval Book*.
    Philadelphia: University of Pennsylvania Press, 1992.

Strohm, Paul. *Hochon's Arrow: The Social Imagination of Fourteenth-Century Texts.* Princeton: Princeton University Press, 1992.

———. "Politics and Poetics: Usk and Chaucer." In *Literary Practice and Social Change in Britain: 1380–1530,* ed. Lee Patterson, 83–112. Berkeley: University of California Press, 1990.

———. *Social Chaucer.* Cambridge: Harvard University Press, 1989.

Stroud, Theodore. "Boethius' Influence on Chaucer's *Troilus.*" *Modern Philology* 49 (1951): 1–9.

Sweeney, Eileen C. *Logic, Theology and Poetry in Boethius, Abelard, and Alan of Lille.* New York: Palgrave, 2006.

Thomas, Arvind. "What's Myrie about the Prose of the Parson's Tale?" *Chaucer Review* 46 (2012): 419–438.

Townsend, David. "The Current Questions and Future Prospects of Medieval Latin Studies." In *The Oxford Handbook of Medieval Latin Literature,* ed. Ralph Hexter and David Townsend, 3–24. Oxford: Oxford University Press, 2012.

Trilling, Renée R. *The Aesthetics of Nostalgia: Historical Representation in Old English Verse.* Toronto: University of Toronto Press, 2009.

Turner, Marion. "'Certaynly his Sayinges Can I Nat Amende': Thomas Usk and *Troilus and Criseyde.*" *Chaucer Review* 37 (2002): 26–39.

Utley, Francis L. "Scene-Division in Chaucer's *Troilus and Criseyde.*" In *Studies in Medieval Literature in Honor of Professor Albert Croll Baugh,* ed. MacEdward Leach, 109–38. Philadelphia: University of Pennsylvania Press, 1961.

Wallace, David. *Chaucer and the Early Writings of Boccaccio.* Chaucer Studies, 12. London: Boydell and Brewer, 1985.

Walling, Amanda. "'In Hir Tellyng Difference': Gender, Authority, and Interpretation in the *Tale of Melibee.*'" *Chaucer Review* 40 (2005): 163–81.

Waswo, Richard. "The Narrator of *Troilus and Criseyde.*" *English Literary History* 50 (1983): 1–25.

Watt, Diane. *Amoral Gower: Language, Sex and Politics.* Minneapolis: University of Minnesota Press, 2003.

Wetherbee, Winthrop. *Chaucer and the Poets: An Essay on Troilus and Criseyde.* Ithaca: Cornell University Press, 1984.

———. "Classical and Boethian Tradition in *Confessio Amantis.*" In *A Companion to Gower,* ed. Siân Echard, 181–96. Cambridge, UK: Brewer, 2004.

———. "Latin Structure and Vernacular Space: Gower, Chaucer and the Boethian Tradition." In *Chaucer and Gower: Difference, Mutuality, Exchange,* ed. R. F. Yeager, 7–35. ELS Monograph Series, 51. Victoria, B.C.: English Literary Studies, 1991.

———. *Platonism and Poetry in the Twelfth Century: The Literary Influence of the School of Chartres.* Princeton: Princeton University Press, 1972.

Wilson, R. M. "On the Continuity of English Prose." In *Mélanges de linguistique et de philologie Fernand Mossé in memoriam,* 486–94. Paris: Didier, 1959.

Wimsatt, James. "Realism in *Troilus and Criseyde.*" In *Essays on Troilus and Criseyde,* ed. Mary Salu, 43–56. Woodbridge, Suffolk, UK: Brewer, 1991.

Windeatt, Barry. "Classical and Medieval Elements in Chaucer's *Troilus*." In *The European Tragedy of Troilus*, ed. Piero Boitani, 111–31. Oxford: Clarendon Press, 1989.

Winstead, Karen. "'I am al other to yow than yee weene': Hoccleve, Women, and the Series." *Philological Quarterly* 72 (1993): 143–55.

Wogan-Browne, Jocelyn, ed. *The Idea of the Vernacular*. University Park, PA: Pennsylvania State University Press, 1999.

Wolfson, Susan. "Reading for Form." *MLQ* 61 (2000): 1–16.

Young, Karl. "Chaucer's 'Troilus and Criseyde' as Romance." *PMLA* 53 (1938): 38–63.

Ziolkowski, Jan. *Alan of Lille's Grammar of Sex: The Meaning of Grammar to a Twelfth-Century Intellectual*. Speculum Monographs, 10. Cambridge, MA: Medieval Academy of America, 1985.

Printed in Great Britain
by Amazon

70224702R00158